MW00668282

Fundamentals of Chinese Characters

Seal Script   漢字基礎

Clerical Script   漢字基礎

Regular Script   漢字基礎

Normalized Script   汉字基础

Semi-cursive Script   汉字基础

Cursive Script   汉字基础

Fundamentals of Chinese Characters

John Jing-hua Yin 印京华

University of Vermont

Illustrations by Zhao Xin

Yale University Press

New Haven and London

Copyright © 2006 by Yale University
All rights reserved.
This book may not be reproduced, in whole or in part, including
illustrations, in any form (beyond that copying permitted by Sections
107 and 108 of the U.S. Copyright Law and except by reviewers for the
public press), without written permission from the publishers.

Publisher: Mary Jane Peluso
Development Editor: Brie Kluytenaar
Manuscript Editor: Annie Imbornoni
Production Controller: Aldo Cupo
Cover Designer: James J. Johnson
Marketing Manager: Timothy Shea

Printed in the United States of America

Library of Congress Cataloging-in-Publication Data

Yin, John Jing-hua, 1955-
   Fundamentals of Chinese characters / John Jing-hua Yin : illustrations
by Zhao Xin =   [Han zi ji chu / Yin Jinghua]
    p. cm.
   Parallel title in Chinese characters.
   Includes bibliographical references and index.
   ISBN-13: 978-0-300-10945-0 (pbk.)
   ISBN-10: 0-300-10945-8 (pbk.)
   1. Chinese characters. 2. Chinese language—Writing. I. Title: Han zi
ji chu. II. Title.
   PL1171.Y57 2006
   895.1′82421—dc22

                          2005057778

A catalogue record for this book is available from the British Library.

The paper in this book meets the guidelines for permanence and
durability of the Committee on Production Guidelines for Book Longevity
of the Council on Library Resources.

Contents 目录

Chapter 14 第十四章 Characters Formed with Semantic and Phonetic Components: Picto-Phonetic Characters 由形旁和声旁合成的汉字: 形声字

Acknowledgments 致谢

I would like to thank my students first, as many of the ideas used in this book came from them. They have always tried to overcome the difficulties encountered in learning the Chinese language. They put a great deal of time and energy into learning Chinese and their frustrations over the limited results have spurred me to search for a more effective and efficient yet enjoyable approach to Chinese language teaching. This book is the result of my students' desires to learn the Chinese language well. I thank the Freeman Foundation for the generosity that provided financial support for my research related to the formulation of the theoretical basis for the approach used in this book. I thank Professor Mingde Zhao of the Chinese Central University of Minority Nationalities for sharing with me his insights on the nature of Chinese characters and his experiences in teaching them. My heartfelt thanks go to Professor Hongqing Yang of Pengcheng University of China, who kindly presented me a copy of the Chinese Character Fast Recognition Dictionary, which he and his wife spent years compiling. Their dictionary was very instrumental in helping me find information on many characters covered in this book. I also thank Professor Dasui Li of Peking University for sharing his study findings on the concept and definition of explanative characters. My special thanks go to the reviewers of my manuscript, including Professor Wei Hong, Purdue University; Professor Shengli Feng, Harvard University; Professor Chao Fen Sun, Stanford University; Professor Ming Chao Gui, University of Oklahoma; and Professor Xiaobin Jian, the College of William and Mary. I am deeply grateful for their time and expertise expended in evaluating the book, and more important, for their recognition of the academic and educational value of this book. I can never thank enough my colleague Professor Peter Seybolt of the University of Vermont. He has given me advice and provided the firmest and most tangible support in all possible ways during the whole process of my writing the book. After I finished the first manuscript of the book, he carefully read through it and refined my writing. He also proofread the final manuscript. Without his support, writing this book would have been difficult. I am grateful to my other colleagues, Ms. Chunyan Chen and Ms. Pam Lin, who substituted for me or assisted me in teaching my regular Chinese classes so that I could spend more time on writing. My heartfelt gratitude also goes to my parents, sisters, and my mother-in-law, who are never short of moral support and whom I can always depend on. At my request, my father wrote all the characters covered in this book as well as the title of the book in his beautiful cursive style despite being 83 years old. My two sisters helped to get the Chinese font that I needed and helped me find Mr. Xin Zhao, the talented artist who did the vivid illustrations for all the basic characters in the book. I want to thank Yale University Press staff, including Annie Imbornoni, Brie Kluytenaar, and Gretchen Rings, for guiding me through the publication procedures. Last but not least, I want to say thanks to my family. Rose and Jason always knew that their dad should not be disturbed while he was writing. Diana possesses all the qualities I could dream of during the whole process of writing this book. Without her taking care of the whole family and managing the house, I would have had no time and no place to write at home; without her being the first listener of my ideas, this project would not have flourished. She has been not only caring but also inspirational. This book, after all, is a product not of one person, but of the joint efforts of many people.

Introduction 前言

Rationales for the book

When learning a foreign language, we generally learn to listen and speak first and then learn to read and write words we can understand and speak. After all, this is the natural sequence of acquiring one's own native language, and it might seem to be the most efficient and effective approach to learning a foreign language. Teachers of Chinese as a foreign language have been using this approach for the past few decades. Consequently, students of Chinese in American universities learn to understand and speak Chinese first and then learn to read and write Chinese. In other words, you usually learn to write what you can say and rarely learn to write what you cannot say.

However, written Chinese is very different from alphabetic languages such as English in that the Chinese logographic writing system uses characters, which do not provide beginners with any clues as to pronunciation. Conversely, being able to speak a Chinese word does not help beginners know how that word is written. Unfortunately, the approach commonly adopted in the past several decades has been to teach students to write the characters for what they have just learned to speak. Therefore, the characters for the most commonly used daily expressions in Chinese are also taught in the first few lessons. The characters in such frequently used daily expressions as "Hello" (你好), "How are you" (你好吗), "I am fine" (我很好), and "Thanks" (谢谢) have quite complicated written structures. Teaching students how to write these characters is like teaching students who have no knowledge of the English alphabet how to spell a multisyllabic English word. Teaching Chinese characters in this way violates the pedagogical principle of teaching the easy first and proceeding gradually and systematically to the difficult. This approach presents students with a bigger challenge than is necessary, making the learning of Chinese characters a very difficult and painful process. In the past few decades, only a few very talented and hardworking students have met the challenge and survived; most students unfortunately get discouraged and discontinue their efforts to learn Chinese. A new approach that accommodates the unique features of the Chinese writing system must be found to improve the effectiveness and efficiency of Chinese language teaching.

The new approach that I have been contemplating and experimenting with is to "proceed separately and strike together," which can be referred to as the Dual-Track Approach. The idea is to offer a separate course on Chinese characters alongside the regular elementary Chinese course, with each course having its own focus in the beginning (i.e., the first semester). Thus, spoken Chinese can be taught without being hampered by the written forms that are usually presented in a regular Chinese language course, and fundamental knowledge of Chinese characters can be taught systematically according to the intrinsic regularity of Chinese characters and in compliance with the pedagogical principle of going from the easy to the difficult. Later (i.e., in the second semester), when students have mastered a couple hundred basic Chinese characters and several dozen radicals, and when students have become familiar with Chinese sounds and the tonal system and have learned some useful daily expressions, they will be ready to learn to speak and write the same thing at the same time.

On the Chinese characters track, characters should be taught according to their intrinsic regularity as shown below:

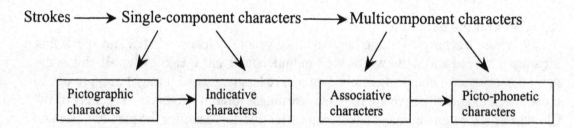

To implement this new approach, I have found no suitable and adequate book on the market. I have written this book in the hope that it will make it possible to teach and learn the fundamentals of Chinese characters using this new approach. A lot of the materials included in the book have been used in the Chinese characters course I have offered since the fall of 2002 at the University of Vermont. I also conducted an experimental study at the end of the fall semester in 2002. The resulting statistical analysis showed that students who took the Chinese characters course (one third of whom had never learned Chinese before and did not take the regular Chinese language course at the same time during the semester) did significantly better in a test on Chinese radical recognition and application than those who took only a regular Chinese language course.[1]

We should not burden the students who have no Chinese language background with the task of memorizing the pronunciation of each character. Forcing them to memorize the pronunciation of each character in the beginning creates cognitive overload and prevents students from quickly accumulating the basic characters needed to continue to learn more characters. I have found that my students can quickly establish the link between the shape and the meaning of many basic characters without being bothered with learning how to pronounce them. The advantages of offering a separate course on Chinese characters have been or are beginning to be recognized by many of my colleagues in the field of Chinese language teaching. This book will assist Chinese language instructors offering a course of this kind at their universities to help their students learn Chinese characters with ease and confidence.

Structure of the book

Taking a new approach, the book presents Chinese characters according to their intrinsic regularity rather than the sequence of the characters used as follow-ups in teaching spoken Chinese. The book focuses on the connections between the shapes and meanings of basic Chinese characters and makes it possible for students to learn to identify the meanings of these characters from their shapes without bothering to learn their pronunciations at the elementary level.

The book first provides basic knowledge of the history (Chapter 1) and the characteristics of Chinese characters (Chapter 2). This allows instructors to present a whole picture of Chinese characters at the beginning of the course. The book then introduces the strokes and correct stroke order for writing characters by focusing on 14

---

[1] The paper reporting the result of the statistics analysis, entitled "The Necessity and Practice of Offering a Course on Chinese Characters at the Beginning Level," was presented at the 4th International Conference on Chinese Language Pedagogy, held in Kunming on July 2-4, 2004, and was published in the 2004 Supplementary Issue of the *Journal of Yunnan Normal University (Teaching and Research on Chinese as a Foreign Language Edition)* on pp. 98-101.

characters used as numbers (Chapter 3). In the next five chapters (Chapters 4-8), 100 basic pictographic single-component characters as well as the strokes and correct stroke order are introduced. Based on these characters, 20 indicative characters are presented next (Chapter 9). Then 15 characters for directions and positions, containing not only pictographic and indicative characters but also phonetic loan characters, are presented (Chapter 10), serving as the transition from learning single-component characters to learning multicomponent characters. In the next four chapters (Chapters 11-14), 80 multicomponent characters are presented, exemplifying how the characters introduced in the previous chapters can be used as components in forming multicomponent characters. These include 20 associative characters (Chapter 11) formed by two or more basic characters, 20 reduced forms of basic characters used as semantic components (Chapter 12), another 20 commonly used semantic components (Chapter 13), and 20 picto-phonetic characters (Chapter 14). The problematic and more-complex strokes, the basic structures of multicomponent characters, and the methods used to simplify the traditional forms of some Chinese characters are also discussed (Chapters 9-14). As the conclusion of the book, Chapter 15 addresses four important questions related to learning Chinese characters after using this book.

The book not only provides students with a fundamental knowledge of 229 basic characters (including 120 of the most frequently used and most productive single-component characters, 80 of the most frequently used multicomponent model characters, and 29 frequently used characters for numbers, positions, and directions) but also gives them interactive exercises designed to help them retain the knowledge they get from each chapter and acquire the skills of recognizing and writing these characters.

For each of the characters covered in the book, its forms in the oracle-bone and bronze inscriptions, in the seal, clerical, regular, and normalized scripts, and in the semi-cursive and cursive scripts are presented after the explanation of the character. If a character has more than one form in the oracle-bone and bronze inscriptions, usually only the earliest one is presented. If no form of a character in the oracle-bone or bronze inscriptions has yet been discovered, there will be a blank in the box for that form of the character. The purpose of presenting the various forms for each character is to help students gain a sense of the historical development of a character. Although the semi-cursive and cursive styles were developed concurrently with the regular script, they did not become printing types later on as the regular script did. They have remained handwritten forms used for daily practical purposes; in addition, they have been a form of art (calligraphy). Therefore, the semi-cursive and cursive styles for each character are also presented for students to learn to recognize, appreciate, and imitate.

Recognizing that students have different Chinese language backgrounds, learning purposes, and motivations as well as abilities, each of the chapters (Chapters 3-14) that introduce Chinese characters has five sections to address the needs of different learners. The more Chinese language background students have, the more sections in each of these chapters they should take on. While the first section (i.e., Fundamental Knowledge) is the minimum for everybody, the next two sections (i.e., Challenge 1 and Challenge 2) are for more serious students with no Chinese language background, and the last two sections (i.e., Challenge 3 and Challenge 4) are extra, for students who have already had some Chinese language background. Instructors and independent learners can decide if only the first, the first three, or all of the five sections in each chapter should be used.

Suggestions for instructors using this book

With a good understanding of the rationale and the structure of the book as well as of one's own students, an instructor may already know very well how this book can be best used. The following suggestions are provided for instructors.

Offer an independent course of 1-3 credits on Chinese characters alongside a regular elementary Chinese language course in the very first semester. If scheduling a separate course on Chinese characters is difficult, then set aside one Chinese language class time each week to learn Chinese characters with this book.

The first section (Fundamental Knowledge) of Chapters 3-14 focuses on the connection between the meaning and the shape of each character by using illustrations and etymological explanations. This section is designed to help students recognize the meaning of each basic character from its shape. For true beginners (i.e., students without any Chinese language background), instructors may choose to use this first section in Chapters 3-14 and then let students take on Challenge 1, which requires them to be able to write these characters. We can also consolidate what students have just learned by asking them to take on Challenge 2, which has exercises that require students to apply their knowledge.

Students who have no Chinese background are encouraged, but should never be required, to take on Challenges 3 and 4 unless they have learned the Chinese sound system and know *pinyin*, the Romanized Chinese alphabet.

As there are also a good number of students who can already speak a little Chinese but are not able to read and write Chinese characters, each of the chapters (except Chapters 1, 2, and 15) has two additional sections that provide more knowledge about the characters as well as pronunciation and writing exercises. These sections may be used to challenge more ambitious students. Challenging students does not mean making Chinese characters more difficult and painful for them to learn. To facilitate learning I have composed a four-line verse with all the characters introduced in each respective chapter. The character verses can be used to help those students with some Chinese speaking skills to appreciate and enjoy the sounds of the language as well as establish the link between the shape and the sound of each character with ease.

This book will also benefit independent learners without a Chinese language background. Simply reading it will also help students at all levels to learn and appreciate Chinese characters.

Chapter 1 第一章
The History of Chinese Characters 汉字的历史

To learn the Chinese language seriously, to understand it precisely, and to appreciate it fully, one needs to learn its written forms: Chinese characters.

To learn Chinese characters well, it is helpful to know the ways in which characters were constructed and the historical developments characters have undergone.

I. The Ways in Which Characters Were Constructed 汉字的创制

Chinese characters, unlike the writing system of any alphabetical language, are formed with no letters or combination of letters to represent the sounds of the Chinese language. Rather, they are symbols constructed and used to convey meanings as well as sounds that indicate meanings. Although we still do not know exactly how long Chinese characters have been in existence, we do know that Chinese characters have had a history as a highly developed writing system for no less than 3,300 years.

In the earliest known stages of written Chinese, there were six kinds of Chinese characters: 1) pictographic characters, 2) indicative characters, 3) associative characters, 4) picto-phonetic characters, 5) explanative characters, and 6) phonetic loan characters. The first five kinds (1, 2, 3, 4, and 5) are categorized according to the ways characters were created, and the last one (6) complemented the other methods by borrowing existing characters to refer to things that no characters had been created for.

The following table summarizes the six categories of Chinese character construction:

Table 1: *Six Categories of Chinese Character Construction*

	Categories	Explanations	Examples*	
1	Pictographic Characters	Characters created by drawing a sketch to depict a material object	人 person	木 tree
2	Indicative Characters	Characters created by 1) drawing an abstract sign to indicate an abstract concept or 2) adding or changing a stroke to an existing pictographic character to indicate a new concept	上 upper	本 root
3	Associative Characters	Characters created by combining two or more pictographic components to infer a new meaning	木 + 木 = 林 tree + tree = woods	人 + 木 = 休 person + tree = rest
4	Picto-phonetic Characters	Characters created by combining a pictographic component that represents a meaning category and another component that indicates the sound of the whole character	氵 + 林 = 淋 water+(sound)=shower	氵 + 木 = 沐 water + (sound) = wash

5	Explanative Characters	Characters created with a pictographic component to help explain the meaning added to another component that represents both the sound and meaning of the whole character	木 + 支 = 枝 tree + branch = branch (sound)	氵 + 益 = 溢 water + spill = spill (sound)
6	Phonetic Loan Characters	Characters originally created for one concept but borrowed to represent another concept with the same pronunciation	六 six (originally "hut")	北 north (originally "back")

* The examples given in this table use modern Chinese characters, which have become more logographic than pictographic. Please refer to Table 2 on page 5 for the historical development of Chinese characters.

These six kinds of Chinese characters, which were summarized and exemplified by Xu Shen in his *An Analysis and Explanation of Characters* (《说文解字》) at the beginning of the first century AD, reflect the earliest stages of the creation and use of Chinese characters.

The first major way of creating Chinese characters that came into use was the pictographic method. The human body or body parts as well as things that can be observed in nature were depicted in simple drawings based on their most conspicuous and differentiated traits. However, an abstract concept is not expressed easily by drawing a picture, so the indicative method, in which a symbol was added to a drawing to indicate the concept, was adopted. When a meaning could be sensed or deduced by combining two existing pictographs, a combined form was produced to save the trouble of creating a new pictograph. This method of combing two existing pictographs is called the associative method. When a meaning could not be expressed by creating a character with the associative method, then the picto-phonetic method was deployed. The picto-phonetic method forms a character with a pictograph as one part to indicate the major category of meaning and another part to indicate the pronunciation of the whole character. When a pictographic component representing both the sound and the meaning could not express the meaning clearly enough, another pictographic component was added to clarify or differentiate the meaning of the whole character from others. This method is the explanative method. The explanative method was also deployed when a character was borrowed (but never returned) to mean something else simply because this borrowed character had the same pronunciation as the new idea, which as yet had no character to express it. These borrowed characters are called phonetic loan characters.

The picto-phonetic method has been the most productive in creating characters. Because the explanative method has not been clearly understood for many years and because a lot of work to distinguish explanative characters from picto-phonetic characters has still not been satisfactorily done, many explanative characters are confused with picto-phonetic characters. Nevertheless, it is widely accepted that over 90 percent of the characters used today are picto-phonetic in a broad sense. Of course, because of developments and changes in the language over the past few thousand years, in modern Chinese no more than 30 percent of the picto-phonetic characters contain a phonetic component that can accurately represent the pronunciation of the whole character.

Regardless of how a character was created, when created it almost always had the trait of a pictograph one way or another. Over thousands of years, the pictographic essence slowly faded and is no longer visually obvious in modern Chinese characters. Now, formed with various kinds of lines, dots, and hooks, Chinese characters are highly symbolic. They mostly appear as logographs rather than pictographs. In other words, they look more like symbols than drawings.

II. The Development of Chinese Characters 汉字的发展

The history of the Chinese characters can be divided into two major periods: ancient writing and modern writing. Associated with these two periods, there are six major writing styles, starting from the earliest systematic form of Chinese characters inscribed on oracle bones from about 3,300 years ago.

During the ancient writing stage, characters we can still see today were inscribed on tortoise shells and animal bones and cast or inscribed on bronze bells and vessels. Chinese characters inscribed on tortoise shells and animal bones are often referred to as "oracle-bone inscriptions," and those cast or inscribed on bronze bells and vessels are often called "bronze inscriptions." Oracle-bone inscriptions date to the Shang Dynasty (1711-1066 BC) in China while bronze inscriptions were common in the Zhou Dynasty (1066-256 BC). The characters' size, positioning, complexity, and textual format in the oracle-bone inscriptions are inconsistent, but the size and the textual format in the bronze inscriptions are more fixed. In bronze inscriptions, the characters are more symmetrical and the strokes are simpler.

Toward the end of the Zhou Dynasty, the Qin State began to use a new script both to write on bamboo strips and pieces of silk and to inscribe onto rocks or precious stones. This script is called the "seal script," which is still used for inscribing names on a seal. After the Qin State conquered the other six states during the Warring States Period (475-221 BC), unified China, and established the Qin Dynasty (221-206 BC), the seal script was decreed as the standard of writing for the whole country. In the seal script, the positioning of characters and complexity of forms became consistent, and all the characters were roughly square in shape. However, the character strokes became lengthened, curved, and complicated.

Because a large of number of documents had to be written or copied as part of the administrative work after the unification of China, the seal script with its lengthened and curved strokes was quite time-consuming and cumbersome. Among local officials at the lower levels of the government who dealt with relatively unimportant documents, a new script was created to save time. This new script continued to be developed in the Han Dynasty (206 BC-220 AD) and became the officially approved formal way of writing. This script is now referred to as the "official script" or "clerical script" (隶书).

The clerical script is very different from the seal script as there are four basic simplifications and modifications for convenience and speed of writing as well as for tidiness: 1) the curved strokes in the seal script became somewhat straighter, 2) the overall number of strokes was reduced, 3) some different components were merged into one, and 4) some components were modified and simplified. The change from the seal script to the clerical script is often referred to as the "official change" or "clerical change" (隶变). This change, the largest transformation of Chinese character structure, dropped the pictographic appearance of Chinese characters almost completely and established the foundation of the structures for the modern Chinese characters. Thus, in the history of

Chinese character development, the clerical script is viewed as the turning point dividing ancient writing and modern writing.

The Ancient Writing Period (古体字时期), from the earliest known oracle-bone inscriptions in the late Shang Dynasty to the development of the seal script, lasted about 1,160 years, and the Modern Writing Period (今体字时期), from the time of the clerical change to the present, has lasted more than 2,200 years. This period of time in the history of Chinese character development is still considered modern because the structures of Chinese characters have remained the same from the clerical change until today.

Although the structures of Chinese characters have not changed since the clerical change, the strokes of Chinese characters have undergone two major changes: regularization (楷化) and normalization (规范化).

Toward the end of the Han Dynasty (206 BC-220 AD), strokes with an undulate end, which was a common feature of characters in the clerical script, became smooth and straight in the regular script (楷书), and some thick curvy lines seen in the clerical script changed to hooks in the regular script. This change is known as "regularization" (楷化). As the strokes were relatively smoother, straighter, and clearer in the regular script, it was easier to read and write and became widespread. The invention of printing helped the regular script, used as one of the major printing types, become widely accepted as the standard form of Chinese writing. Such calligraphers as Zhong Yao in the Three Kingdoms Period (220-280 AD), Wang Xizhi and Wang Xianzhi in the Eastern Jin Dynasty (317-420 AD), Ouyang Xun, Yan Zhenqing, and Liu Gongquan in the Tang Dynasty (618-907), Su Shi, Huang Tingjian, and Mi Fu in the Song Dynasty (960-1279 AD), and Zhao Mengfu in the Yuan Dynasty (1279-1368 AD), among others, also contributed to making the regular script the standard for young students to admire, imitate, learn, and master. The regular script has been the standard of Chinese writing for more than 1,800 years, with the semi-cursive and cursive styles developing concurrently. However, as there are many variations of the semi-cursive and cursive styles, they have never become standardized printing types. Instead, they have been used for everyday communication and appreciated as a form of art.

Although the regular script changed the appearance of strokes in the clerical script, many characters remained complicated. Some characters have variations resulting from many centuries of use, during which time character variants with fewer strokes and simpler structures were created for convenience. Other characters have variations arising from a lack of uniformity among printing types after the invention of printing. Although these alternative forms of characters were popularly used for years, they were never officially recognized or accepted as the "standard forms of characters" (正体字) up to the 1950's.

In the first three and half decades of the 20th century, attempts to accept these "nonstandard forms of characters" (俗体字) officially and to continue to simplify more Chinese characters were made, but they failed. However, these efforts laid the foundation for the language reform that took place in the second half of the 20th century. After World War II and the civil war in China in the late 1940's, the systemization, simplification, and standardization of Chinese characters was finally on the agenda of the Chinese government. A special government organization, first called the Committee for Chinese Language Reform and later the National Language Commission, was established in 1954 to direct and oversee the normalization of Chinese characters.

Table 2: *Historical Development of Chinese Characters*

Major Periods		Major Forms	Most Popular Time	Characteristics	Examples
Ancient Writing Period 古体字时期		Oracle-Bone Inscription 甲骨文	The Shang Dynasty (1711-1066 BC)	Character size, positioning, form complexity, and textual format are not consistent.	person tree water fire / cart horse bird cloud
		Bronze Inscription 金文	The Zhou Dynasty (1066-256 BC)	Character positioning and form complexity continue to be inconsistent, but the size and the textual format are more fixed. Strokes are simpler, and characters are more symmetrical.	
		Seal Script 篆书	The late Zhou Dynasty and the Qin Dynasty (221-206 BC)	Many variant forms of characters are eliminated. Character positioning and form complexity become consistent. Many of the strokes are lengthened, curved, and complicated, and all the characters are roughly square in shape.	
Modern Writing Period 今体字时期	Traditional Form 传统字	Clerical Script 隶书	The Qin Dynasty and the Han Dynasty (206 BC-220 AD)	Character strokes are less curved, the number of strokes is reduced, and many of the components are modified and simplified. Pictographic shapes are completely dropped. Characters have become writing symbols.	人木水火 車馬鳥雲
		Regular Script 楷书	From the late Han Dynasty to 1955	Character strokes are smoother and straighter than those in the clerical script. They are clear and easy to read and write.	人木水火 車馬鳥雲
	Normalized Form 规范字		From 1955 to the present	1,027 character variants are eliminated. The number of strokes in 2,235 of the characters is systematically reduced. The forms of characters for printing types and the stroke order are standardized.	人木水火 车马鸟云

In 1955, to systemize Chinese characters, the "List of the First Group of Standardized Forms of Variant Characters" was officially published. Among the 810 sets of characters, with 2 to 6 variants in each set, 1,027 variant characters (异体字) were abolished, and the remaining characters have been referred to as "the standard forms of characters" (正体字) since then.

In 1956, after several years of discussion, revision, and consultation, the "Scheme for Simplifying Chinese Characters" was officially published. In 1964, the "Complete List of Simplified Characters" was officially published, and it was republished in 1986. The list has 2,235 simplified characters in total, and 1,116 of them are frequently used today in daily life. In fact, among the 2,235 simplified characters, only 482 of them are basic. The remaining 1,753 characters in the list are all derivatives of these 482 basic simplified characters. Among the 482 basic ones, about 20 percent were newly created in the 1950's, while the other 80 percent were created beginning over several thousand years ago.

In 1964, in an effort to standardize the printed forms of Chinese characters, the "List of Chinese Character Forms for General Printing" was officially published. The list has provided the standardized printed forms for 6,196 generally used characters.

In 1988, the "List of Frequently Used Characters in Modern Chinese," which includes 3,500 characters, was officially published, and later in the same year, the "List of Generally Used Characters in Modern Chinese" was also officially published. This second list contains 7,000 characters, which include the 3,500 frequently used ones contained in the first list.

In 1997, "Standard Stroke Order for Generally Used Characters in Modern Chinese" was officially published.

After 50 years of simplifying, systemizing, and standardizing work on Chinese characters, they are considered normalized. The "normalized forms of Chinese characters"(规范汉字) consist of two major types: 1) the inherited characters (传承字), that is, the Chinese characters that were created and officially accepted before the 20th century and had the same structure since the "clerical change" without being simplified until today, and 2) the simplified characters (简化字), or those Chinese characters that have been simplified, systemized, or standardized since the 1950's. The original forms of the characters, before being simplified or replaced by today's simple forms, are often referred to as "complex characters" (繁体字). The complex characters together with the inherited characters constitute the "traditional forms of Chinese characters" (传统汉字).

Modern Chinese characters (现代汉字), which is another term referring to the normalized forms of Chinese characters, are officially recognized and used in Mainland China, Singapore, and Malaysia as well as at the United Nations, while the traditional forms of Chinese characters are still in use in Taiwan, Hong Kong, and Macao as well as among some Chinese communities outside China.

Among modern Chinese characters, about 75 percent are inherited characters, about 5 percent are newly created characters or characters that have been borrowed to represent new modern meanings, and about 20 percent are simplified characters.

The history of the development of Chinese characters in terms of the evolution of forms over the past several thousand years has demonstrated three general trends in the process.

First, Chinese characters used to be drawings depicting objects and have slowly become more-abstract writing symbols. Second, Chinese characters started with the pictographic method as the major way of character construction and have ended up using more and more abstract symbols developed from pictographs as phonetic symbols in new characters. Third, Chinese characters used to have a lot of pictographic symbols that were complicated to write, but they have now become logographs that are much easier to write than before.

In this book, we will focus on the inherited characters, but we will also look at the simplified characters and their counterparts in the traditional forms.

Table 3: *Definitions for Terms About Chinese Characters*

Terms	Definitions	Examples
Inherited characters 传承字	Characters that were created and officially accepted before the 20th century, the structures of which have remained the same since the "clerical change"	日月水火 sun, moon, water, fire
Simplified characters 简化字	Characters that have been simplified, systemized, or standardized since the 1950's and have been officially accepted	车马它泪 cart, horse, it, tears
Complex characters 繁体字	Characters that have been replaced by the simplified characters	車馬牠淚 cart, horse, it, tears
Traditional Chinese Characters 传统汉字	Characters that consist of a) inherited characters and b) complex characters that have been simplified	a) 日月水火 b) 車馬牠淚
Normalized Chinese Characters 规范汉字	Characters that consist of a) inherited characters and b) simplified characters	a) 日月水火 b) 车马它泪
Modern Chinese Characters 现代汉字	Another term for "normalized Chinese characters"	Same as above

III. Chapter Review Exercises 本章复习

Choose the best answers to fill in the blanks.
1. Chinese characters became a mature writing system _____.
   a. at least 3,000 years ago
   b. about 2,000 years ago
   c. about 1,000 years ago
   d. about 500 years ago

2. _____ is not one of the six categories of character construction.
   a. Pictograph
   b. Associative
   c. Simplification
   d. Indicative

3. A character that was constructed with the associative method would combine
    _____.
    a. a phonetic component and a pictographic component
    b. two phonetic components
    c. a pictographic component and another abstract symbol
    d. two pictographic components

4. Ninety percent of modern Chinese characters are considered _____.
    a. picto-phonetic compounds
    b. pictographs
    c. associative compounds
    d. phonetic loans

5. The formula that can best represent the explanative method is _____.
    a. a semantic component + another semantic component
    b. a semantic component + a phonetic component
    c. a semantic component that is also phonetic + another semantic component
    d. a pictographic component + an abstract symbol

6. Modern Chinese characters are _____.
    a. mostly picture-like, and their meanings can be figured out from their
        shapes
    b. highly symbolic, and their meanings can only be understood through
        learning
    c. mostly phonetic symbols
    d. all simplified in the second half of the 20th century

7. The earliest form of Chinese characters recognized as a mature system is
    _____.
    a. the oracle-bone inscription
    b. the bronze inscription
    c. the seal script
    d. the clerical script

8. The development of Chinese characters entered the Modern Writing Period from
    the Ancient Writing Period when _____ came into use.
    a. the seal script
    b. the bronze inscription
    c. the regular script
    d. the clerical script

9. The Modern Writing Period started as early as about 2,000 years ago, but it is still
    considered modern because _____.
    a. the history of Chinese characters is so long that 2,000 years or so is a
        relatively short period of time

    b. the basic structures of Chinese characters have remained the same since then, although the shapes of strokes have changed a lot

    c. the shapes of strokes in characters have remained the same since then, although the basic structures of characters have changed a lot

    d. most of the characters still mean the same today as they did 2,000 years ago.

10. One prominent difference between the clerical script and the regular script is _____.

    a. the meanings expressed by characters

    b. the structures of characters

    c. the number of strokes in characters

    d. the shapes of strokes in characters

11. _____ of the officially accepted simplified characters in the 1950's are the creations of that time, and the rest were the creations of the past few thousand years before the 1950's.

    a. None

    b. 20 percent

    c. 50 percent

    d. 80 percent

12. The normalized forms of characters mainly consist of _____.

    a. traditional characters and simplified characters

    b. traditional characters and inherited characters

    c. inherited characters and simplified characters

    d. inherited characters and complex characters

13. Another term that has been used to refer to the normalized forms of characters is _____.

    a. "modern Chinese characters"

    b. "traditional Chinese characters"

    c. "simplified Chinese characters"

    d. "inherited Chinese characters"

14. The simplified characters are widely used _____.

    a. in mainland China only

    b. in Taiwan only

    c. in Taiwan, Hong Kong, and Macao as well as some Chinese communities outside China

    d. in mainland China, Singapore, and Malaysia as well as the United Nations

15. _____ of modern Chinese characters are inherited characters.

    a. 50 percent

    b. 60 percent

    c. 70 percent

    d. 75 percent

16. The transition _____ is not a general trend in the history of the development of Chinese characters.

    a. from concrete visual symbols depicting material objects to abstract writing symbols

    b. from phonetic symbols to ideographic characters

    c. from complicated pictographs to simple writing symbols

    d. from pictographs expressing concepts to picto-phonetic symbols indicating meanings and sound

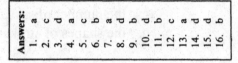

Answers:
1. a
2. c
3. d
4. a
5. c
6. b
7. a
8. d
9. b
10. d
11. b
12. c
13. a
14. d
15. d
16. b

Chapter 2 第二章
Characteristics of Chinese Characters 汉字的特点

In the previous chapter, you learned the six formations of Chinese characters and a brief history of Chinese characters. In this chapter, you will look at some other major characteristics of Chinese characters, which will help you to learn them with confidence.

I. One Character, One Phonetic Syllable 一个汉字，一个音节

A Chinese character is an independent symbol that expresses a meaning. What makes the pronunciation of a character easy is the fact that the pronunciation of any character in Chinese is monosyllabic: one character represents one phonetic syllable. A phonetic syllable is a segment of pronunciation that contains one vowel sound with or without one or more consonant sounds. Vowel sounds are loud and clear. When they are pronounced, the airflow from the lungs vibrates the vocal chords, and the shape of the mouth and the position of the tongue make the different sounds. For example, in English, the letters a, e, i, o, and u are often used to represent the vowel sounds in a word. In the English word "go," the vowel sound is represented by the letter o, and as there is only one vowel sound, there is only one syllable. In the word "wonderful," the letters o, e, and u represent three vowel sounds; therefore, there are three syllables: won • der • ful. Besides vowel sounds, there are consonant sounds, such as g, w, n, d, r, f, and l in the words "go" and "wonderful." The consonant sounds are not as loud as vowel sounds because when they are produced, one part of your mouth (the lips, the teeth, the tongue, the soft palate, and so on) is used to block the airflow from the lungs. Many consonant sounds do not even require the vibration of the vocal chords; they are voiceless, such as f in the word "wonderful." In Chinese, it does not matter what a character means, and it does matter whether the character is a word by itself or a morpheme (part of word), it is always pronounced with one syllable.

II. The Sound System for Chinese Characters 汉字的发音系统

If one character is pronounced as one syllable, then how is a Chinese syllable formed? Like a syllable in English, a syllable in Chinese always has a vowel sound with or without one or more consonant sounds. Although Chinese has some different vowel and consonant sounds from English, what makes the Chinese sound system really different from that of English is the fact that except for two nasal sounds and one retroflex sound, no consonant sounds appear at the end of a syllable in Chinese. Instead, a vowel, a combination of a vowel and a nasal sound, or a retroflex sound always forms the ending of a Chinese syllable. In Chinese, consonants appear at the beginning of a syllable. For this reason, Chinese consonants are often referred to as "initials" and Chinese vowels as "finals." The vowel and nasal combinations that appear at the end of a syllable are referred to as "nasal finals," and the retroflex sound that ends a syllable is called the "retroflex final."

Since Chinese characters do not spell out their initials and finals with letters or combinations of letters as does an alphabetical language such as English, a phonetic notation system has to be used to know how a character is pronounced. The most widely used system throughout the world for studying Chinese and for noting the pronunciation of Chinese characters is the Chinese Phonetic Alphabet (*pinyin*), which employs 26 Latin letters that are the same as those in the English alphabet. This phonetic notation system will be used throughout the book.

In the Chinese sound system, there are 21 initials and 40 finals.

1) 21 initials: *b, p, m, f, d, t, n, l, g, k, h, zh, ch, sh, r, j, q, x, z, c,* and *s*
2) 40 finals:

- 9 simple finals: *a, o, e, ê, i, -i [ɿ], -i [ʅ], u,* and *ü*
- 14 compound finals: *ai, ei, ao, ou, ia, io, ie, iao, iou, ue, uo, uai, uei,* and *üe*
- 16 nasal finals: *an, en, ang, eng, ian, in, iang, ing, ong, uan, uen, uang, ueng, üan, ün, iong*
- 1 retroflex final: *er*

These 21 initials and 40 finals, as well as a possible zero initial, form 410 different syllables in the "common speech" of the Chinese language, which is often referred to as Mandarin Chinese (see Tables 5-8). Native English speakers can quickly master the pronunciation of most of the sounds in Chinese. Only five sounds may present some challenges to some people. Four of them are initials: *j, q, x,* and *r*. The last one is the umlaut sound *ü*, which English does not have. However, by knowing the tongue position and by practicing a bit, all native English speakers can produce these sounds well, or at least approximate these sounds so closely that their communication in Chinese will not be hindered.

What really makes the Chinese sound system challenging is the tones. Each syllable in Chinese has as many as four different tones. The first tone is a high-pitched level tone and is represented by a horizontal bar (‾) over the vowel letter or the most salient vowel letter in a syllable. The second tone is a rising tone, and its tone mark is a rightward up-going line (´). The third tone is a dipping tone. It starts low and goes even lower before going up. The third tone is indicated by a small tick (ˇ). The fourth tone is a falling tone, and its tone mark (`) is a short line going downward to the right. The following table shows the pitch heights of these four tones:

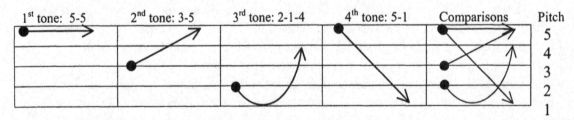

Table 4: *Pitch Heights for the Four Tones in Chinese*

The meaning of a syllable is different with different tones, and different characters are used to represent different meanings. For example, *dā* means "to build" and is represented by 搭; *dá* means "to answer" and is represented by 答; *dǎ* has the meaning of "to hit" and its character is 打; and *dà* means "big" and is represented by 大. If the tone

Table 5: *Table of Syllables with Finals a, o, e and Finals That Begin with a, o, and e.*

	a [a]	o [ɔ]	e [ɤ]	ê [ɛ]	er [əɻ/ɐɻ]	ai [aɪ]	ei [eɪ]	ao [aʊ]	ou [ou]	an [an]	en [ən]	ang [aŋ]	eng [ɤŋ]
Ø	1234 a	1234 o	1234 e	1234 ê	234 er	1234 ai	2 ei	1234 ao	1 34 ou	1 34 an	1 4 en	12 4 ang	1 eng
b [p]	1234 ba	1234 bo				1234 bai	1 34 bei	1234 bao		1 34 ban	1 34 ben	1 34 bang	1234 beng
p [pʰ]	12 4 pa	1234 po				1234 pai	12 4 pei	1234 pao	1 pou	12 4 pan	12 4 pen	1234 pang	1234 peng
m [m]	1234 ma	1234 mo	me			234 mai	234 mei	1234 mao	23 mou	1234 man	12 4 men	23 mang	1234 meng
f [f]	1234 fa	2 fo					1234 fei		3 fou	1234 fan	1234 fen	1234 fang	1234 feng
d [t]	1234 da		2 de			1 34 dai	3 dei	1234 dao	1 34 dou	1 34 dan	4 den	1 34 dang	1 34 deng
t [tʰ]	1 34 ta		4 te			12 4 tai		1234 tao	12 4 tou	1234 tan		1234 tang	12 teng
n [n]	1234 na		2 4 ne			34 nai	34 nei	234 nao	4 nou	234 nan	4 nen	234 nang	2 neng
l [l]	1234 la	lo	4 le			2 4 lai	1234 lei	1234 lao	1234 lou	234 lan		234 lang	234 leng
g [k]	1234 ga		1234 ge			1 34 gai	3 gei	1 34 gao	1 34 gou	1 34 gan	1 4 gen	1 34 gang	1 34 geng
k [kʰ]	1 3 ka		1234 ke			1 34 kai	1 kei	34 kao	1 34 kou	1 34 kan	3 ken	12 4 kang	1 keng
h [x]	123 ha		12 4 he			1234 hai	1 hei	1234 hao	1234 hou	1234 han	234 hen	12 4 hang	12 4 heng
zh [tʂ]	1234 zha		1234 zhe			1234 zhai	4 zhei	1234 zhao	1234 zhou	1 34 zhan	1 34 zhen	1 34 zhang	1 34 zheng
ch [tʂʰ]	1234 cha		1 34 che			12 chai		123 chao	1234 chou	1234 chan	12 4 chen	1234 chang	1234 cheng
sh [ʂ]	1234 sha		1234 she			1 34 shai	2 shei	1234 shao	1234 shou	1 34 shan	1234 shen	1 34 shang	1234 sheng
r [ʐ]			34 re					234 rao	2 4 rou	23 ran	234 ren	1234 rang	12 reng
z [ts]	12 za		2 4 ze			1 34 zai	2 zei	1234 zao	1 34 zou	1234 zan	3 zen	1 4 zang	1 4 zeng
c [tsʰ]	1 ca		4 ce			1234 cai	4 cei	123 cao	4 cou	1234 can	12 cen	1 3 cang	2 4 ceng
s [s]	1 34 sa		4 se			1 4 sai		1 34 sao	1 34 sou	1 34 san	1 sen	1 34 sang	1 seng
j [tɕ]													
q [tɕʰ]													
x [ɕ]													

Table 6: Table of Syllables with i or ī Combinations as Finals

	-i [ɿ]	-i [ʅ]	i [i]	ia [ia]	io [iɔ]	ie [iɛ]	iao [iau]	iou [iou]	ian [iɛn]	in [in]	iang [iaŋ]	ing [iŋ/iəŋ]
Ø			1234 yi	1234 ya	1 yo	1234 ye	1234 yao	1234 you	1234 yan	1234 yin	1234 yang	1234 ying
b [p]			1234 bi			1234 bie	1 34 biao		1 34 bian	1 4 bin		1 34 bing
p [pʰ]			1234 pi			1 3 pie	1234 piao		12 4 pian	1234 pin		12 ping
m [m]			1234 mi			1 4 mie	234 miao	4 miu	234 mian	23 min		234 ming
f [f]												
d [t]			1234 di			12 die	1 4 diao	1 diu	1 34 dian			1 34 ding
t [tʰ]			1234 ti			1 34 tie	1234 tiao		1234 tian			123 ting
n [n]			234 ni			1 4 nie	34 niao	1234 niu	1234 nian	2 nin	2 4 niang	234 ning
l [l]			234 li	3 lia		34 lie	1234 liao	1234 liu	234 lian	234 lin	234 liang	1234 ling
g [k]												
k [kʰ]												
h [x]												
zh [tʂ]		1234 zhi										
ch [tʂʰ]		1234 chi										
sh [ʂ]		1234 shi										
r [ʐ]		4 ri										
z [ts]	1 34 zi											
c [tsʰ]	1234 ci											
s [s]	1 34 si											
j [tɕ]			1234 ji	1234 jia		1234 jie	1234 jiao	1 34 jiu	1 34 jian	1 34 jin	1 34 jiang	1 34 jing
q [tɕʰ]			1234 qi	1 34 qia		1234 qie	1234 qiao	12 qiu	1234 qian	1234 qin	1234 qiang	1234 qing
x [ɕ]			1234 xi	124 xia		1234 xie	1234 xiao	1 34 xiu	1234 xian	1 4 xin	1234 xiang	1234 xing

Table 7: *Table of Syllables with u or u Combinations as Finals*

	u [u]	ua [ua]	uo [uɔ]	uai [uaɪ]	uei [ueɪ]	uan [uan]	uen [uən]	uang [uaŋ]	ueng [uɤŋ]	ong [ʊŋ]
Ø	1234 wu	1234 wa	1 34 wo	1 34 wai	1234 wei	1234 wan	1234 wen	1234 wang	1 4 weng	
b [p]	234 bu									
p [pʰ]	1234 pu									
m [m]	234 mu									
f [f]	1234 fu									
d [t]	1234 du		1234 duo		1 4 dui	1 34 duan	1 34 dun			1 34 dong
t [tʰ]	1234 tu		1234 tuo		1234 tui	12 tuan	12 4 tun			1234 tong
n [n]	234 nu		2 4 nuo			3 nuan				2 4 nong
l [l]	234 lu		1234 luo			234 luan	12 4 lun			234 long
g [k]	1234 gu	1 34 gua	1234 guo	1 34 guai	1 34 gui	1 34 guan	34 gun	1 34 guang		1 34 gong
k [kʰ]	1 34 ku	1 34 kua	4 kuo	34 kuai	1234 kui	1 3 kuan	1 34 kun	12 4 kuang		1 34 kong
h [x]	1234 hu	12 4 hua	1234 huo	2 4 huai	1234 hui	1234 huan	12 4 hun	1234 huang		1234 hong
zh [tʂ]	1234 zhu	1 3 zhua	12 zhuo	1 34 zhuai	1234 zhui	1 34 zhuan	1 3 zhun	1 4 zhuang		1 34 zhong
ch [tʂʰ]	1234 chu	1 chua	1 4 chuo	1 34 chuai	12 chui	1234 chuan	123 chun	1234 chuang		1234 chong
sh [ʂ]	1234 shu	1 3 shua	1 4 shuo	1 34 shuai	234 shui	1 4 shuan	34 shun	1 3 shuang		
r [ʐ]	234 ru		4 ruo		34 rui	3 ruan	4 run			23 rong
z [ts]	234 zu		1234 zuo		34 zui	1 34 zuan	1 zun			1 34 zong
c [tsʰ]	1 4 cu		1 34 cuo		1 4 cui	12 4 cuan	1234 cun			12 cong
s [s]	12 4 su		1 3 suo		1234 sui	1 4 suan	1 3 sun			1 34 song
j [tɕ]										
q [tɕʰ]										
x [ɕ]										

Table 8: *Table of Syllables with ü or ü Combinations as Finals*

	ü [y]	üe [yɛ]	üan [yɛn]	ün [yn]	iong [yʊŋ/iʊŋ]
Ø	1234 yu	1 4 yue	1234 yuan	1234 yun	1234 yong
b [p]					
p [pʰ]					
m [m]					
f [f]					
d [t]					
t [tʰ]					
n [n]	3 nü	4 nüe			
l [l]	234 lü	4 lüe			
g [k]					
k [kʰ]					
h [x]					
zh [tʂ]					
ch [tʂʰ]					
sh [ʂ]					
r [ʐ]					
z [ts]					
c [tsʰ]					
s [s]					
j [tɕ]	1234 ju	12 4 jue	1 34 juan	1 4 jun	3 jiong
q [tɕʰ]	1234 qu	12 4 que	1234 quan	2 qun	2 qiong
x [ɕ]	1234 xu	1234 xue	1234 xuan	12 4 xun	12 xiong

Notes for the above four tables:
1) The International Phonetic Alphabet (IPA) is used in the square brakets "[ ]" to provide a phonetic transcription for each initial and final.
2) All four tables have the 21 initials plus Ø representing the zero initial in the first column.
3) An empty cell indicates that the combination of the initial and the final is impossible.
4) The numbers used in the cells represent the possible tones for the syllable.
5) According to the spelling rules of *pinyin*,
   a. the two dots over *ü* are omitted when *ü* is preceded by *j*, *q*, and *x*;
   b. the second letter in *iou*, *uei*, or *uen* is dropped when they are preceded by an initial;
   c. with no initial, the simple finals *i*, *u, and ü* are spelled as *yi*, *wu*, and *yu*;
   d. with no initial, the first letter *i* in a compound final is replaced by *y*, and the first letter *u* in a compound final is replaced by *w*.

is not pronounced correctly, and the syllable is not in context, it is nearly impossible for listeners to know which *da* the speaker means, except when a corresponding character is written down or shown at the same time.

III. One Syllable, Often Many Different Characters 一个发音，多个汉字

Although it is convenient that each character is pronounced in one syllable, the tones make it a bit complicated. What makes the relationship between characters and the Chinese sound system more complicated is the homonyms. In the Chinese sound system, there are only about 400 different syllables. Even with as many as four different tones for each syllable, the total number of syllables with different tones in use in Chinese is 1,196. On the other hand, the total number of Chinese characters that have been created since ancient times is 54,678, as collected and recorded in the *Giant Dictionary of the Chinese Language* (《汉语大字典》) published in 1990. If we take the 2,500 characters that were found to be the most frequently used and divide by 1,196, which is the total number of different syllables in Mandarin Chinese, we still get about two characters for each syllable on average. In reality, some syllables are represented by more than two of these 2,500 most frequently used characters. Take the syllable *yi* as an example. The first tone syllable *yī* has four characters (一 衣 医 依); the second tone syllable *yí* has six characters (仪 宜 姨 移 遗 疑); the third tone syllable *yǐ* has six characters (乙 已 以 蚁 倚 椅); and the fourth syllable *yì* has sixteen characters (亿 义 艺 忆 议 亦 异 役 译 易 疫 益 谊 意 毅 翼). It would be impossible to understand what someone means when he or she says *yi* in any of the four tones out of the context.

Y. R. Chao, a Chinese linguist, composed a story called "The History of Mr. Shi Eating Lions" in classical Chinese.[1] It presents an extreme case of the homonymic phenomenon in Chinese by using 34 characters that share the same initial and final with four different tones. It goes like this:

Shīshì Shí Shī Shǐ

Shíshì shīshì shīshì, shì shī, shì shí shí shī. Shì shíshí shì shì shì shī. Shí shí, shì shí shí shì shì. Shì shí, shì shīshì shì shì. Shì shí shì shí shī, shì shīshì, shǐ shì shí shī shìshì. Shì shí shì shí shī shì, shì shíshì. Shíshī shì, shì shì shì shì shíshì. Shíshì shì, shī shí shì shì shíshì. Shí shí, shì shí shì shí shī shī. Shí shí shì shì.

By listening to the story or looking at the story in Chinese alphabetic spellings, no native Chinese speakers would be able to understand it. To understand the story, one has to read it in Chinese characters as follows:

---

[1] See Y. R. Chao's *Language Issues*, Beijing: Commerical Press, 1980, p. 149. （见赵元任：《语言问题》。北京：商务印书馆，1980年，149页。）

施氏食狮史

石室诗士施氏，嗜狮，誓食十狮。氏时时适市视狮。十时，适十狮
适市。是时，适施氏适市。氏视是十狮，恃矢势，使是十狮逝世。
氏拾是十狮尸，适石室。石室湿，氏使侍拭石室。石室拭，氏始试
食是十狮尸。食时，始识是十狮尸，实十石狮尸。试释是事。

The English translation is as follows:

```
The History of Mr. Shi Eating Lions

     Mr. Shi, a poet in a stone room, liked to eat
lions and was determined to eat ten lions. He often
went to the market to see lions. At ten o'clock,
when ten lions were at the market, Mr. Shi was also
at the market. Seeing that there were ten lions, he
used arrows and killed the ten lions. He collected
the ten lion corpses and went to the stone room. The
stone room was wet, and he asked a servant to wipe
the stone room. The stone room was wiped, and he
started to try to eat the ten lion corpses. He did
not realize the ten lion corpuses were really ten
stone lion corpses until he started to eat. Try to
explain this matter.
```

Although this story is not composed in modern Chinese and is a humorously exaggerated homonymic case in the Chinese language, it does exemplify the importance of retaining Chinese characters, and it indicates the difficulty (some would argue impossibility) of using a phonetic system to replace Chinese characters. Now you can understand better the statement at the beginning of the first chapter: "To learn the Chinese language seriously, to understand it precisely, and to appreciate it fully, one needs to learn its written forms: Chinese characters."

IV. Not All Characters Are in Active Use 并非所有汉字都用

The number of Chinese characters has grown over the last few thousand years, as indicated by the major dictionaries that have been compiled during that time. *An Analysis and Explanation of Characters* (《说文解字》) is the earliest dictionary we know of. Xu Shen put it together around 121 AD as a collection of 9,353 characters. *The Kangxi Dictionary* (《康熙字典》), complied by Zhang Yushu, Chen Tingjing, and others in 1716 under the rule of Emperor Kangxi in the Qing Dynasty, includes 47,043 characters. *The Giant Dictionary of the Chinese Language* (《汉语大字典》), complied and published by Xu Zhongshu and others in 1990, records 54,678 characters.

However, the number of characters in general use now is about 7,000. Among the 7,000 characters, as mentioned earlier, the general public now frequently uses only about 3,500 characters, found in the "List of Frequently Used Chinese Characters" published by the National Language Commission of China in 1988. Furthermore, a test done in 1987 by Shanxi University, under the request of the National Language Commission of China, on randomly selected samples of printed materials containing two million characters, shows that 1) the 2,500 most frequently used characters in the first part of the list can account for 97.97 percent of the characters that appeared in the data; 2) the next 1,000 characters in the second part of the list can cover 1.51 percent; and 3) the total coverage rate of the two groups (with 3,500 characters in all) is 99.48 percent.

This means that if someone could recognize the first 2,500 characters in the list, he or she would run into only two unrecognized characters in every one hundred characters that appear in Chinese printed materials similar to the tested data. Having learned the remaining 1,000 characters in the list, he or she would be able to reduce the number of unrecognized characters to one in every one hundred characters seen in the same kind of printed materials.

V. Not All Characters Are Words 汉字不都是词

It is encouraging to realize that knowing 3,500 of the most frequently used characters enables one to recognize 99 percent of the characters that appear in newspapers, magazines, and books for general readers, but that knowledge does not guarantee the reader's understanding because characters are not always words in modern Chinese. One must know the relationship between the characters in a word and the meaning of a word formed by two or more characters. In classical Chinese, most words are only one character. However, in modern Chinese, most words contain two characters; as a result, many of the characters that would be words in classical Chinese are now morphemes that form words in modern Chinese.

In designing the Chinese Language Proficiency Test for learners of Chinese as a foreign language in 1992, the Testing Center of the Office for the National Chinese Language Proficiency Test Committee developed the "General Outline of the Chinese Vocabulary Levels and Graded Chinese Characters" (《汉语水平词汇与汉字等级大纲》). It is based on sixteen different lists of Chinese words (not characters) and includes 8,822 carefully selected words at four levels (see Table 9). The developers predicted that 3,000 of the most frequently used words would cover 86 percent of the language materials for general readers, 5,000 would cover 91 percent, and 8,000 would cover 95 percent. If we look at the number of characters that the selected 8,822 words contain and compare them with the 2,500 most frequently used characters in the "List of Frequently Used Characters" mentioned earlier, we see that the developers' prediction about the vocabulary coverage rate is believable. The 8,822 words in the "General Outline" have been formed with 2,905 characters, of which 2,485 characters overlap with the 2,500 characters that appear in the first part of the "List of Frequently Used Chinese Characters."

Table 9: The Number of Words and Characters at the Four Levels in the "General Outline"

	Level A	Level B	Level C	Level D	Total
Words	1,033	2,018	2,202	3,569	8,822
Characters	800	804	601	700	2,905

Although not all characters are words, knowing the meaning of characters will help one learn the meaning of the words they form. If the best way to increase one's English vocabulary is to learn prefixes, suffixes, and roots, then similarly the most efficient way to increase one's Chinese vocabulary is to learn Chinese characters, especially those most frequently used characters.

VI. The Smallest Units Forming a Character Are Strokes 笔画是汉字的 最小构成单位

As mentioned in Chapter 1, Chinese characters originated as pictographs, but through thousands of years of development and changes, the pictographic essence slowly faded and is not visually obvious in modern Chinese characters, which now are highly symbolic and constructed with various kinds of lines, dots, and hooks. These lines, dots, and hooks are strokes. A stroke is a mark made by a writing instrument, such as a pen, that is put down on a writing object, such as paper, and moved until it is lifted from the writing object. These strokes are arranged in a special way to form characters. Some characters have two or more components, and these components are also formed by strokes. Strokes are the smallest units used to form characters. In modern Chinese characters, there are six basic strokes: the horizontal stroke, the vertical stroke, the left-falling curved stroke, the right-falling curved stroke, the dot, and the rising stroke.

Table 10: The Six Basic Strokes

	Stroke	Name in Chinese	Name in English
1	一	héng	the horizontal
2	丨	shù	the vertical
3	丿	piě	the left-falling curved
4	乀	nà	the right-falling curved
5	丶	diǎn	the dot
6	丿	tí	the rising

If a thousand-mile journey starts with the first step, then a journey to learn Chinese characters should start with these six simple strokes as the first step.

Please try to learn the name of each stroke in Chinese. You will find that it is much easier to name strokes in Chinese than in English, as their names in Chinese are all monosyllabic.

VII. Chapter Review Exercises 本章复习

I. Choose the best answers to fill in the blanks.

1. A vowel is a sound that _____.
   a. is comparatively loud and clear
   b. is weaker and softer than consonants
   c. is often blocked by a part of the mouth when pronounced
   d. can be voiceless

2. A syllable is a segment of pronunciation that contains _____.
   a. no vowels
   b. consonants only
   c. a vowel with or without consonants
   d. two or three vowel sounds

3. In a Chinese syllable, consonants are called initials because _____.
   a. they never appear at the end of a syllable
   b. they mostly appear at the beginning of a syllable
   c. they never appear at the beginning of a syllable
   d. they are not always needed before vowels to form a syllable

4. There are _____ different tones in Chinese.
   a. three
   b. six
   c. two
   d. four

5. Most Chinese sounds are _____ those in English.
   a. completely different from
   b. more difficult to pronounce than
   c. very similar to
   d. harder to learn than

6. Most words in modern Chinese are formed with _____ characters.
   a. one
   b. two
   c. three
   d. four

7. Chinese characters can hardly be replaced by any alphabetical system because
   _____.
   a. homonyms in Chinese may hinder communications without characters
   b. Chinese characters are easy and fun to write
   c. no alphabetical system can represent the tones well
   d. Chinese students do not like to write alphabetized Chinese

8. More than 54,000 Chinese characters have been recorded in a comprehensive Chinese dictionary; however, only _____ are in general use.
    a. 28,000
    b. 21,000
    c. 14,000
    d. 7,000

9. To recognize 97 percent of the characters that appear in printed matter for the general Chinese public, one needs to know at least _____ characters.
    a. 2,000
    b. 2,500
    c. 3,500
    d. 7,000

10. To reach the highest level set by the Testing Center of the Office for the National Chinese Language Proficiency Test Committee, a student of Chinese as a foreign language needs a vocabulary of _____ words.
    a. about 8,000
    b. about 6,000
    c. about 4,000
    d. about 2,000

11. Which of the following statements is wrong?
    a. It is common that several Chinese characters share the same pronunciation.
    b. A Chinese character contains only one syllable.
    c. No alphabetic system can replace the Chinese writing system.
    d. All Chinese characters are words.

12. The smallest units that are used to form Chinese characters are _____.
    a. simple pictures
    b. abstract symbols
    c. strokes
    d. lines

Answers:	
1.	a
2.	c
3.	b
4.	d
5.	c
6.	b
7.	a
8.	d
9.	b
10.	a
11.	d
12.	c

II. Speak and Write.

1. Say the names of the six basic strokes, and then match the names with the strokes on the right:

héng	／
shù	丶
piě	✓
nà	｜
diǎn	一
tí	＼

2. Imitate the models of the basic strokes with a pencil. Pay special attention to the direction of the movement for each stroke.

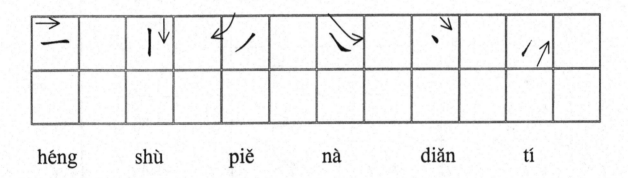

héng　　　shù　　　piě　　　nà　　　diǎn　　　tí

Chapter 3 第三章
Characters for Numbers 数字

I. Fundamental Knowledge 基础知识

A. Shapes and Meanings 见形思义

Numbers 数字	Ancient Character Shape 古字形	Modern Character Shape 今字形	Meaning 字义
1	一	一	one
2	二	二	two
3	三	三	three
4	四	四	four
5	五	五	five
6	六	六	six
7	七	七	seven
8	八	八	eight
9	九	九	nine
10	十	十	ten
100	百	百	hundred
1,000	千	千	thousand
10,000	萬	万	ten thousand
100,000,000	億	亿	hundred million

B. Trace the Roots and Understand with Reason 追根溯源，晓之以理

Chinese characters have undergone changes for thousands of years, and the characters used now are highly abstract symbols. This section provides etymological information to help you understand and memorize the meaning of each Chinese character. The semi-cursive style and the cursive style of each character are also provided. As calligraphic styles, they are viewed as a form of art in China. In everyday life, people also write in one or another kind of semi-cursive or cursive style.

一   One horizontal line represents the meaning "one."

Oracle	Bronze	Seal	Clerical	Regular	Normal-ized	Semi-cursive	Cursive
一	一	一	一	一	一	一	一

二   Two horizontal lines represent the meaning "two."

Oracle	Bronze	Seal	Clerical	Regular	Normal-ized	Semi-cursive	Cursive
二	二	二	二	二	二	二	二

三   Three horizontal lines represent the meaning "three."

Oracle	Bronze	Seal	Clerical	Regular	Normal-ized	Semi-cursive	Cursive
三	三	三	三	三	三	三	三

四   The number four was originally made in the same way as one, two, and three, and was represented by four parallel lines arranged horizontally. However, for an unknown reason, the character that represents a nose with nostrils and means "to breathe" was borrowed to replace the four parallel lines symbolizing four. Therefore, 四 is a phonetic loan.

Oracle	Bronze	Seal	Clerical	Regular	Normal-ized	Semi-cursive	Cursive
亖	𠙹	四	四	四	四	四	四

五   The number five is in the middle of the nine single digits (1-9) and was originally represented by an X, and then by an X between two parallel horizontal lines. Now the back slash stroke has become a horizontal stroke with a downward turn.

Oracle	Bronze	Seal	Clerical	Regular	Normal-ized	Semi-cursive	Cursive
X	区	区	五	五	五	五	五

六   六 originally portrayed a hut. Because the words for "hut" and "six" were pronounced the same in ancient Chinese, the character for "hut" was borrowed to represent "six" as well. It was used so frequently to mean "six" that another character had to be created to refer to its original meaning—"hut." Now this character is used exclusively to mean "six."

Oracle	Bronze	Seal	Clerical	Regular	Normal-ized	Semi-cursive	Cursive
六	六	六	六	六	六	六	六

七   This character has been borrowed to mean "seven." It originally meant "to cut." The idea of cutting was conveyed through the character, which has a horizontal line symbolizing an object such as a stick and a vertical crossing line symbolizing the tool used to break the object into pieces. As the character came to represent "seven," the idea of cutting began to be represented by this character with a knife graph added to its right side: 切.

Oracle	Bronze	Seal	Clerical	Regular	Normal-ized	Semi-cursive	Cursive
十	七	七	七	七	七	七	七

八   Just as 七 originally meant "to cut," 八 originally meant "to divide." After it was borrowed to mean "eight," the idea of dividing was represented by this character with a knife graph added beneath it: 分. Now 八 exclusively means "eight."

Oracle	Bronze	Seal	Clerical	Regular	Normal-ized	Semi-cursive	Cursive
)(	八	)(	八	八	八	八	八

九 九 represents an elbow and upper arm on the bottom right with a raised forearm with fingers at the end on the left. It originally meant "elbow" but was borrowed to mean "nine" because the pronunciations of the words for "nine" and "elbow" were the same in ancient Chinese. Later on, another character was created to mean "elbow."

Oracle	Bronze	Seal	Clerical	Regular	Normal-ized	Semi-cursive	Cursive
𠃑	𠂉	九	九	九	九	九	九

十 While such numbers as one, two, and three were represented by one, two, and three horizontal lines, respectively, "ten" was represented by one vertical line or one vertical line with a dot in the middle recalling a very old way of indicating ten by making a knot on a piece of rope. Later, this dot became a horizontal line across the vertical line; therefore, 十 now means "ten" in Chinese.

Oracle	Bronze	Seal	Clerical	Regular	Normal-ized	Semi-cursive	Cursive
丨	丨	十	十	十	十	十	十

百 The character for "one hundred," 百, was formed by 一 on top and 白 underneath. While 一 represents "one," indicating that this character is a number, 白 depicts a candlelight flame and means "bright" or "white." However, the pronunciation of 白 rather than its meaning contributed to the formation of the character 百. 白 serves as a clue to the pronunciation of the character 百.

Oracle	Bronze	Seal	Clerical	Regular	Normal-ized	Semi-cursive	Cursive
百	百	百	百	百	百	百	百

千 千, which means "one thousand," was created in the same way as 百: one part (一) is associated with the meaning, and the other part (亻) is associated with the pronunciation. However, 亻, meaning "person," does not now help people know the pronunciation of 千, as the pronunciation for 亻 is completely different from that of 千 because of phonological changes that took place over a long period of time.

Oracle	Bronze	Seal	Clerical	Regular	Normalized	Semi-cursive	Cursive
彳	孑	秊	千	千	千	千	δ

万

万 was also created with 一 to indicate that it is a number. The lower part of the character is a variation of "person." However, unlike 千, which has 一 in the middle of "person," 万 has 一 above "person." Although 万 has been used to mean "ten thousand" for about two thousand years, it was not officially recognized and designated to replace its variant form until 1956. The variant form, 萬, is a graph of a scorpion that was borrowed to mean "ten thousand," as it was pronounced the same as "ten thousand" in classical Chinese. As this character was used so frequently to mean "ten thousand," a different character was created for "scorpion."

Oracle	Bronze	Seal	Clerical	Regular	Normalized	Semi-cursive	Cursive
¥	¥	禺	萬	萬	万	万	万

亿

This character, which means "one hundred million," came into existence relatively late, as it does not appear in oracle-bone inscriptions and bronze inscriptions. Perhaps, people did not need such a big number until later. The method of using 一 to indicate that a character is a number, which was done with 百, 千, and 万, was dropped when 亿 was created, probably because no suitable place could be found for 一 in the character, or the pronunciation of "one hundred million" is too close to that of 一. However, 亻 (person) continued to be used as a component of the character. It is on the left side of the character, and 乙 on the right side indicates the pronunciation for the whole character. Before 乙 was used as the phonetic component in the character, 意 had acted as the phonetic component.

Oracle	Bronze	Seal	Clerical	Regular	Normalized	Semi-cursive	Cursive
		億	億	億	亿	亿	亿

C. Recognition Reinforcement 辨认巩固练习

1.　Link each character on the first line with its corresponding meaning in English on the second line:

八　　五　　一　　九　　四　　三　　七　　十　　二　　六

one　two　three　four　five　six　seven　eight　nine　ten

2.　Link each character on the left side with its corresponding meaning in English on the right side:

千　　　　hundred

亿　　　　thousand

万　　　　ten thousand

百　　　　hundred million

3.　Provide the meaning in English for the following characters:

四 _____　　六_____　　九_____　　七_____

万 _____　　百_____　　五_____　　亿_____

三 _____　　八_____　　千_____　　十_____

II. Challenge 1: Write the Characters 挑战一: 知义书形

A. Strokes in Characters 详说笔画

If you are able to recognize all the characters in this chapter, you should then try to write them because this will enhance retention.

In addition, writing characters can be a form of art. By writing characters, you will develop your ability to appreciate Chinese calligraphy aesthetically. However, you should learn to write the regular style first. Learning the regular style is usually viewed as "walking," while the semi-cursive is viewed as "jogging," and the cursive as "running." Trying to run before being able to walk is counterproductive. Before you learn to write well in the regular style, it is enough for you to be able to recognize characters in the semi-cursive style or cursive style.

Chinese characters are formed by various kinds of strokes, and the regular style of a Chinese character is written stroke by stroke. As mentioned in the previous chapter, a stroke is a mark made when a writing instrument is put down on a writing object and is moved until it is lifted from the writing object. After the pointed brush pen was invented as the preferred writing instrument for Chinese characters about two thousand years ago, the strokes in Chinese characters began to become more regularized than those in oracle-bone inscriptions and bronze inscriptions and less curvy than those in the seal script.

Now pencils and pens are the most common writing instrument for Chinese. When you learn how to write characters today, you should by all means use pens or pencils first rather than a brush pen. Later, if you become interested in Chinese calligraphy, you can start to use brush pens.

Thirty-three different strokes are used in modern Chinese characters; however, only six basic strokes are briefly explained and practiced in the previous chapter. Some of these six basic strokes have variant shapes, and each has its own specific name, but for convenience, we will still use the names of the prototype strokes to refer to their variants, and we will not count the variants in the total number of different strokes.

Apart from the six basic strokes, there are also three dependent strokes: the bend, the turn, and the hook. Dependent strokes cannot be used independently; they have to be attached to at least one other kind of stroke to form a complex stroke. The six basic strokes and the three dependent strokes together form all of the twenty-seven complex strokes used in modern Chinese characters. You will not learn them all in this chapter but throughout this book. The following table gives a general idea of all the strokes in modern Chinese characters.

Table 11: All the Strokes in Modern Chinese Characters

Stroke		Basic Strokes						Dependent Strokes		
	Name	héng	shù	piě	nà	diǎn	tí	wān	zhé	gōu
	Example	1¹ ⎯ horizontal	2¹ ∣ vertical	3¹ ╱ left-falling	4¹ ╲ right-falling	5¹ 丶 dot	6¹ ╱ rising	bend	turn	hook
Basic Stroke Variants	Variant 1	1² ⎯ short horizontal	2² ∣ short vertical	3² ╱ vertical left-falling	4² ～ leveled right-falling	5² ╱ left dot				
	Variant 2		2³ ∣ pointed vertical	3³ ╱ small left-falling		5³ ╲ big right dot				
	Variant 3			3⁴ leveled left-falling						
Two Strokes Combined	⎯ +			7 ╱					8 ⌐	9 ⌐
	∣ +						10 ↲	11 ∟	12 ∟	13 ↓
	╱ +				14 ✓				15 ✓	
	wān (bending) +									16 ⟩
	wò (crouching) +									17 ⌣
	xié (slanting) +									18 ╲

Three Strokes Combined	⅂+						19 乙 / 20 乁 / 21 乚	22 ⅂
	⅃+						23 亅	
	L+		24 ㄥ				25 ㄣ	
	L+							26 Ｌ
Four Strokes Combined	∠+		27 ㇌				28 ㇈	
	⅂+L							29¹ ㇄ / 29² 乙
	⅂+＼							30 乀
	⅃+）							31 ㇋
	㇈+							32 ㇉
Five Strokes Combined	㇈+							33 ㇡

* Note: Digits in front of each stroke are used to indicate the number of different kinds of strokes in Chinese characters

First, look at the shapes of the basic strokes. Although fountain pens, ballpoint pens, and pencils have been used more and more as writing instruments for Chinese character in the last hundred years, the strokes in Chinese characters have retained characteristics developed by brush pens, which can be seen by close observation of the regular script of Chinese characters. Is the thickness in each stroke exactly the same all way through? No. The thickness of a stroke varies depending on how a brush pen is used to achieve visual elegance and beauty. The horizontal stroke is thick on both ends and thin in the middle. The dot is pointed on the top left side and round at the bottom right side. The right-falling curved stroke is pointed at both ends but thick toward the lower right side. Different pressures that a writer applies to a brush pen create variations in thickness. Knowing how each stroke is written with a brush pen helps one achieve a similar effect when writing with a hard pen. However, it is difficult to learn to write characters with a brush pen first. An easier way is to pay attention to the direction of the movement of each stroke without worrying about the thickness. When you are familiar with each stroke and can write it easily, you can start to try two basic techniques (pressing and lifting) in the right place during the movement of each stroke. The pressing and lifting techniques will take some time to become automatic.

Table 12: *Writing the Six Basic Chinese Character Strokes*

	Strokes		Stroke Names	Stroke Movement	Writing Techniques
1	—		héng the horizontal	From left to right	Press at both ends
2	丨	丨	shù the vertical	From top to bottom	Press at both ends, or press in the beginning at the top and lift in the end at the bottom

3	✓	piě the left-falling curved	From top to lower left	Start by pressing and curve down to the lower left in a lifting manner
4	＼	nà the right-falling curved	From top to lower right	Start lightly and go down to lower right, pressing the hardest before ending in a lifting manner towards the right
5	丶	diǎn the dot	Down to lower right	Start lightly and end with a pressing pause
6	／	tí the rising	Up to right	Start by pressing the pen, and then lift the pen upward to the right

Write these basic strokes again while saying their names in Chinese:

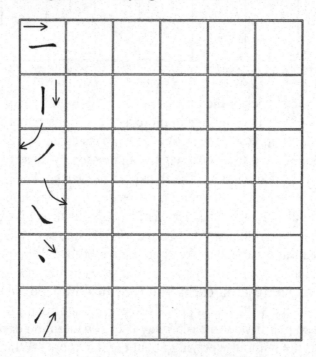

   To write the characters you have learned in this chapter, in addition to the six basic strokes, you need to use the following complex strokes:

フ *héngzhé* (horizontal stroke with a turn), as in 五 百

乛 *héngzhégōu* (horizontal stroke with a turn and a hook), as in 万

乚 *shùwān* (vertical stroke with a bend), as in 四

乚 *shùwāngōu* (vertical stroke with a bend and a hook), as in 七

乛 *héngzhéwāngōu* (horizontal stroke with a turn, a bend, and a hook), as in 九

乙 (a variant of *héngzhéwāngōu*), as in 亿

Write these strokes, and pay attention to the direction of the stroke movement as indicated.

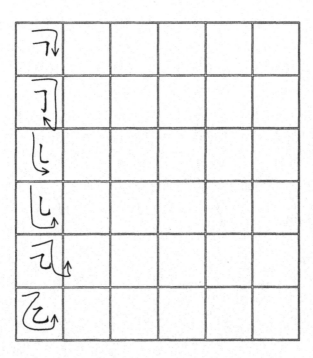

B. Rules for Stroke Order 笔顺规则

If there are more than two strokes in a Chinese character, which stroke should be written first? There are rules for conventional stroke order that help us to balance Chinese characters. The knowledge of stroke order also helps us appreciate other handwritten forms of Chinese.

Stroke Order Rule (1): *From top to bottom.* The strokes at the top of a character should be written before those at the bottom.

For example: 三 (three):　　一 二 三

Stroke Order Rule (2): *From left to right.* The strokes on the left side of a character should be written before those on the right.

For example: 八 (eight): 丿 八

With these two rules in mind, how should 六 (six) be written? Write the character stroke by stroke in the boxes provided below, and compare your strokes with the upside-down answers provided below.

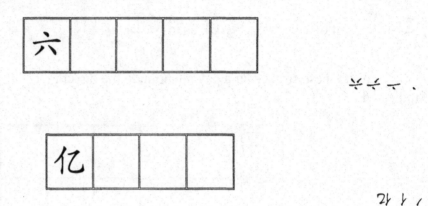

What about 亿?

Stroke Order Rule (3): *The horizontal before the vertical or the left-falling.* The horizontal stroke should be written before the vertical stroke or the left-falling stroke if they cross each other.

For example: 十: 一 十

How should 千 (thousand) be written? Write the character stroke by stroke, and compare your strokes with the upside-down answers provided below.

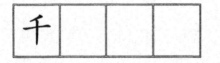

As the short left-falling stroke does not cross the vertical or the horizontal stroke and is at the top, it should be written first according to Rule (1), the horizontal stroke is second, and the vertical is last according to Rule (3).

Stroke Order Rule (4): *The enclosing strokes first, then the enclosed, and finally the sealing horizontal stroke.* The enclosing strokes, which form the sides and top of the frame, should be written first. Strokes inside the frame should be written next, and then the closing stroke, which is usually a horizontal stroke at the bottom of the frame.

For example: 四: 丨 冂 冈 冈 四

How should 百 (hundred) be written? Write the character stroke by stroke, and compare your strokes with the upside-down answers provided below.

C. Write with a Pencil 动手动笔

With knowledge of the strokes and stroke order rules, you are ready to write all the characters in this chapter.

You should always pay attention to the overall shape of each character and learn to write each character proportionally by following the conventional stroke order and by imitating the model characters as closely as possible. Dotted lines inside each box will help you write a proportionally balanced character.

The only way to acquire the ability to write characters is actually to write them. Just as in learning to swim, one ought to jump into water that is deep enough to swim and shallow enough not to get drowned. Just talking about swimming will not enable one to swim. Therefore, let's jump into the water of Chinese characters and swim.

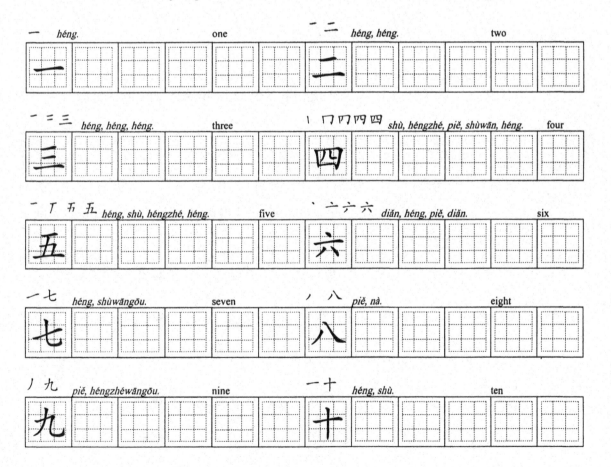

一ナT万百百
héng, piě, shù, héngzhé, héng, héng.　　　hundred

ノ二千
piě, héng, shù.　　　thousand

百						千					

一ブ万
héng, héngzhégōu, piě.　　　ten thousand

ノ亻亿
piě, shù, héngzhéwāngōu .　　　hundred million

万						亿					

Computer technologies have developed so much that both hardware and software for Chinese word processing are readily available. Some people may wonder whether the keyboard will replace pens and pencils for writing Chinese characters; however, pens and pencils are still needed and widely used for writing in English, elementary school students still learn to write using pens and pencils, and learners of English as a foreign language still learn to write in English with pens and pencils, so the answer to whether the keyboard will replace pens and pencils for writing Chinese characters is clear.

III. Challenge 2: Apply Your Knowledge 挑战二: 举一反三

A. Know Many Things by Learning One 闻一知十

1. 十 is ten, and 一 is one. Put them together， 十一 is eleven. What about the following? Fill in the blanks with English and Chinese translations.

   十二 _____   十四 _____   十六_____

   thirteen _____   fifteen _____   seventeen _____

2. 二十 is twenty. What about the following? Fill in the blanks with English or Chinese translations.

   三十 _____   forty _____   五十 _____

   sixty _____   八十 _____   ninety _____

3. Can you figure out what these mean?

   一百 _____   二百 _____   三百 _____

   四千_____   五千_____   六千 _____

七万_____   八万_____   九万_____

4. One million is 一百万 in Chinese, ten million is 一千万, and one hundred million can be 一万万; however, Chinese people prefer to use 一亿 instead.

    What is the English for 五十亿?

    _____

    What about 一亿二千三百四十五万六千七百八十九?

    _____

B. Be Perceptive of the Slightest Differences 明察秋毫

1. Which character in each group have you not yet learned? Circle it.
    a. Group 1
        i. 三   ii. 千   iii. 十   iv. 工

    b. Group 2
        i. 四   ii. 万   iii. 西   iv. 亿

    c. Group 3
        i. 王   ii. 五   iii. 百   iv. 七

    d. Group 4
        i. 六   ii. 九   iii. 八   iv. 人

    Answers:
    a. iv. b. iii. c. i. d. iv.

2. Can you add one stroke to make another character you have learned?
    a. Make as many characters as possible by adding only one stroke
        i. 一

        Answer: 刂 丫 十

        ii. 丿

        Answer: 〈 九

    b. Make characters with one or two more strokes by adding one stroke at a time
        i. 一

Answer: ┼ ┼┼
or: ╷╷ ╷╷╷

3. Which stroke is that?

a. Which character has the stroke *hénzhégōu* (⌐) in it?
    i. 五   ii. 六   iii. 亿   iv. 万

b. Which characters has the stroke *hénzhéwāngōu* (⌐) in it?
    i. 九   ii. 七   iii. 八   iv. 五

c. Which character does NOT have the stroke *hénzhé* (⌐) in it?
    i. 四   ii. 五   iii. 千   iv. 百

d. How many *hén* (一) strokes are in the character 五?
    i. One   ii. Two   iii. Three   iv. Four

e. How many *diǎn* (丶) strokes are there in the character 六?
    i. Four   ii. Three   iii. Two   iv. One

f. Which stroke is *shùwān* (⌐) in the character 四?
    i. The 2nd   ii. The 3rd   iii. The 4th   iv. The 5th

Answers:
a. iv.   b. i.   c. iii.   d. ii.   e. iii.   f. iii.

C. Be Aware of the Complex Counterpart 学简知繁

The traditional forms of Chinese characters, as you learned in Chapter 1, are made up of two elements: inherited characters and complex characters. These complex forms of characters, the simplified counterparts of which have been officially accepted as modern Chinese characters, are still in use in Taiwan, Hong Kong, Macao, and some Chinese communities outside China. In addition, most historical books were written and printed with the complex forms of characters. These forms can also be seen at any historical site in China. Although we will not challenge you to learn the character forms used in the seal script or an earlier form as they are rarely used except in historical or archeological studies or in calligraphy or fine art, we will give you the option to learn to recognize and write the complex forms of the characters in this and subsequent chapters. If you do not want to learn the complex forms now, at the beginning stage, you may skip this section and go on to the next.

1. Comparison. In this chapter, there are only two simplified characters: 万 and 亿. Their corresponding complex forms are 萬 and 億.

	Simplified Form	Complex Form	Meaning
1	万	萬	ten thousand
2	亿	億	hundred million

2. Explanation.

萬. As mentioned earlier, 萬 was originally a graph of a scorpion:

The character was borrowed to mean "ten thousand" as it was pronounced the same as "ten thousand" in ancient Chinese.

億. Like its simplified counterpart 亿, 億 is also a picto-phonetic character. 亻 means "person," implying that the character is used to count the number of people, and 意 represents the sound of the whole character.

3. Writing. Writing these two characters in their complex forms may help you recognize and memorize them, although a more effective way to recognize and memorize them is to be familiar with their overall shapes and to know all their components. As you continue to learn in the next few chapters, the accumulation of knowledge about the commonly used components in Chinese characters will help you memorize characters more effectively. Now, follow the models and write, paying attention to the structure of the characters.

一 十 艹 艹 苎 苧 苎 苩 苩 萬 萬 萬 萬

héng, shù, héng, piě, shù, héngzhé, héng, héng, shù, héngzhégōu, shù, tí, diǎn. ten thousand

萬

丿 亻 亻 仁 仁 仁 仁 倅 倅 倅 偣 億 億 億

piě, shù, diǎn, héng, diǎn, piě, héng, shù, héngzhé, héng, héng, diǎn, wògōu, diǎn, diǎn. hundred million

億

IV. Challenge 3: Pronounce the Characters 挑战三：见形发音

In an alphabetical language, a letter usually represents one or more sounds, and most of the time, it is predictable what letters or combinations of letters represent a certain sound. In Chinese, except for picto-phonetic and explanative characters, no characters provide clues to pronunciation. Even those picto-phonetic and explanative characters that contain a component to indicate the pronunciation do not follow a simple and organized system. An educated Chinese speaker may predict the pronunciation of an unknown character by its phonetic component but will be correct only about 50 percent of the time. Of the 3,500 frequently used Chinese characters, only 30 percent (i.e., about 1,050 characters) contain components that are representative of the pronunciation of the whole characters, but still, the tones of many components are not the same as those of the characters. In order to take advantage of the phonetic components of these 30 percent, one still has to learn these components (which are in fact also characters) one by one so as to establish the link between the shape of a component and a particular Chinese syllable. Therefore, unlike an alphabetical language that uses a small number of letters or combination of letters to represent the sounds of the language, the Chinese language uses thousands of characters as phonetic components in other characters to indicate pronunciation, and with only 30 percent accuracy. Therefore, the more you manage to establish the link between shape and pronunciation, the better you will be able to predict the pronunciation of an unfamiliar character.

Establishing the link between the shape and pronunciation of the first few hundred characters you read will be quite challenging if you have not learned to speak Chinese previously, or if you are learning to speak Chinese at the same time. This is not to say that it is impossible. The following verse, containing all the characters introduced in this chapter, has been specially written to help you listen and read out loud. If you read it out loud as accurately and as frequently as possible, you will be able to memorize the verse as a whole piece, and each character will fall into its own position in the verse. Thus, the memorization of the verse will help you access the meaning, pronunciation, and shape of a character more efficiently. Of course, if you are not ready for this challenge, you can skip this section and go to the next section to practice writing characters or go on to the next chapter to learn to recognize more Chinese characters. As you learn to speak and read Chinese more easily, the ability to recognize characters will also help you, and you can return to this section later.

1. Listen and read (choose the form you prefer):

(In the traditional form)

Yī èr sān, sān èr yī,
一二三，三二一，

Yī èr sān sì wǔ liù qī,
一二三四五六七，

Bā jiǔ shí, shí jiǔ bā,
八九十，十九八，

Bā jiǔ shí bǎi qiān wàn yì.
八九十百千萬億。

(In the normalized form)

Yī èr sān, sān èr yī,
一二三，三二一，

Yī èr sān sì wǔ liù qī,
一二三四五六七，

Bā jiǔ shí, shí jiǔ bā,
八九十，十九八，

Bā jiǔ shí bǎi qiān wàn yì.
八九十百千万亿。

2. Read aloud by looking only at the characters:

(In the traditional form)	*(In the normalized form)*
一二三，三二一，	一二三，三二一，
一二三四五六七，	一二三四五六七，
八九十，十九八，	八九十，十九八，
八九十百千萬億。	八九十百千万亿。

3. Read the following characters aloud with your teacher or someone who can help with your pronunciation:

a. 一二三四五六七八九十，十九八七六五四三二一

b. 十一，十二，十三，十四，十五，十六，十七，十八，十九

c. 二十，三十，四十，五十，六十，七十，八十，九十

d. 一百，二百，三百，四百，五百，六百，七百，八百，九百

e. 一千，二千，三千，四千，五千，六千，七千，八千，九千

f. 一万，二万，三万，四万，五万，六万，七万，八万，九万

g. 十万，二十万，三十万，四十万，五十万，

　　六十万，七十万，八十万，九十万

h. 一百万，二百万，三百万，四百万，五百万，

　　六百万，七百万，八百万，九百万

i. 一千万，二千万，三千万，四千万，五千万，

　　六千万，七千万，八千万，九千万

j. 一亿，二亿，三亿，四亿，五亿，六亿，七亿，八亿，九亿，十亿

V. Challenge 4: Dictation 挑战四：听音书形知义

1. By now, you should be able to recite the character verse for this chapter. Write the verse in Chinese characters and the meaning of each character in the spaces provided below:

Yī	èr	sān	,	sān	èr	yī	,

Yī	èr	sān	sì	wǔ	liù	qī	,

Bā	jiǔ	shí	,	shí	jiǔ	bā	,

Bā	jiǔ	shí	bǎi	qiān	wàn	yì	.

2. Look at the *pinyin*, say it aloud, and write the appropriate character in the first box and the meaning in English in the second.

pinyin	*character*	*meaning*	*pinyin*	*character*	*meaning*
sān			wǔ		
qī			bā		

shí			liù		
èr			yī		
qiān			bǎi		
yì			wàn		
sì			jiǔ		

3. Have your instructor dictate the characters or words covered in this chapter.

Chapter 4 第四章
Basic Characters for Nature and Plants
与自然及植物有关的基本汉字

I. Fundamental Knowledge 基础知识

A. Shapes and Meanings 见形思义

	Drawing 图	Ancient Character Shape 古字形	Modern Character Shape 今字形	Meaning 字义
1.		日	日	sun
2.			月	moon
3.		川	水	water
4.		火	火	fire
5.		土	土	soil
6.		山	山	mountain
7.		川	川	river/valley
8.		王	玉	jade

9.		戶	石	rock
10.		田	田	farmland/field
11.		金	金	metal
12.		木	木	wood
13.		竹	竹	bamboo
14.		禾	禾	crop
15.		艸	艸	grass
16.		米	米	rice
17.		气	气	air
18.		云	云	cloud
19.		雨	雨	rain

| 20. | 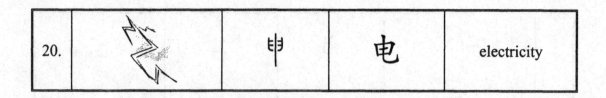 | 申 | 电 | electricity |

B. Trace the Roots and Understand with Reason 追根溯源，晓之以理

日 By looking only at the shape of this character, one can hardly tell that it represents the "sun." The character in the bronze inscription was a circle with a dot in the center. After the clerical change for ease of writing, the circular stroke became straight lines.

Oracle	Bronze	Seal	Clerical	Regular	Normalized	Semi-cursive	Cursive
⊡	⊙	日	日	日	日	日	∂

月 Although the moon can also be round, most of the time it is in the form of a crescent. Therefore, the crescent shape is the most conspicuous feature associated with the moon, and the character was formed according to it. The modern form 月 represents not only the "moon" but also "meat" when it is used as a component to form other Chinese characters related to meat or flesh.

	Bronze	Seal	Clerical	Regular	Normalized	Semi-cursive	Cursive
	)	D	月	月	月	月	3

水 Before the clerical change, the character 水 had a winding line in the middle indicating the flow of water, with dots on both sides representing drops of water. The character represents "water."

Oracle	Bronze	Seal	Clerical	Regular	Normalized	Semi-cursive	Cursive
⅍	川	川	水	水	水	水	为

火 Meaning "fire," this character in the oracle-bone inscription period depicts a flame. Then in the bronze inscription period, it started to be formed with lines and dots.

Oracle	Bronze	Seal	Clerical	Regular	Normal-ized	Semi-cursive	Cursive
火	火	火	火	火	火	火	火

土   In the oracle-bone inscription period, 土 was depicted as a clod above the ground. From the bronze inscription period to the present, it has represented the idea of "soil" or "earth."

Oracle	Bronze	Seal	Clerical	Regular	Normal-ized	Semi-cursive	Cursive
土	土	土	土	土	土	土	土

山   山 is depicted as several mountain peaks in the oracle-bone and bronze inscriptions. The modern character is a simplified depiction of "mountain."

Oracle	Bronze	Seal	Clerical	Regular	Normal-ized	Semi-cursive	Cursive
山	山	山	山	山	山	山	山

川   In the oracle-bone inscriptions, 川 looked like a river, with three dots representing water running between two lines that stand for river banks. In the bronze inscriptions, the three dots became a line; thus there were three curvy lines. The original meaning of the character is "river," and its derived meaning is "valley."

Oracle	Bronze	Seal	Clerical	Regular	Normal-ized	Semi-cursive	Cursive
川	川	川	川	川	川	川	川

玉   玉 means "jade." In the oracle-bone inscriptions, it was depicted as several jade ornaments linked together with a string. Notice that the three horizontal strokes were of the same length in the bronze inscriptions and in the seal script. However, beginning with the clerical script, the horizontal strokes were no longer the same length, and a dot was added to distinguish it from the character 王, which means "king."

Oracle	Bronze	Seal	Clerical	Regular	Normal-ized	Semi-cursive	Cursive
王	王	王	玉	玉	玉	玉	玉

石 The idea of "rock" was pictured as a piece of rock that falls from a cliff, as is sometimes seen after a rainy day when pieces of rock slip from a nearby mountain to the road.

Oracle	Bronze	Seal	Clerical	Regular	Normal-ized	Semi-cursive	Cursive
石	石	石	石	石	石	石	石

田 This character depicts a piece of farmland, in which crisscrossed ridges have been built for irrigation. As can be seen, the character has not changed much over three thousand years. It is translated as "farmland" in English.

Oracle	Bronze	Seal	Clerical	Regular	Normal-ized	Semi-cursive	Cursive
田	田	田	田	田	田	田	田

金 The earliest form of this character in the bronze inscriptions had two big dots on the left, indicating two pieces of metal, and a furnace on the right. Alternatively, the element on the right could have been a tool or weapon made of metal: the top is the shape of an arrowhead and the bottom an axe.   In the seal script, the form of the character changed. The two dots indicating pieces of metal now appeared in the earth (土) in the lower part of the character, and the top part resembled the character 今, which indicated the pronunciation of the whole character.

Oracle	Bronze	Seal	Clerical	Regular	Normal-ized	Semi-cursive	Cursive
	金	金	金	金	金	金	金

木 木 originally represented "tree," as depicted in the oracle-bone and bronze inscriptions. In modern Chinese, it mostly refers to "wood," and a different character is used for "tree."

Oracle	Bronze	Seal	Clerical	Regular	Normal-ized	Semi-cursive	Cursive
木	木	木	木	木	木	木	求

竹   竹 represents "bamboo." The earliest form of this character, in the bronze inscriptions, looked like two bamboo stems with leaves.

Oracle	Bronze	Seal	Clerical	Regular	Normal-ized	Semi-cursive	Cursive
	竹	竹	竹	竹	竹	竹	竹

禾   A heavy head of grain bending on a stalk was the prototype for the character 禾 in the bronze inscriptions. It represented "standing grain." In modern Chinese characters, the heavy head became a short left-falling stroke.

Oracle	Bronze	Seal	Clerical	Regular	Normal-ized	Semi-cursive	Cursive
禾	禾	禾	禾	禾	禾	禾	禾

艸   艸 originally came from 中, which was doubled and meant "young grass with stalks and leaves." However, this character is rarely used in modern Chinese. Instead, the character 草 is used to refer to "grass." 艸 was transformed into ⺾, which is used as a component in other characters related to "grass" or "herbaceous plants."

Oracle	Bronze	Seal	Clerical	Regular	Normal-ized	Semi-cursive	Cursive
屮	屮屮	艸	艸	艸	⺾	艸	艸

米   米 means "rice." In the oracle-bone inscriptions, the idea of "rice" was represented by scattered dots indicating grains of rice and by a horizontal stroke that indicates a sieve, which differentiates this character from other characters that also have scattered dots to mean to water.

Oracle	Bronze	Seal	Clerical	Regular	Normal-ized	Semi-cursive	Cursive
川	米	米	米	米	米	米	米

气　　In the oracle-bone inscriptions, 气 is three lines, indicating airflow. To differentiate it from the character 三 for three, two lines became curved in the bronze inscriptions. The phonetic component 气 and the semantic component 米 formed another character, 氣, to refer to "sacrificial grains and animals" or "animal feed." However, 氣 was somehow used more and more often to mean "air" in place of 气 until 1956 when 气 was officially reinstated to mean "air" again.

Oracle	Bronze	Seal	Clerical	Regular	Normal-ized	Semi-cursive	Cursive
三	气	气	氣	氣	气	气	气

云　　In the oracle-bone and bronze inscriptions, 云 had two horizontal strokes, indicating layers of clouds, and a curved line representing a cirrus. For a long time, 云 was borrowed as a phonetic loan word meaning "to say." At the same time, 雨 as added on top of 云 to create the character 雲, meaning "cloud." In the normalized form, 雨 is omitted, and the character 云 has resumed its original meaning, "cloud."

Oracle	Bronze	Seal	Clerical	Regular	Normal-ized	Semi-cursive	Cursive
云	云	雲	雲	雲	云	云	云

雨　　In its earliest form in the bronze inscription period, the character meaning "rain" had a horizontal stroke representing the sky and dots representing rain drops. However, the character has gradually changed its form since the bronze inscription period.

Oracle	Bronze	Seal	Clerical	Regular	Normal-ized	Semi-cursive	Cursive
雨	雨	雨	雨	雨	雨	雨	雨

电   电 means "electricity." Originally it was used to refer to "lightning," as depicted in the oracle-bone inscriptions. Lightning is often seen when it is raining; therefore, in the bronze inscriptions, the character has two parts, with "rain" on top and a depiction of lightning below. In the normalized form that began to be used in 1956, the top part was omitted, and the vertical stroke in the lower part is extended upward.

Oracle	Bronze	Seal	Clerical	Regular	Normal-ized	Semi-cursive	Cursive
𩃬	電	電	電	電	电	电	电

C. Recognition Reinforcement 辨认巩固练习

1.   Go back to the beginning of this chapter. Look at the drawings and the characters. Then cover the drawings and try to remember the meaning of each character.

2.   Link each character on the first line with its corresponding meaning in English on the second line.

    a. 火   水   月   土   日

      sun   mountain   moon   water   fire   soil

    b. 玉   田   山   石   川

      mountain   river   soil   jade   rock   farmland

    c. 艸   竹   金   禾   木

      wood   bamboo   sky   grass   standing grain   metal

    d. 雨   云   米   气   电

      air   electricity   cloud   wood   rain   rice

3.   There are ten characters on the left side and eleven words in English on the right side. Put the letter for each character in the blank next to the corresponding English word. In each group, there is an extra blank that should be left empty.

Group 1:

a. 田

b. 日

c. 电

d. 雨

e. 月

f. 水

g. 土

h. 竹

i. 金

j. 石

_____ water

_____ rock

_____ electricity

_____ rain

_____ farmland

_____ sun

_____ metal

_____ bamboo

_____ soil

_____ fire

_____ moon

Group 2:

a. 气

b. 火

c. 云

d. 川

e. 艸

f. 米

g. 玉

h. 禾

i. 山

j. 木

_____ river

_____ grass

_____ wood

_____ rice

_____ water

_____ cloud

_____ jade

_____ standing grain

_____ mountain

_____ fire

_____ air

4.   Provide the meaning in English for each of the following characters:

日_____   月_____   水_____   火_____   土_____

山_____   川_____   玉_____   石_____   田_____

金_____   木_____   竹_____   禾_____   艸_____

米_____   气_____   云_____   雨_____   电_____

II. Challenge 1: Write the Characters 挑战一: 知义书形

A. Strokes in Characters 详说笔画

So far, you have learned these strokes:

1) Basic strokes:

一 *héng*   丨 *shù*   丿 *piě*   乀 *nà*   丶 *diǎn*   ㇀ *tí*

2) Complex strokes:

乛 *héngzhé*   ㇆ *héngzhégōu*   乚 *shùwān*

乚 *shùwāngōu*   ㇈ 乙 *héngzhéwāngōu*

To write the characters in this chapter, you need to use some of the strokes listed above, as well as the following complex strokes:

乛 *héngpiě* (a horizontal stroke connected with a left-falling stroke), as in 水

乚 *shùzhé* (a vertical stroke with a turn), as in 山

亅 *shùgōu* (a vertical stroke with a hook), as in 竹

乙 *héngzhéxiégōu* (a horizontal stroke with a turn, a slant, and a hook), as in 气

㇜ *piězhé* (a left-falling stroke with a turn), as in 云

Write these strokes, and pay attention to the direction of the stroke movement as indicated.

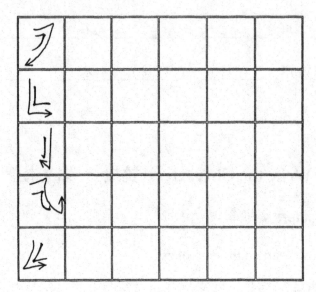

You probably have noticed that *zhé* (a turn) turns either down or right; there are no other possible directions for *zhé*. Therefore, *shùzhé* is a vertical stroke connected with a horizontal stroke that always goes to the right, never to the left. What about *piězhé* (a left-falling stroke with a turn)? It is a left-falling stroke connected with a horizontal stroke that also goes to the right. *Zhé* is a stroke that is connected with either *héng* (a horizontal stroke) or *shù* (a vertical stroke). *Héng* is always written from left to right, and *shù* is always written from top to bottom. Then it is easy to understand why *zhé* goes either rightward or downward depending on the stroke to which it is connected.

B. Rules for Stroke Order 笔顺规则

You have learned four stroke order rules:

Stroke Order Rule (1): *From top to bottom*
Stroke Order Rule (2): *From left to right*
Stroke Order Rule (3): *Horizontal before vertical or left-falling*
Stroke Order Rule (4): *Enclosing strokes first, then the enclosed, and finally the sealing horizontal stroke*

You will now learn a few more rules that will be applied to writing characters in this chapter:

Stroke Order Rule (5): *Left-falling before right-falling.* When the left-falling stroke and the right-falling stroke come together in a character, write the left-falling stroke first and then write the right-falling stroke.

For example: 木 (tree): 一 十 才 木

What about 禾? Can you try to write it using the correct stroke order?

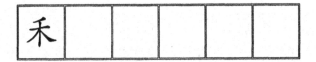

禾 | | | | |

𡿨 禾 禾 干 一

Stroke Order Rule (6): *Vertical stroke in the middle before the strokes on both sides.* When a vertical stroke or the stroke containing a vertical segment in the prominent middle position does not cross other strokes, it should be written first.

For example: 水 (water): 亅 丬 㐅 水

Can you apply this rule to the writing of 山?

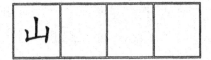

山 | | |

𠃊 𠃌 丨

C. Write with a Pencil 动手动笔

With knowledge of the new complex strokes and the new stroke order rules, you are ready to write all the characters in this chapter.

Pay attention to the overall shape of each character, and learn to write each character according to the conventional stroke order. Imitate the model character as closely as possible at first. Then try to write the character without referring to the model while writing.

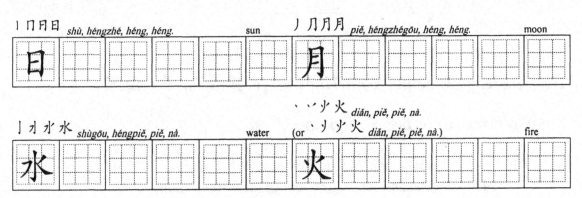

丨 冂 日 日 *shù, héngzhé, héng, héng.*   sun   丿 刀 月 月 *piě, héngzhégōu, héng, héng.*   moon

日

月

丨 丬 㐅 水 *shùgōu, héngpiě, piě, nà.*   water   丶 丷 少 火 *diǎn, piě, piě, nà.*
(or 丶 丿 少 火 *diǎn, piě, piě, nà.*)   fire

水

火

一十土 *héng, shù, héng.* soil
土

丨山山 *shù, shùzhé, shù.* mountain
山

丿川川 *piě, shù, shù.* river
川

一二千王玉 *héng, héng, shù, héng, diǎn.* jade
玉

一丁石石石 *héng, piě, shù, héngzhé, héng.* rock
石

丨冂冂田田 *shù, héngzhé, héng, shù, héng.* farmland
田

丿人人合合全全金金 *piě, nà, héng, héng, shù, diǎn, piě, héng.* metal/gold
金

一十才木 *héng, shù, piě, nà.* wood
木

丿𠂉牛牛竹竹 *piě, héng, shù, piě, héng, shùgōu.* bamboo
竹

一二千禾禾 *piě, héng, shù, piě, nà.* standing grain
禾

丨丨丷艹艹艹 *shùzhé, shù, piě, shùzhé, shù, shù.* grass
艹

丶丷丷半米米 *diǎn, piě, héng, shù, piě, nà.* rice
米

丿𠂉气气 *piě, héng, héng, héngzhéxiégōu.* air
气

一二云云 *héng, héng, piězhé, diǎn.* cloud
云

一冖冂雨雨雨雨雨 *héng, shù, héngzhégōu, shù, diǎn, diǎn, diǎn, diǎn.* rain
雨

丨冂冂日电 *shù, héngzhé, héng, héng, shùwānggōu.* electricity
电

III. Challenge 2: Apply Your Knowledge 挑战二: 举一反三

A. Know Many Things by Learning One 闻一知十

1. 一月 is January, and 二月 is February. What month is each of the following? Fill in the blanks with English and Chinese translations.

四月 _____   九月 _____   十一月_____

July _____   October _____   December _____

2. 一月一日 is the first day of January, or January 1st, and 一月三十一日 is January 31. What is the date for each of the following?

五月六日 _____   July 4th _____

八月十五日 _____   February 14th _____

十二月二十五日 _____   October 1st _____

3. Compounding is a major method of forming words and phrases with characters in modern Chinese. Here are some words and phrases formed by some of the characters in this chapter. Can you figure out what they mean?

a. 石山   _____ volcano

b. 土山   _____ irrigated paddy field

c. 火山   _____ jade stone

d. 水田   _____ rain water

e. 雨水   _____ stone mountain

f. 玉石   _____dirt mountain

B. Be Perceptive of the Slightest Differences 明察秋毫

1. Which character in each group have you not yet learned? Circle it.
    a. Group 1
        i.金   ii. 水   iii. 火   iv. 大

    b. Group 2
        i. 日   ii. 目   iii. 月   iv. 百

    c. Group 3
        i. 田   ii. 电   iii. 里   iv. 雨

    d. Group 4
        i. 长   ii. 米   iii. 木   iv. 禾

e. Group 5
   i. 石   ii. 右   iii. 九   iv. 气

f. Group 6
   i. 土   ii. 山   iii. 玉   iv. 士

Answers:
a. iv.
b. ii.
c. iii.
d. i.
e. ii.
f. iv.

2. Which character in each group is different?
   a. Which character does not have a *héng* as the first stroke?
      i. 土   ii. 玉   iii. 金   iv. 石

   b. Which character does not have a *piě* as the first stroke?
      i. 竹   ii. 火   iii. 禾   iv. 气

   c. Which character does not have a *shù* as the first stroke?
      i. 木   ii. 日   iii. 山   iv. 电

   d. Which character does not have a *nà* as the last stroke?
      i. 米   ii. 水   iii. 火   iv. 气

   e. Which character does not have a *diǎn* as the last stroke?
      i. 米   ii. 雨   iii. 玉   iv. 云

   f. Which character contains a *héngzhégōu* stroke?
      i. 石   ii. 月   iii. 气   iv. 电

   g. Which character contains a *piězhé* stroke?
      i. 山   ii. 艹   iii. 云   iv. 水

   h. Which character contains a *héngzhéxiégōu* stroke?
      i. 竹   ii. 万   iii. 水   iv. 气

Answers:
a. iii.
b. ii.
c. iv.
d. i.
e. ii.
f. iii.
g. iv.
h. iv.

3. How many strokes are there?
   a. Which character has just three strokes?
      i. 日   ii. 月   iii. 山   iv. 水

   b. Which character has just four strokes?
      i. 石   ii. 云   iii. 玉   iv. 电

    c. Which character has just five strokes?
          i. 田   ii. 金   iii. 米   iv. 川

    d. Which character has just six strokes?
          i. 禾   ii. 电   iii. 水   iv. 艸

    e. Which character has just eight strokes?
          i. 雨   ii. 米   iii. 百   iv. 石

Answers: a. iii b. ii c. i d. iv e. i

C. Be Aware of the Complex Counterpart 学简知繁

    If you do not want to learn the complex forms now, at the beginning stage, you may skip this section and go on to the next one.

1. Comparison. In this chapter, there are three simplified characters: 气， 电， and 云. Their complex forms are 氣， 電， and 雲.

	Simplified Form	Complex Form	Meaning
1	气	氣	air
2	电	電	electricity
3	云	雲	cloud

2. Explanation.

氣. The character for "air" in the oracle-bone and bronze inscriptions does not have the component 米. The character 氣 was originally used to refer to "sacrificial grains or animals" or "animal feed." When it was popularly used to refer to "air," the character 餼 was created by adding the component 食, which means "food," to 氣 to refer to the original meaning of 氣. In the normalized form, 气 is back in use to mean "air," and 饩, the simplified form of 餼, is used to mean what 氣 originally referred to. The character 氣 now continues to be used in the traditional form to mean "air."

電. The earliest form of this character is found in oracle-bone inscriptions, and is similar to the lower half of the character. It represents "lightning during a thunderstorm." To make it easier to understand, in the bronze inscriptions the character began to have 雨 as a component at the top to indicate that this is a phenomenon associated with "rain."

雲. Like the character 電, the earliest form of 雲 (cloud) does not have 雨 as the component at the top. In the oracle-bone and the bronze inscriptions, the character has only two horizontal lines and one curved line to represent layers of cloud and a cirrus cloud. In the seal script, we begin to see the 雨 component added to the top.

3. Writing. In its traditional form, each of the three characters is composed of two components. Before writing them, you must observe the differences in the strokes of a particular component both before and after it becomes part of a compound character. For example, 氣 is composed of 气 and 米; however, if you look at the last stroke of the 米 component in the character 氣, what difference can you see? The last stroke of the 米 component in 氣 is a *diǎn* (the dot stroke) rather than a *nà* (the right-falling stroke). This stroke change is to accommodate the other components in the character in order to keep all parts proportionally balanced and achieve the overall integrity of the character. Now if you compare the 雨 component in 電 and 雲 with the character 雨 itself, is there any difference in strokes?

雨   電雲

> Answer: The *héngzhégōu* stroke in the character 雨 becomes a *hénggōu* in the component. The *shù* stroke on the left becomes a dot.

丿 丄 乍 气 气 氕 氧 氣 氣 氣

piě, héng, héngzhéxiégōu; diǎn, piě, héng, shù, piě, diǎn.   air

氣

一 广 厂 币 乕 乕 乕 霛 雲 雪 雷 電

héng, diǎn, hénggōu, shù, diǎn, diǎn, diǎn, diǎn; shù, héngzhé, héng, héng, shùwāngōu.   electricity

電

一 广 厂 币 乕 乕 乕 雲 雲 雲 雲

héng, diǎn, hénggōu, shù, diǎn, diǎn, diǎn, diǎn; héng, héng, piězhé, diǎn.   cloud

雲

IV. Challenge 3: Pronounce the Characters 挑战三: 见形发音

You know what to expect in this section if you have taken the third challenge in Chapter 3. Again, a verse containing all the characters introduced in this chapter is specially written to help you listen and read aloud. Listening is the most important input. A good musician has an ear for tunes. A good language learner must develop an ear for the pronunciation of the target language. Only when you have listened attentively to the reading of the verse are you ready to read it aloud. Ask your instructor to make a recording of the verse. Listen to it several times, and then read it aloud as accurately and as frequently as possible. You should memorize the verse as a whole piece. The memorization of the verse will facilitate access to the meaning, pronunciation, and shape of a character more efficiently.

If you are not ready for this challenge yet, you can skip this section and go to the next section to practice writing characters or go on to the next chapter to learn to recognize more Chinese characters. As you learn to speak and read Chinese more easily, the ability to recognize characters will also help you. You can return to this section later.

1. Listen and read (choose the form you prefer):

(In the traditional form)   *(In the normalized form)*

Rì yuè shuǐ huǒ tǔ,   Rì yuè shuǐ huǒ tǔ,
日月水火土,   日月水火土,

Shān chuān yù shí tián,   Shān chuān yù shí tián,
山川玉石田,   山川玉石田,

Jīn mù zhú hé cǎo,   Jīn mù zhú hé cǎo,
金木竹禾艸,   金木竹禾艸,

Mǐ qì yún yǔ diàn.   Mǐ qì yún yǔ diàn.
米氣雲雨電。   米气云雨电。

2. Read aloud by looking only at the characters:

(In the traditional form)   *(In the normalized form)*

日月水火土,   日月水火土,
山川玉石田,   山川玉石田,
金木竹禾艸,   金木竹禾艸,
米氣雲雨電。   米气云雨电。

3. Guess the answers to the following riddles using the characters in the list. Answer the riddle in Chinese aloud to yourself or to someone who can help with pronunciation, and write the character in the box and its *pinyin* transliteration outside the box after each riddle. Note that in each group there are nine riddles for nine of the ten characters in the list.

Group 1: 日月水火土山川玉石田

a) It is something that people drink.

b) It is a square when written, and it is round when seen. It stays longer in summer and shorter in winter.

c) Some people like to climb it; the tallest one in the world is Mount Everest.

d) It is usually green but sometimes whitish. People in China like to make an ornament of it.

e) It can be seen at night along with stars.

f) It is hot, and people always have to guard their houses from it.

g) It is the place where people work and get agricultural produce.

h) It is often between mountains and has water in it.

i) It is beneath us, and Chinese people in the old days worshipped it.

Group 2: 金木竹禾艹米气云雨电

a) It is what giant pandas love to eat.

b) It is white and people like to cook and eat it.

c) If you are not careful, you may get a shock from it.

d) It is what people harvest when it grows and becomes ripe.

e) It is solid and becomes liquid only when heated at a very high temperature.

f) It has green leaves, is seldom taller than human beings, and is usually not wanted in farmland.

g) It has green leaves and provides shade for people.

h) It is usually white and light, but when it becomes dark and thick, it comes down as raindrops.

i) It is colorless and is all around us.

V. Challenge 4: Dictation 挑战四: 听音书形知义

1. By now, you should be able to recite the character verse for this chapter. Write the verse in Chinese characters and the meaning of each character in the spaces provided below:

Rì	yuè	shuǐ	huǒ	tǔ	,

Shān	chuān	yù	shí	tián	,

Jīn	mù	zhú	hé	cǎo	,

Mǐ	qì	yún	yǔ	diàn	.

2. Look at the *pinyin*, say it aloud, and write the appropriate character in the first box and the meaning in English in the second.

pinyin	character	meaning	pinyin	character	meaning
shí			qì		
shuǐ			jīn		
yuè			tǔ		
shān			tián		
huǒ			cǎo		
yù			diàn		
chuān			mǐ		
rì			mù		
hé			zhú		
yún			yǔ		

3. Have your instructor dictate the characters or words covered in Chapter 4.

Chapter 5 第五章
Basic Characters for People and Parts of the Body (Part 1)
与人及人体有关的基本汉字（一）

I. Fundamental Knowledge 基础知识

A. Shapes and Meanings 见形思义

	Drawing 图	Ancient Character Shape 古字形	Modern Character Shape 今字形	Meaning 字义
1.			人	person
2.			儿	child
3.			母	mother
4.			子	baby
5.			女	woman
6.			大	big
7.			小	small
8.			长	long

9.		自	自	self
10.		立	立	stand
11.		口	口	mouth
12.		目	目	eye
13.		手	手	hand
14.		足	足	foot
15.		身	身	body
16.		心	心	heart
17.		耳	耳	ear
18.		舌	舌	tongue
19.		牙	牙	tooth

| 20. | 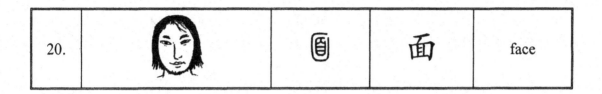 | 圓 | 面 | face |

B. Trace the Roots and Understand with Reason 追根溯源，晓之以理

人　This character represents a human being. In the oracle-bone inscriptions, it is a side view of a person. Now it can also be used to refer to mankind.

Oracle	Bronze	Seal	Clerical	Regular	Normal-ized	Semi-cursive	Cursive
勹	勹	尺	人	人	人	人	人

儿　儿 means "child." The older form of this character is 兒. It has 臼 on top of 儿 to represent a wide-open mouth of a crying or laughing child. In the simplified form of 兒, 臼 is omitted. The form 儿 in fact has existed for about two thousand years, but it has been used as the variant form of 人. It was first used to mean "child" in the 1850's and was officially accepted as a character to mean "child" in 1956.

Oracle	Bronze	Seal	Clerical	Regular	Normal-ized	Semi-cursive	Cursive
𠑹	𠑹	兒	兒	兒	儿	儿	儿

母　母 represents "mother." The character in the oracle-bone inscriptions showed a woman on her knees. Because mothers breast-feed their babies, there are two dots indicating breasts in the character to help convey the concept of "mother." Since the change to the clerical script, the two dots representing breasts are still there in the character, but one can hardly know what they mean if not taught.

Oracle	Bronze	Seal	Clerical	Regular	Normal-ized	Semi-cursive	Cursive
𢆶	𢆶	𠙥	母	母	母	母	母

子　The earliest form of the character as seen in the oracle-bone inscriptions, the bronze inscriptions, and the seal script depicted a baby with a head, two arms, and one leg. A baby cannot walk or even stand, and its legs are often swaddled, so depicting it with one leg instead of two legs is more effective to get across the idea of a "baby."

Oracle	Bronze	Seal	Clerical	Regular	Normal-ized	Semi-cursive	Cursive
𜸕	𜸕	𜸕	子	子	子	子	孑

女 女 means "woman." The earliest form of this character looked like a person kneeling down, resembling the earliest form of the character for "mother." A woman surely has breasts, but the two dots representing breasts are used only to convey the concept of "mother." To distinguish "woman" from "mother," the two dots are omitted in the character for "woman."

Oracle	Bronze	Seal	Clerical	Regular	Normal-ized	Semi-cursive	Cursive
𠨍	𠨍	𠨍	女	女	女	女	𛀁

大 When a baby grows up, he becomes big. The character 大 depicts a man standing with two arms stretched out, referring to the idea of "being big."

Oracle	Bronze	Seal	Clerical	Regular	Normal-ized	Semi-cursive	Cursive
大	大	大	大	大	大	大	大

小 The opposite of "big" is "small." The idea of "being small" is conveyed by three small particles in the earliest form of the character 小.

Oracle	Bronze	Seal	Clerical	Regular	Normal-ized	Semi-cursive	Cursive
小	小	川	小	小	小	小	小

长 This character means "long." The idea of "being long" is expressed by the hair of an elderly person. As hair was not cut in ancient times, generally speaking, the older one was, the longer the hair. The character in the clerical script had three horizontal strokes to signify long hair. However, in the cursive style, the three horizontal strokes were replaced by one left-falling stroke, and another short left-falling stroke was also omitted. The regularized cursive style became the official form in 1956.

Oracle	Bronze	Seal	Clerical	Regular	Normal-ized	Semi-cursive	Cursive

自 was originally used to represent a "nose" in the oracle-bone inscriptions. Later, it came to mean "self," to the extent that a new character, 鼻, had to be created to mean "nose." Now, the character 自 is used exclusively to mean "self."

Oracle	Bronze	Seal	Clerical	Regular	Normal-ized	Semi-cursive	Cursive

立 In the oracle-bone and bronze inscriptions, this character depicts a big person standing on the ground to indicate "standing."

Oracle	Bronze	Seal	Clerical	Regular	Normal-ized	Semi-cursive	Cursive

口 This character depicts the shape of an open mouth and means "mouth." An extended meaning also commonly used is "opening."

Oracle	Bronze	Seal	Clerical	Regular	Normal-ized	Semi-cursive	Cursive

目 In the oracle-bone and bronze inscriptions, the character depicted an eye. However, the eye has been rotated vertically since the time of the seal script.

Oracle	Bronze	Seal	Clerical	Regular	Normal-ized	Semi-cursive	Cursive

手   手 means "hand." In its earliest form, it was depicted as five fingers with the lower part of the arm.

Oracle	Bronze	Seal	Clerical	Regular	Normal-ized	Semi-cursive	Cursive
	⼿	⼿	手	手	手	手	

足   In the oracle-bone and bronze inscriptions, the three toes and heel in the lower part of the character represented the foot, and the square or circle at the top of the character indicated part of the leg. This character, an image of a foot under a leg means "foot."

Oracle	Bronze	Seal	Clerical	Regular	Normal-ized	Semi-cursive	Cursive
			足	足	足	足	

身   The prototype of 身 depicted a pregnant person in the oracle-bone and bronze inscriptions and meant "pregnancy," with a dot representing the fetus. Later, it was used to mean "body."

Oracle	Bronze	Seal	Clerical	Regular	Normal-ized	Semi-cursive	Cursive
			身	身	身	身	

心   In the oracle-bone inscriptions, the character was in the shape of a heart. Although the shape of the character has changed a lot, its original meaning, "heart," has remained the same.

Oracle	Bronze	Seal	Clerical	Regular	Normal-ized	Semi-cursive	Cursive
			心	心	心	心	

耳   In the oracle-bone and bronze inscriptions, the character was a vivid image of an ear. However, since the time of the seal script, the shape of the character by itself can hardly reveal the meaning it represents, "ear."

Oracle	Bronze	Seal	Clerical	Regular	Normal-ized	Semi-cursive	Cursive
𦣻	𦣻	耳	耳	耳	耳	耳	牙

舌   The lower part of this character is 口, which means "mouth," and the upper part depicts the tongue extended. The whole character means "tongue."

Oracle	Bronze	Seal	Clerical	Regular	Normal-ized	Semi-cursive	Cursive
舌	舌	舌	舌	舌	舌	舌	舌

牙   牙 represents "tooth." Its earliest form showed the shape of the upper tooth interlocked with a lower tooth.

Oracle	Bronze	Seal	Clerical	Regular	Normal-ized	Semi-cursive	Cursive
牙	牙	牙	牙	牙	牙	牙	牙

面   The earliest form of this character was an eye inside the outline of a face. It is now used to refer to the whole front of the head, or "face."

Oracle	Bronze	Seal	Clerical	Regular	Normal-ized	Semi-cursive	Cursive
面		面	面	面	面	面	面

C. Recognition Reinforcement 辨认巩固练习

1.   Go back to the beginning of this chapter. Look at the drawings and the characters. Then cover the drawings and try to remember the meaning of each character.

2.   Link each character on the first line with its corresponding meaning in English on the second line.

     e. 人   儿   母   子   女

     child   woman   baby   person   mother   big

f. 大   小   长   自   立

   small big stand long self person

g. 口   目   手   足   身

   foot hand mouth body eye heart

h. 心   耳   舌   牙   面

   ear tooth heart face tongue eye

3.   There are ten characters on the left side and eleven words in English on the right side. Put the letter for each character in the blank next to the corresponding English word. In each group, there is an extra blank that should be left empty.

Group 1:

    a. 自

    b. 儿   _____small

                          _____mother

    c. 小   _____big

    d. 女   _____stand

    e. 子   _____person

    f. 人   _____child

                            _____baby

    g. 立   _____woman

    h. 长   _____self

    i. 母   _____long

    j. 大   _____foot

Group 2:

    a. 心   _____ear

    b. 口   _____face

                            _____body

    c. 足

d. 舌   _____tooth

e. 手   _____heart

f. 面   _____foot

g. 身   _____mouth

h. 耳   _____tongue

i. 目   _____hand

                                                      _____eye

j. 牙   _____self

4.   Provide the meaning in English for each of the following characters:

人_____ 儿_____ 母_____ 子_____ 女_____

大_____ 小_____ 长_____ 自_____ 立_____

口_____ 目_____ 手_____ 足_____ 身_____

心_____ 耳_____ 舌_____ 牙_____ 面_____

II. Challenge 1: Write the Characters 挑战一：知义书形

A. Strokes in Characters 详说笔画

So far, you have learned these strokes:

1) Basic strokes:

一 *héng*   丨 *shù*   丿 *piě*   乀 *nà*   丶 *diǎn*   ⺀ *tí*

2) Complex strokes:

⺄ *héngzhé*   ⺄ *héngzhégōu*   乚 *shùwān*   乚 *shùzhé*

乚 *shùwāngōu*   乁 乙 *héngzhéwāngōu*   乁 *héngzhéxiégōu*

亅 *shùgōu*   乛 *héngpiě*   乚 *piězhé*

To write the characters in this chapter, you need to use some of the strokes listed above, as well as the following complex strokes:

)   *wāngōu* (a bending stroke with a hook), as in 子 手

く   *piědiǎn* (a left-falling stroke with a big dot), as in 女

亅   *shùtí* (a vertical stroke with a right rising stroke), as in 长

乚   *wògōu* (a crouching stroke with a hook), as in 心

Write these strokes, and pay attention to the direction of the stroke movement as indicated.

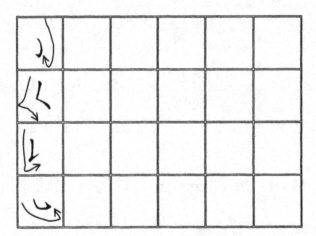

You may wonder why *shùtí* is not called *shùgōu* as it is also a vertical stroke with a hook. There are two reasons. First, the stroke that forms the hook in *shùtí* is *tí*, and second, to call this complex stroke *shùgōu* does not differentiate it from the complex stroke that has the hook on the left side of the vertical stroke. Now, when *shùtí* is mentioned, you know that it is a vertical stroke with a hook on the right side.

B. Rules for Stroke Order 笔顺规则

You have learned six stroke order rules:

Stroke Order Rule (1): *From top to bottom*
Stroke Order Rule (2): *From left to right*
Stroke Order Rule (3): *Horizontal before vertical or left-falling*

Stroke Order Rule (4): *Enclosing strokes first, then the enclosed, and finally the sealing horizontal stroke*

Stroke Order Rule (5): *Left-falling before right-falling*

Stroke Order Rule (6): *Vertical stroke in the middle before the strokes on both sides*

However, these rules are not absolute, but relative and mutually conditioned. For example, Stroke Order Rule (3) requires us to write the horizontal stroke before the vertical when they are together in a character, but if the horizontal stroke does not cross the vertical stroke and is on its left side, then the vertical stroke goes before the horizontal stroke. Therefore, in the lower part of the character 足, the stroke order is 丶 冖 口 甲 甲 甲 足. Sometimes, after years of writing, people find that one way of writing is easier than another, even though it does not comply with the stroke order rules. Therefore, there are also exceptions to the rules. For example, if you follow Stroke Order Rule (3), there is no exception in writing the character 大 as 一 ナ 大. However, writing the character 女 is an exception because the conventional way of writing 女 does not start with the horizontal stroke. It goes like this: 〈 女 女. You may find it easier to write out a well-balanced 女 this way than having the horizontal stroke first. Another example is the character 子. The horizontal stroke is drawn last: 乛 了 子.

Sometimes there can also be more than one proper way of writing a character. Although there are not many characters that can be classified into this group, there are a few you should be aware of. For example, for the character 母, the standardized stroke order is 乚 口 日 母 母; however, another popular stroke order is 乚 口 丹 母 母. Another example is the character 火. Its most popular stroke order is 丶 丿 丬 火, which complies with Stroke Order Rule (2), but the standard stroke order for 火 is 丶 丶 丬 火. In this book, the standard stroke order for a character is given first, followed by a popular alternative. You are encouraged to use the standard stroke order while being aware of the popular alternative.

C. Write with a Pencil 动手动笔

With knowledge of more complex strokes and a more sophisticated knowledge of stroke order rules, you are ready to write all the characters in this chapter.

Pay attention to the overall shape of each character and learn to write each character according to the standard stroke order. Writing a newly learned character in a rush without thinking is a waste of time. To help remember the right way to write a character, imitate the model character as closely as possible. Then try to write the character without referring to the model.

丿 人 *piě, nà.*　　　　　　　　person　　丿 几 *piě, shùwāngōu.*　　　　　　child

乙乜母母母 *shùzhé, héngzhégōu, diǎn, héng, diǎn.*
(or 乙乜母母母 *shùzhé, héngzhégōu, héng, diǎn, diǎn.)* mother

了了子 *héngpiě, wānggōu, héng.* baby

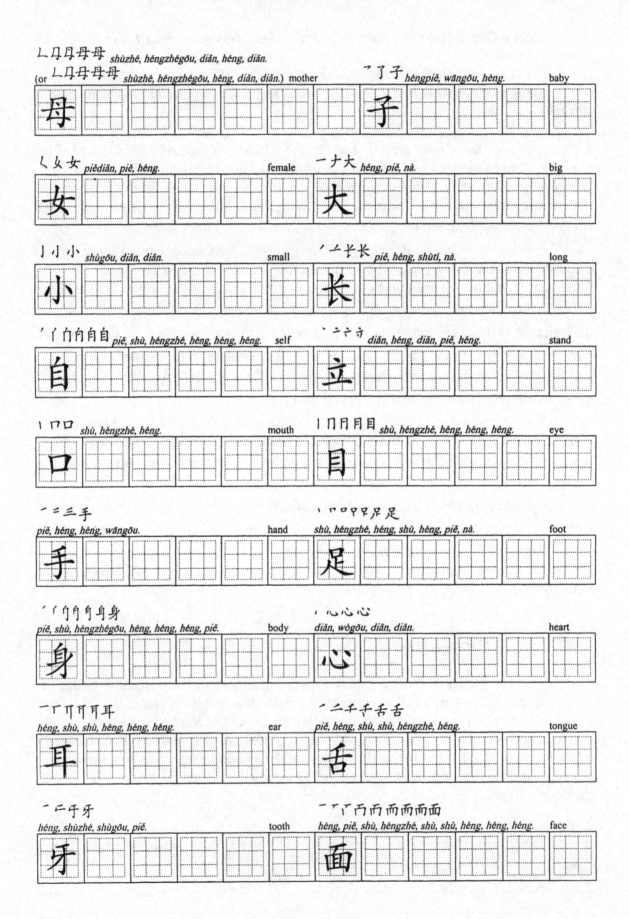

乙女女 *piědiǎn, piě, héng.* female

一ナ大 *héng, piě, nà.* big

亅小小 *shùgōu, diǎn, diǎn.* small

ノ一长长 *piě, héng, shùtí, nà.* long

ノイ白白自自 *piě, shù, héngzhé, héng, héng, héng.* self

丶二寸立 *diǎn, héng, diǎn, piě, héng.* stand

丨口口 *shù, héngzhé, héng.* mouth

丨门门目目 *shù, héngzhé, héng, héng, héng.* eye

一二三手 *piě, héng, héng, wānggōu.* hand

丨口口甲甲足足 *shù, héngzhé, héng, shù, héng, piě, nà.* foot

ノイ白白自身身 *piě, shù, héngzhégōu, héng, héng, héng, piě.* body

丶心心心 *diǎn, wògōu, diǎn, diǎn.* heart

一丅丌丌丌耳 *héng, shù, shù, héng, héng, héng.* ear

ノ二千千舌舌 *piě, héng, shù, shù, héngzhé, héng.* tongue

一二干牙 *héng, shùzhé, shùgōu, piě.* tooth

一丆丆丆而而而面面 *héng, piě, shù, héngzhé, shù, shù, héng, héng, héng.* face

III. Challenge 2: Apply Your Knowledge 挑战二: 举一反三

A. Know Many Things by Learning One 闻一知十

1. When 儿 and 子 are put together, the new word 儿子, meaning "son," is formed. The eldest son in a family is called 大儿子, and the youngest son is called 小儿子. Can you figure out the following? Fill in the blanks with English and Chinese translations.

   二儿子 _____   大女儿 _____

   三儿子_____   二女儿 _____

   the 4th son _____   三女儿 _____

   the 5th son _____   the youngest daughter _____

2. The original meaning of 面 is "face." One of its extended meanings is "side." If something has only one side, we can say 一面. How many sides does each of the following have? Write out the answers in Chinese characters.

   hexahedron (6) _____   octahedron (8) _____

   tetrahedron (4) _____   decahedron (10) _____

   heptahedron (7) _____   dodecahedron (12) _____

3. In modern Chinese, most of the words are formed with two characters. Here are some words formed by characters in this and previous chapters. Can you figure out what they mean?

   a. 小心   _____ luck at card playing

   b. 舌面   _____ be fond of gossip

   c. 自立   _____ body and mind

   d. 长舌   _____ be careful

   e. 手气   _____ the surface of the tongue

   f. 身心   _____ be independent

B. Be Perceptive of the Slightest Differences 明察秋毫

1. Which character in each group have you not yet learned? Circle it.
    a. Group 1
       i. 人   ii. 大   iii. 八   iv. 文

    b. Group 2
       i. 口   ii. 目   iii. 页   iv. 百

    c. Group 3
       i. 首   ii. 电   iii. 面   iv. 雨

    d. Group 4
       i. 长   ii. 欠   iii. 女   iv. 禾

    e. Group 5
       i. 足   ii. 舌   iii. 尸   iv. 石

    f. Group 6
       i. 土   ii. 立   iii. 五   iv. 王

Answers: a. iv. b. iii. c. ii. d. ii. e. iii. f. iv.

2. Which character in each group is different?
    a. Which character does not have a *héng* as the last stroke?
       i. 子   ii. 女   iii. 手   iv. 耳

    b. Which character does not have a *piě* as the first stroke?
       i. 人   ii. 大   iii. 长   iv. 手

    c. Which character does not have a *shù* as the first stroke?
       i. 儿   ii. 口   iii. 目   iv. 足

    d. Which character does not have a *nà* as the last stroke?
       i. 大   ii. 长   iii. 足   iv. 女

    e. Which character does not have a *diǎn* as the first stroke?
       i. 母   ii. 小   iii. 立   iv. 心

    f. Which character contains a *wāngōu* stroke?
       i. 小   ii. 手   iii. 身   iv. 长

    g.   Which character contains a *shùtí* stroke?

       i. 牙   ii. 子   iii. 长   iv. 母

    h.   Which character contains a *wògōu* stroke?

       i. 足   ii. 万   iii. 气   iv. 心

Answers: a. iii. b. ii. c. i. d. iv. e. i. f. ii. g. iii. h. iv.

3.   How many strokes are there?

    a.   Which character has more than three strokes?

       i. 子   ii. 女   iii. 手   iv. 小

    b.   Which character has more than four strokes?

       i. 牙   ii. 目   iii. 长   iv. 心

    c.   Which character has just five strokes?

       i. 母   ii. 自   iii. 耳   iv. 牙

    d.   Which character has just six strokes?

       i. 足   ii. 长   iii. 母   iv. 舌

    e.   Which character has just seven strokes?

       i. 身   ii. 面   iii. 立   iv. 耳

Answers: a. iii. b. ii. c. i. d. iv. e. i.

C. Be Aware of the Complex Counterpart 学简知繁

If you do not want to learn the complex forms now at the beginning stage, you may skip this section and go on to the next one.

1. Comparison. In this chapter, there are two simplified characters: 儿 and 长. Their complex forms are 兒 and 長.

	Simplified Form	Complex Form	Meaning
1	儿	兒	child
2	长	長	long

2. Explanation.

兒. The traditional form of the character consists of two parts. The lower part indicates a pair of legs while the upper part indicates a wide-open mouth, crying or laughing. It signifies a child.

長. The traditional form of the character depicts a person with very long hair, suggesting the idea of "being long."

3. Writing. It does not matter whether it is in the traditional form or in the normalized form, the basic stroke order rules apply to all Chinese characters. Write these two characters in their traditional form.

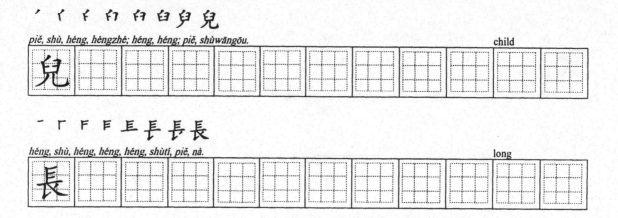

IV. Challenge 3: Pronounce the Characters 挑战三: 见形发音

To succeed in the challenge, you must learn the verse so thoroughly that eventually you will be able to recite it. If you do not have a recording of the verse, then ask your instructor to make one for you. Only when you have listened repeatedly to the verse will you be ready to read it aloud. Read it aloud as accurately and as frequently as possible until you are able to memorize it. Memorization of the verse will help you remember the meaning, pronunciation, and shape of the characters more efficiently.

Again, if you are not ready for this challenge, you can skip this section and go to the next section to practice writing characters or go on to the next chapter to learn to recognize more Chinese characters. You can return to this section later.

1. Listen and read (choose the form you prefer):

(In the traditional form)   *(In the normalized form)*

Rén ér mǔ zǐ nǚ,   Rén ér mǔ zǐ nǚ,
人兒母子女,   人儿母子女,

Dà xiǎo cháng zì lì,
大小長自立，

Kǒu mù shǒu zú shēn,
口目手足身，

Xīn ěr shé yá miàn.
心耳舌牙面。

Dà xiǎo cháng zì lì
大小长自立，

Kǒu mù shǒu zú shēn,
口目手足身，

Xīn ěr shé yá miàn.
心耳舌牙面。

2.　Read aloud by looking only at the characters:

(In the traditional form)

人兒母子女，

大小長自立，

口目手足身，

心耳舌牙面。

(In the normalized form)

人儿母子女，

大小长自立，

口目手足身，

心耳舌牙面。

3.　Guess the answers to the following riddles using the characters in the list. Answer the riddle in Chinese aloud to yourself or to someone who can help with pronunciation, and write the character in the box and its *pinyin* transliteration outside the box after each riddle. Note that in each group there are nine riddles for nine of the ten characters in the list.

Group 1: 人儿母子女大小长自立

a) It is the opposite of "big."

b) It is the most intelligent animal on the earth.

c) It is too young to walk and is often swaddled.

d) It is the person who gives birth.

e) It is the action that a person can take with his/her legs straight on the ground to support his/her body. ☐

f) It is the opposite of "short." ☐

g) It is someone pointing at his/her own nose. ☐

h) It is the sex of a person who cannot properly be called "he." ☐

i) It is a very young person running around. ☐

Group 2: 口目手足身心耳舌牙面

a) It is what a person sees with. ☐

b) It is what a person uses to walk, run, and kick. ☐

c) It is below the nose and a receptacle for food. ☐

d) It is what a person chews with when eating. ☐

e) Everyone has two to do things with. ☐

f) They have never met each other, but together they enable people to hear. ☐

g) It works like a pump and sends nutrition to all parts of the body. ☐

h) It contains all the major inner organs. ☐

i) It is soft, but it can also be sharp and hurt people's feelings.

V. Challenge 4: Dictation 挑战四: 听音书形知义

1. By now, you should be able to recite the character verse for this chapter. Write the verse in Chinese characters and the meaning of each character in the spaces provided below:

Rén	ér	mǔ	zǐ	nǔ	,

Dà	xiǎo	cháng	zì	lì	,

Kǒu	mù	shǒu	zú	shēn	,

Xīn	ěr	shé	yá	miàn	.

2. Look at the *pinyin*, say it aloud, and write the appropriate character in the first box and the meaning in English in the second.

pinyin	*character*	*meaning*	*pinyin*	*character*	*meaning*
dà			shǒu		
ér			yá		

mǔ				kǒu		
zì				ěr		
rén				shé		
xiǎo				zú		
cháng				nǚ		
zǐ				lì		
xīn				shēn		
mù				miàn		

3. Have your instructor dictate the characters or words covered in Chapter 5.

Chapter 6 第六章
Basic Characters for People and Parts of the Body (Part 2)
与人及人体有关的基本汉字（二）

I. Fundamental Knowledge 基础知识

A. Shapes and Meanings 见形思义

	Drawing 图	Ancient Character Form 古字形	Modern Character Form 今字形	Meaning 字义
1.		士	士	adult
2.		王	王	ruler
3.			父	father
4.			文	writing
5.			言	speech
6.			又	hand / again
7.			交	cross/intersect
8.			止	foot / cease

9.		𠨍	艮	look back
10.		見	见	see
11.		鬼	鬼	ghost/devil
12.		𦣻	首	head
13.		頁	页	head / page
14.		示	示	altar table / show
15.		元	元	head / dollar
16.		歹	歹	broken bone / bad
17.		肉	肉	flesh
18.		尸	尸	corpse
19.		骨	骨	bone

20.			欠	yawn / lack

B. Trace the Roots and Understand with Reason 追根溯源，晓之以理

士   This character, meaning "adult," is formed by 十 (ten) and 一 (one), implying that a person can do things well from the beginning (one) to the end (ten). Some scholars also interpret the oldest form of this character in the oracle-bone inscriptions as a depiction of an erect male reproductive organ, implying a grown-up, or adult. Please note the difference between this character and 土 (soil). The horizontal stroke at the bottom of 士 (adult) is shorter than the one at the bottom of 土 (soil).

Oracle	Bronze	Seal	Clerical	Regular	Normal-ized	Semi-cursive	Cursive
1	土	士	士	士	士	士	士

王   The earliest forms of the character 王 in the oracle-bone and bronze inscriptions depicted the shape of a battle axe or tomahawk, which was a powerful weapon in ancient times. In ancient times, a ruler, usually also the military commander, would use this powerful weapon to fight the enemies and urge the soldiers forward. This weapon became the symbol of power, and began to be used to symbolize the highest ruler of a land.

Oracle	Bronze	Seal	Clerical	Regular	Normal-ized	Semi-cursive	Cursive
大	王	王	王	王	王	王	王

父   As depicted in its earliest forms in the oracle-bone and bronze inscriptions, as well as in the seal script, this character was a hand holding a tool or weapon. Since it was the responsibility of men to fight in battles or work in the fields, this character became the symbol of "man." Later on, it also took on the meaning of "father."

Oracle	Bronze	Seal	Clerical	Regular	Normal-ized	Semi-cursive	Cursive
父	父	父	父	父	父	父	父

文　The earliest forms of the character 文 in the oracle-bone and bronze inscriptions represented a person with designs tattooed on the upper body. The character, therefore, originally referred to a person with tattoos, and the meaning "writing" was derived later.

Oracle	Bronze	Seal	Clerical	Regular	Normal-ized	Semi-cursive	Cursive
			文	文	文	文	文

言　If you compare the forms of the character 言 (　 　) with those of the character 舌 (　 　) in the oracle-bone and bronze inscriptions, you will see that the difference between them was just a short horizontal stroke added to the top of the tongue, indicating that the tongue was in use. Therefore, the meaning of the character is "speech" or "speak."

Oracle	Bronze	Seal	Clerical	Regular	Normal-ized	Semi-cursive	Cursive
			言	言	言	言	言

又　The earliest forms of the character in the oracle-bone and bronze inscriptions, as well as in the seal script, looked like a hand reaching to the right. For simplicity, instead of five fingers, only three were depicted in the character. The original meaning of the character was "right hand" or "hand," and later it was borrowed to describe a repeated action (again). However, used as a component in other characters, 又 still means "hand," and it is also used to replace relatively more complicated components when simplifying some complex traditional characters.

Oracle	Bronze	Seal	Clerical	Regular	Normal-ized	Semi-cursive	Cursive
			又	又	又	又	又

交　The earliest forms of 交 in the oracle-bone and bronze inscriptions, as well as in the seal script, were a sketch of a person with legs crossed. Therefore, the primary meaning of this character is "cross" or "intersect."

Oracle	Bronze	Seal	Clerical	Regular	Normal-ized	Semi-cursive	Cursive
			交	交	交	交	交

止   This character in the oracle-bone inscriptions looked like a footprint, and it was originally used to mean "foot." Many other characters with 止 as a component are all related to foot. Because of the concept of "the foot that stays in place," 止 has taken on the meaning "to cease."

Oracle	Bronze	Seal	Clerical	Regular	Normal-ized	Semi-cursive	Cursive
			止	止	止	止	

艮   The earliest forms of 艮 in the oracle-bone and bronze inscriptions, as well as in the seal script, represented a person with a big eye looking back. After the clerical change, one could no longer see that image. The bottom of the part for "eye" was broken up, and the part for "person" also changed its shape. Although the meaning of the character 艮 is still "to look back," it has several different extended meanings, such as "blunt" and "defying." It is most often seen as a component in other characters.

Oracle	Bronze	Seal	Clerical	Regular	Normal-ized	Semi-cursive	Cursive
			艮	艮	艮	艮	

见   The character 见 means "to see." In the oracle-bone and bronze inscriptions, the character was represented by a person with a big eye on top. The eye became 目 in the seal script and the clerical script, as well as in the regular script. The normalized form of the character comes from the cursive form, which eliminates the three short horizontal strokes in 目 by extending the left-falling stroke.

Oracle	Bronze	Seal	Clerical	Regular	Normal-ized	Semi-cursive	Cursive
			見	見	见	见	

鬼　The character 鬼 means "ghost," which is what a person becomes after death, according to traditional belief. In the oracle-bone inscriptions, the character represented a person with a monstrous head. Starting from the time of the seal script, 厶, which indicates "the nether world," has been added to the character, and thus we now have 鬼 as the character for "ghost."　鬼 also means "devil."

Oracle	Bronze	Seal	Clerical	Regular	Normal-ized	Semi-cursive	Cursive
畏	鬼	鬼	鬼	鬼	鬼	鬼	鬼

首　In the oracle-bone inscriptions, this character had the shape of the head of a beast. In the bronze inscriptions, the character was formed with components representing an eye and hair. In the seal script, the character appears to have been formed by a component representing the hair and another indicating the nose, which may also mean "self." Although the formation of the character has undergone all these changes, the primary meaning of the character remains "the head."

Oracle	Bronze	Seal	Clerical	Regular	Normal-ized	Semi-cursive	Cursive
首	首	首	首	首	首	首	首

页　The character 页 has the same primary meaning as 首; however, unlike 首, the character 页 originally referred only to the head of a human being. This can be seen in its form in the oracle-bone inscriptions, which represented a person's head with an eye and hair. Although the upper part of the character changed its form from a head to an eye and then to a nose, the lower part, which is in the shape of human legs, remained in place (please refer to the different forms of the characters below). In the simplified form of the character, the left-falling stroke is extended upward to represent the three eliminated horizontal strokes. Characters containing 页 as a component are still related to the head, but 页 itself has been borrowed to mean "page," that is, "one side of a sheet of paper." The character 頭, which was formed by 頁 meaning "head" plus a phonetic component, 豆, was then created and used to mean "head." In 1935, the cursive way of writing the character 頭 as 头 was for the first time proposed to replace 頭; however, it was not officially accepted as a normalized form until 1956. Now, 头 is the character commonly used to mean "head," whereas 页 is used to mean "page."

Oracle	Bronze	Seal	Clerical	Regular	Normal-ized	Semi-cursive	Cursive
𤽐	𦣻	𩑣	頁	頁	页	頁	頁

示   People in ancient times often called on deities for guidance and protection by placing sacrificial offerings on a stone table or altar. The earliest form of this character in the oracle-bone inscriptions depicts this sacrificial offering table. Therefore, the original meaning of the character 示 is "stone table for sacrificial offerings."   Sacrificial ceremonies were intended to show the gods the devotion of the supplicants; thus, the character 示 has also taken on the meaning of "show."

Oracle	Bronze	Seal	Clerical	Regular	Normal-ized	Semi-cursive	Cursive
示		示	示	示	示	示	示

元   This is the third character that originally meant "head." Because the head is the most important and most prominent part of the human body, it should not be a surprise that several characters were created to depict this part of the body. The character in the oracle-bone inscriptions has a person as the lower part and two horizontal strokes to indicate the head and its position. The form of the character has not changed much. However, in modern Chinese, it has been borrowed to refer to a Chinese unit of currency.

Oracle	Bronze	Seal	Clerical	Regular	Normal-ized	Semi-cursive	Cursive
元	元	元	元	元	元	元	元

歹   The character 歹 has a variant form 歺 , which more closely resembles the forms of the character in the oracle-bone inscriptions and in the seal script. 歺 represented a bone that is broken after the meat is scraped away. The character 歹 , therefore, has taken on the meaning of "bad" or "vicious."

Oracle	Bronze	Seal	Clerical	Regular	Normal-ized	Semi-cursive	Cursive
歺		歺	歹	歹	歹	歹	歹

肉   The earliest form of this character in the oracle-bone inscriptions resembled a piece of meat with ribs.   The character 肉 is primarily used to mean "the flesh of animals."   When it becomes a component of another character, it often takes the form 月, which is close to its form in the seal script and looks the same as the character for "moon," but it indicates "flesh."   The character 骨 meaning "bone," which is to be discussed below, is a good example of a compound character formed with 月.

Oracle	Bronze	Seal	Clerical	Regular	Normal-ized	Semi-cursive	Cursive
夕		月	肉	肉	肉	肉	肉

尸   The character 尸 in the oracle-bone and bronze inscriptions looked like a sitting person seen from the side.   In ancient times, 示 (the stone table for sacrificial offerings) was used during the sacrificial ceremonies for deities, whereas 尸 was used during sacrificial ceremonies for ancestors or relatives.   尸 depicts a person sitting on high who accepts the sacrifice and worship in the name of the dead during the sacrificial ceremonies.   Later a memorial tablet or a portrait of the dead was substituted for the person sitting on high.   To make the meaning of "corpse" clear, the character 死 (歹 [broken bone] + 匕 [upside down person] = 死 [death]) was added under 尸.   As the practice mentioned above is no longer in existence, 尸 rather than 屍 is now used as a normalized form to mean "a corpse."

Oracle	Bronze	Seal	Clerical	Regular	Normal-ized	Semi-cursive	Cursive
夕	乀	尸	屍	屍	尸	尸	丂

骨   The character 骨 has two parts: 冎 meaning "bare bones" and 月 meaning "flesh."   The earliest form of 骨 in the oracle-bone inscriptions depicted bones without flesh.   Later, 月 (flesh) was added to mean "bones in flesh," distinguishing 骨 from 冎, which meant "bare bones."   However, in modern Chinese, 冎 is no longer used as a character, and 骨 is, therefore, used to mean either "bare bones" or "bones in flesh."

Oracle	Bronze	Seal	Clerical	Regular	Normal-ized	Semi-cursive	Cursive
冎		骨	骨	骨	骨	骨	骨

欠   This character in its earliest form in the oracle-bone inscriptions depicted a person kneeling with a wide-open mouth. It is believed that this represented a person in the act of yawning since the meaning of the character is "yawning." After the clerical change, the wide-open mouth is not obvious from the shape of the character; however, characters with 欠 as a component are all related to opening the mouth and exhaling. When one yawns, it means one is tired and short of energy. Therefore, the extended meaning of 欠, which is commonly used in modern Chinese, is "to lack."

Oracle	Bronze	Seal	Clerical	Regular	Normal-ized	Semi-cursive	Cursive
𨈆		欥	欠	欠	欠	欠	欠

C. Recognition Reinforcement 辨认巩固练习

1. Go back to the beginning of this chapter. Look at the drawings and the characters. Then cover the drawings and try to remember the meaning of each character.

2. Link each character on the first line with its corresponding meaning in English on the second line:

a.   士   王   父   文   言

     writing   father   ruler   speech   adult

b.   又   交   止   艮   见

     look back   cease   again   see   intersect

c.   鬼   首   页   示   元

     head   dollar   ghost   page   show

d.   歹   肉   尸   骨   欠

     bad   corpse   yawn   flesh   bone

3. There are ten characters on the left side and eleven words in English on the right side.   Put the letter for each character in the blank next to the corresponding English word.   In each group, there is an extra blank that should be left empty.

Group 1:

a. 王

b. 交

c. 艮

d. 父

e. 见

f. 文

g. 士

h. 言

i. 又

j. 止

_____speech

_____adult

_____writing

_____again

_____ head

_____cease

_____ruler

_____see

_____look back

_____father

_____intersect

Group 2:

a. 尸

b. 首

c. 骨

d. 鬼

e. 欠

f. 页

g. 歹

h. 示

i. 肉

j. 元

_____bad

_____yawn

_____flesh

_____corpse

_____dollar

_____show

_____see

_____bone

_____ghost

_____page

_____head

4．Provide the meaning in English for each of the following characters:

士＿＿＿＿＿　　王＿＿＿＿＿　　父＿＿＿＿＿　　文＿＿＿＿＿　　言＿＿＿＿＿

又＿＿＿＿＿　　交＿＿＿＿＿　　止＿＿＿＿＿　　艮＿＿＿＿＿　　见＿＿＿＿＿

鬼＿＿＿＿＿　　首＿＿＿＿＿　　页＿＿＿＿＿　　示＿＿＿＿＿　　元＿＿＿＿＿

歹＿＿＿＿＿　　肉＿＿＿＿＿　　尸＿＿＿＿＿　　骨＿＿＿＿＿　　欠＿＿＿＿＿

II. Challenge 1: Write the Characters 挑战一：知义书形

A. Strokes in Characters 详说笔画

The strokes listed below are the ones you have learned so far:

1) Basic strokes:

一 *héng* 　｜ *shù* 　丿 *piě* 　乀 *nà* 　丶 *diǎn* 　⟋ *tí*

2) Complex strokes:

⊃ *héngzhé*　　⊐ *héngzhégōu*　　乚 *shùwān*　　∟ *shùzhé*

乚 *shùwāngōu*　　乚 乙 *héngzhéwāngōu*　　乁 *héngzhéxiégōu*

亅 *shùgōu*　　㇙ *shùtí*　　㇉ *wāngōu*　　㇃ *wògōu*

㇕ *héngpiě*　　乚 *piězhé*　　乀 *piědiǎn*

Two characters in this chapter contain a complex stroke you have not learned before:

乛　　*hénggōu* (a horizontal stroke with a hook), as in 　骨 欠

Write this stroke, and pay attention to the direction of the stroke movement as indicated.

乛					

Now, let's also review the strokes you have learned in the previous chapters. Before you do the following exercises, it would be helpful to spend some time looking at the basic strokes and complex strokes listed at the beginning of this section and say their names in Chinese out loud several times in order to keep them in mind. If you can keep their names in mind, you will be able to talk about how to write a character with your Chinese teacher or a Chinese friend easily.

Exercise 1: What are the six basic strokes? Say their names in Chinese out loud and fill in the blanks with their names in *pinyin*. Try to remember the tones and put the tone marks on them.

一 _____   丨 _____

丿 _____   乀 _____

乀 _____   丿 _____

Exercise 2: The complex strokes in each of the following pairs are somewhat similar to each other. In what way are they different? Write their names in *pinyin* (with tone marks) to show that you know the difference.

1) ㄱ _____   ㄱ _____

2) ㄴ _____   ㄴ _____

3) ㄴ _____   ㄴ _____

4) ㄥ _____   乁 _____

5) 亅 _____   ㇏ _____

6) ㇀ _____   ㇀ _____

7) ㇆ _____   ㇆ _____

8) ㇄ _____   ㇅ _____

9) ㇆ _____   ㇀ _____

B. *Rules for Stroke Order 笔顺规则*

You have already learned the six stroke order rules, and as mentioned in Chapter 5, these rules are not absolute but relative and mutually conditioned. The best way to learn stroke order is to write a new character by applying your knowledge of the stroke order first and then comparing it with the standard stroke order for that character. The number of empty boxes provided indicates the number of strokes the character in the first box has. Write one stroke after another cumulatively in the empty boxes provided as the example given below shows. Try to determine the reason for any difference in the stroke order or the number of strokes.

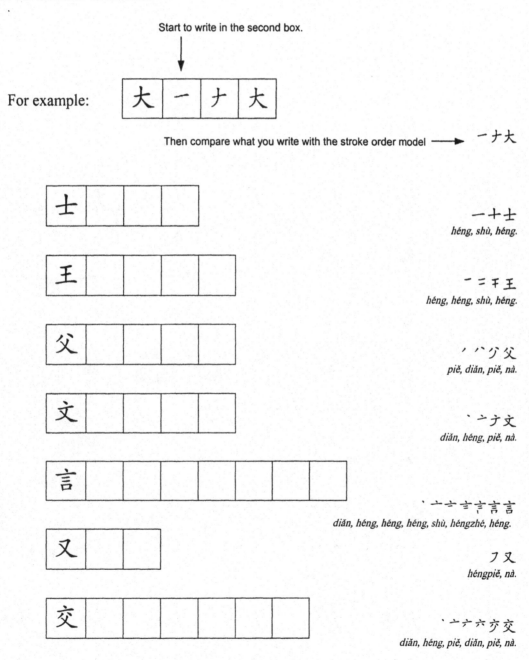

Start to write in the second box.

For example:

Then compare what you write with the stroke order model ⟶ 一 ナ 大

一 十 士
héng, shù, héng.

一 二 千 王
héng, héng, shù, héng.

ノ ハ 夕 父
piě, diǎn, piě, nà.

、 一 ナ 文
diǎn, héng, piě, nà.

、 一 一 言 言 言
diǎn, héng, héng, héng, shù, héngzhé, héng.

フ 又
héngpiě, nà.

、 一 六 六 夯 交
diǎn, héng, piě, diǎn, piě, nà.

止

丨卜止止
shù, héng, shù, héng.

艮

フ⁊ヨ∃艮艮
héngzhé, héng, héng, shùtí, piě, nà.

见

丨冂贝见
shù, héngzhé, piě, shùwāngōu.

鬼

丿亻冖甶白甶鬼鬼鬼
piě, shù, héngzhé, héng, héng, piě, shùwāngōu, piězhé, diǎn.

首

丶丷丷㐌㐌首首首首
diǎn, piě, héng, piě, shù, héngzhé, héng, héng, héng.

页

一丆丆页页页
héng, piě, shù, héngzhé, piě, diǎn.

示

一二于示示
héng, héng, shùgōu, diǎn, diǎn.

元

一二亍元
héng, héng, piě, shùwāngōu.

歹

一丆歹歹
héng, piě, héngpiě, diǎn.

肉

丨冂内内肉肉
shù, héngzhégōu, piě, diǎn, piě, diǎn.

尸

フコ尸
héngzhé, héng, piě.

骨 | | | | | | | |

丶 冂 冎 冎 咼 骨 骨 骨 骨

shù, héngzhé, héngzhé, diǎn, hénggōu, shù, héngzhégōu, héng, héng.

欠 | | |

丿 勹 ケ 欠

piě, hénggōu, piě, nà.

C. Write with a Pencil 动手动笔

Now that you know the meaning of each character as well as the standard stroke order, you need to pay attention to the balance and proportion of each character. To help learners write well-balanced characters, teachers often provide model characters in three kinds of patterned writing boxes:

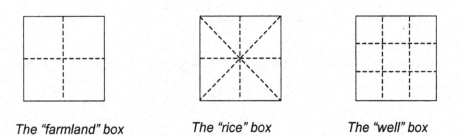

The "farmland" box　　　　The "rice" box　　　　The "well" box

The name for each writing box is based on the overall appearance of the box or the pattern of the dotted lines inside the box. How is the character "farmland" written? Isn't it 田? Does the pattern of the dotted lines in the "rice" box resemble the Chinese character for "rice"? How do you write it? Isn't it 米? The "well" box obviously takes after the Chinese character for "well," which is 井, a character you will learn in Chapter 8. The "well" box is also called the "nine palaces" box because there are nine small boxes regarded as palaces. We are using the "well" boxes in this book. The ultimate goal, however, is for you to be able to write well-balanced characters without these lines.

If one can write well-balanced Chinese characters, one is assumed to be observant, careful, patient, and willing to work hard. Otherwise, one is thought to be sloppy, careless, impatient, and lazy. In China, there is the saying: the characters resemble the person who wrote them. Therefore, a person in China is often judged by the characters he or she writes in addition to his or her words and deeds.

一 十 士
héng, shù, héng.　　　　adult　　　　一 二 干 王　*héng, héng, shù, héng.*　　　ruler

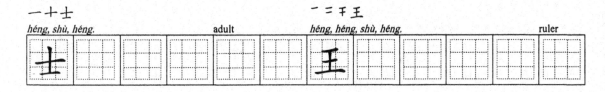

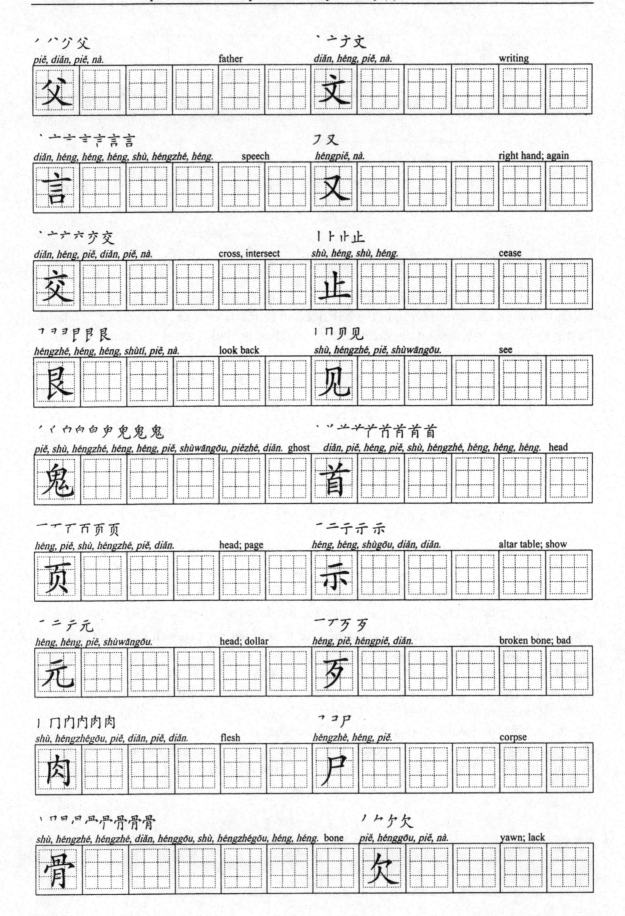

丿 八 ⺈ 父
piě, diǎn, piě, nà. father

父

丶 亠 ㇀ 文
diǎn, héng, piě, nà. writing

文

丶 亠 亠 言 言 言 言
diǎn, héng, héng, héng, shù, héngzhé, héng. speech

言

㇇ 又
héngpiě, nà. right hand; again

又

丶 亠 亠 六 交 交
diǎn, héng, piě, diǎn, piě, nà. cross, intersect

交

丨 卜 止 止
shù, héng, shù, héng. cease

止

㇕ ㇕ ㇕ 𠃍 艮 艮
héngzhé, héng, héng, shùtí, piě, nà. look back

艮

丨 冂 贝 见
shù, héngzhé, piě, shùwāngōu. see

见

丿 亻 白 白 白 由 鬼 鬼 鬼
piě, shù, héngzhé, héng, héng, piě, shùwāngōu, piězhé, diǎn. ghost

鬼

丶 丷 䒑 䒑 丆 首 首 首 首
diǎn, piě, héng, piě, shù, héngzhé, héng, héng, héng. head

首

一 丆 丆 百 页 页
héng, piě, shù, héngzhé, piě, diǎn. head; page

页

一 二 亍 亍 示
héng, héng, shùgōu, diǎn, diǎn. altar table; show

示

一 二 テ 元
héng, héng, piě, shùwāngōu. head; dollar

元

一 丆 歹 歹
héng, piě, héngpiě, diǎn. broken bone; bad

歹

丨 冂 内 内 肉 肉
shù, héngzhégōu, piě, diǎn, piě, diǎn. flesh

肉

㇕ ㇕ 尸
héngzhé, héng, piě. corpse

尸

丨 冂 冎 冎 冎 骨 骨 骨 骨
shù, héngzhé, héngzhé, diǎn, hénggōu, shù, héngzhégōu, héng, héng. bone

骨

丿 ⺈ 欠 欠
piě, hénggōu, piě, nà. yawn; lack

欠

III. Challenge 2: Apply Your Knowledge　挑战二: 举一反三

A. Know Many Things by Learning One 闻一知十

1. 元 and 页 are two characters that are often used for their extended meanings in modern Chinese. 元 is now used to refer to a monetary unit (dollar), and 页 is used to indicate a page of a book. When they are preceded with numerals, can you figure out what they mean? Translate the English phrases into Chinese and the Chinese characters into English.

六元 _____　　七页 _____

nine dollars _____　　ten pages _____

2. The following four characters you have learned in this chapter have something to do either with 目 (eye) or with 手 (hand). Can you categorize them into two groups?

又　　艮　　父　　见

目　　_____　　_____　　_____

手　　_____　　_____　　_____

3. In modern Chinese, most words are formed with two characters. Here are some words formed with some of the characters learned in this chapter and previous chapters. What do they mean?

a. 女士　　_____ parents

b. 父母　　_____ kindred

c. 元首　　_____ madam

d. 文言　　_____ skeleton

e. 尸骨　　_____ head of a state

f. 骨肉　　_____ literary Chinese language

B. Be Perceptive of the Slightest Differences 明察秋毫

1. Which character in each group have you not yet learned? Circle it.
    a. Group 1
        i. 文   ii. 大   iii. 父   iv. 犬

    b. Group 2
        i. 页   ii. 目   iii. 贝   iv. 见

    c. Group 3
        i. 鱼   ii. 首   iii. 面   iv. 雨

    d. Group 4
        i. 艮   ii. 衣   iii. 女   iv. 欠

    e. Group 5
        i. 足   ii. 元   iii. 瓜   iv. 尸

    f. Group 6
        i. 示   ii. 止   iii. 王   iv. 羊

Answers: a. iv. b. iii. i. c. ii iii iii iv. d. e. f.

2. Which of the characters in each group is different?
    a. Which character does not have a *héng* as the last stroke?
        i. 王   ii. 言   iii. 尸   iv. 止

    b. Which character does not have a *piě* as the first stroke?
        i. 父   ii. 文   iii. 鬼   iv. 欠

    c. Which character does not have a *shù* as the first stroke?
        i. 士   ii. 见   iii. 肉   iv. 骨

    d. Which character does not have a *nà* as the last stroke?
        i. 又   ii. 艮   iii. 欠   iv. 页

    e. Which character does not have a *diǎn* as the first stroke?
        i. 父   ii. 首   iii. 言   iv. 交

    f. Which character does not contain a *shùwānggōu* stroke?
        i. 见   ii. 骨   iii. 元   iv. 鬼

g. Which character contains a *shùtí* stroke?
    i. 示　　ii. 见　　iii. 艮　　iv. 欠

h. Which character contains a *héngpiě* stroke?
    i. 文　　ii. 鬼　　iii. 尸　　iv. 歹

Answers: a. iii. b. ii. c. i. d. iv. e. i. f. ii. g. iii. h. iv.

3. How many strokes are there?
  a. Which character has more than three strokes?
    i. 士　　ii. 又　　iii. 歹　　iv. 尸

  b. Which character has more than four strokes?
    i. 见　　ii. 示　　iii. 王　　iv. 元

  c. Which character has just two strokes?
    i. 又　　ii. 士　　iii. 文　　iv. 欠

  d. Which character has just seven strokes?
    i. 言　　ii. 艮　　iii. 肉　　iv. 首

  e. Which character does not have nine strokes?
    i. 鬼　　ii. 首　　iii. 骨　　iv. 肉

Answers: a. iii. b. ii. c. i. d. i. e. iv.

C. Be Aware of the Complex Counterpart 学简知繁

If you do not want to learn the complex forms now at the beginning stage, you may skip this section and go on to the next one.

1. Comparison. In this chapter, there are three simplified characters: 见, 页, and 尸. Their complex forms are 見, 頁, and 屍.

	Simplified Form	Complex Form	Meaning
1	见	見	see
2	页	頁	page

3	尸	屍	corpse

2. Explanation.

見. This traditional form of the character consists of two parts. The lower part represents a pair of legs while the upper part represents a big vertical eye, signifying the action of seeing.

頁. This traditional form of the character is formed with a pair of "legs" at the bottom, with a "nose" over the "legs" plus a horizontal stroke representing the top of a person. The character originally refers to the head of a human being and is used now to mean a "page of a book."

屍. This character has two major components: 尸 and 死. 尸 is a person sitting on high during a sacrificial ceremony to accept the sacrifice and worship in the name of the dead, and 死 means "death." The combination of these two components in the character 屍 produces the meaning of "corpse."

For explanations of their simplified counterparts, please refer to Section B in Part I in this chapter.

3. Writing. Write these three characters in their traditional form.

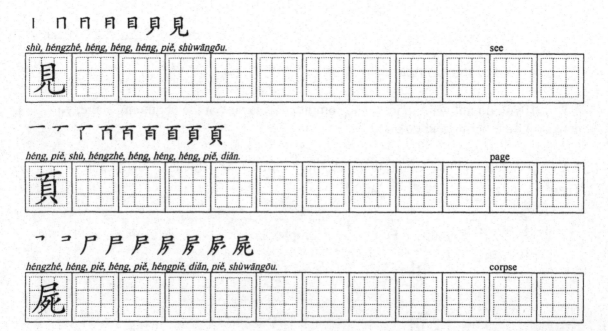

丨 冂 冂 冃 目 貝 見

shù, héngzhé, héng, héng, héng, piě, shùwāngōu.   see

一 冖 冖 丆 百 百 百 頁 頁

héng, piě, shù, héngzhé, héng, héng, héng, piě, diǎn.   page

㇀ ㇇ 尸 尸 屍 屍 屍 屍 屍

héngzhé, héng, piě, héng, piě, héngpiě, diǎn, piě, shùwāngōu.   corpse

IV. Challenge 3: Pronounce the Characters 挑战三：见形发音

Challenge 3 demands that you establish the link between the shape of a character and its pronunciation. As the shape of a character does not provide a clue to the pronunciation of the character, it will be a real challenge for you. To take on the challenge successfully, you will need to listen to a recording of the verse written with the characters in this chapter. If you do not have a recording of the verse, then ask your instructor to make one for you. Only when you have repeatedly listened to the verse will you be ready to read it aloud. Read it aloud as accurately and as frequently as possible until you are able to memorize it. Memorization of the verse will help you remember the meaning, pronunciation, and shape of the characters in the verse more efficiently.

If you are not ready for this challenge, you can skip this section and go to the next section to practice writing characters or go on to the next chapter to learn to recognize more Chinese characters. You can return to this section later.

1. Listen and read (choose the form you prefer):

(In the traditional form)

Shì wǎng fù wén yán,
士王父文言，

Yòu jiāo zhǐ gèn jiàn,
又交止艮見，

Guǐ shǒu yè shì yuán,
鬼首頁示元，

Dǎi ròu shī gǔ qiàn.
歹肉屍骨欠。

(In the normalized form)

Shì wǎng fù wén yán,
士王父文言，

Yòu jiāo zhǐ gèn jiàn,
又交止艮见，

Guǐ shǒu yè shì yuán,
鬼首页示元，

Dǎi ròu shī gǔ qiàn.
歹肉尸骨欠。

2. Read aloud by looking only at the characters:

(In the traditional form)

士王父文言，

又交止艮見，

鬼首頁元示，

歹肉屍骨欠。

(In the normalized form)

士王父文言，

又交止艮见，

鬼首页元示，

歹肉尸骨欠。

3. Guess the answers to the following riddles using the characters in the list. Answer the riddle in Chinese aloud to yourself or to someone who can help with pronunciation, and write the character in the box and its *pinyin* transliteration outside the box after each riddle. Note that in each group there are nine riddles for nine of the ten characters in the list.

Group 1: 又交止艮见士王父文言

a) It is an action requiring use of the eye.

b) It is the man who gave you life.

c) It is in the shape of a footprint but is used to convey the concept "to stop."

d) It is what you use your mouth and tongue to make.

e) It is an action you turn around and use your eyes to do.

f) It is in the shape of the right hand but is borrowed to mean "again" for a repeated action.

g) It is the most powerful person in a kingdom.

h) The character is the result of ten plus one.

i) It depicts the upper body with tattoos and now conveys the idea of "writing."

Group 2: 鬼首页示元歹肉尸骨欠

a) It is what some people believe a person becomes after death.

b) It originally referred to an action we often take when we feel sleepy, but now its extended meaning is "lack."

c) It symbolizes a human head, but it is used to refer to a side of paper.

d) It indicates a human head, but it is often used for a monetary unit now.

e) It is hard and forms the structure of one's body.

f) It is soft and is all over one's body.

g) It is the body of a dead person.

h) It is in the shape of an altar, and it means "to show."

i) It depicts a piece of broken bone, and it implies the concept "bad."

V. Challenge 4: Dictation 挑战四: 听音书形知义

1. By now, you should be able to recite the character verse for this chapter. Write the verse in Chinese characters and the meaning of each character in the spaces provided below:

Shì	wǎng	fù	wén	yán	,

Yòu	jiāo	zhǐ	gěn	jiàn	,

Guǐ	shǒu	yè	shì	yuán	,

Dǎi	ròu	shī	gǔ	qiàn	.

2. Look at the *pinyin*, say it aloud, and write the character in the first box and the meaning in English in the second. If two characters have the same pronunciation, a clue to the English meaning is given.

pinyin	character	meaning	pinyin	character	meaning
yòu			fù		
shǒu			dǎi		
shī			shì		ad____
yán			jiāo		
guǐ			yè		
ròu			gǔ		
jiàn			wáng		
wén			zhǐ		

shì　　　　　al____　　yuán

gěn　　　　　　　　　qiàn

3. Have your instructor dictate the characters or words covered in Chapter 6.

Chapter 7 第七章
Basic Characters for Animals, Food, and Clothing
表示动物、食物、衣物的基本汉字

I. Fundamental Knowledge 基础知识

A. Shapes and Meanings 见形思义

	Drawing 图	Ancient Character Shape 古字形	Modern Character Shape 今字形	Meaning 字义
1.		半	牛	ox/cow
2.		羊	羊	sheep/goat
3.		馬	马	horse
4.		犬	犬	dog
5.		象	象	elephant
6.		鳥	鸟	bird
7.		隹	佳	short-tailed bird
8.		貝	贝	shell

9.		龟	虫	insect
10.		魚	鱼	fish
11.		角	角	horn
12.		爪	爪	claw/hand
13.		毛	毛	hair/fur
14.		羽	羽	feather
15.		皮	皮	skin/leather
16.		瓜	瓜	melon
17.		果	果	fruit
18.		巾	巾	towel
19.		絲	丝	silk

| 20. | 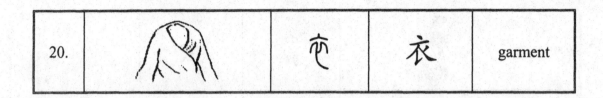 | 衣 | 衣 | garment |

B. Trace the Roots and Understand with Reason 追根溯源，晓之以理

牛 This character means "ox," which is one of the earliest domesticated animals. The oldest form of the character depicted the upward-pointing horns as the most salient feature of an ox. However, after the clerical change, the part that used to indicate the horns became a left-falling stroke and a horizontal stroke. This character is also used to mean "cow."

Oracle	Bronze	Seal	Clerical	Regular	Normal-ized	Semi-cursive	Cursive
牛	牛	牛	牛	牛	牛	牛	牛

羊 This character represents "sheep," another of the earliest domesticated animals. The earliest form of this character in the oracle-bone inscriptions again depicted the most salient part of the animal: the head of a goat with curving horns. This character is also used to mean "goat."

Oracle	Bronze	Seal	Clerical	Regular	Normal-ized	Semi-cursive	Cursive
羊	羊	羊	羊	羊	羊	羊	羊

马 This character refers to still another of the earliest domesticated animals—the horse. In its earliest form in the oracle-bone inscriptions, the whole horse was sketched out. In the bronze inscriptions, the eye and mane are emphasized. The character in its normalized form keeps only the contour of the regular form.

Oracle	Bronze	Seal	Clerical	Regular	Normal-ized	Semi-cursive	Cursive
馬	馬	馬	馬	馬	马	马	马

犬 The regular form of this character is 大 with an additional dot on the upper right side. The character 大 depicts a giant and means "big"; however, 犬 has nothing to do with "giant." It refers to one of the earliest domesticated animals kept and used by man for hunting. Its earliest form in the oracle-bone inscriptions was actually a drawing of a dog, emphasizing the tail. Only after the clerical change, did the character begin to take the form that it is still used today.

Oracle	Bronze	Seal	Clerical	Regular	Normal-ized	Semi-cursive	Cursive

象   The earliest form of this character in the oracle-bone inscriptions was a sketch of an elephant with its head at the top and tail at the bottom and with its trunk as the prominent feature. Without looking at the earliest forms of this character, we can hardly know, from the more recent forms of the character, that the character means "elephant."

Oracle	Bronze	Seal	Clerical	Regular	Normal-ized	Semi-cursive	Cursive

鸟   From its form in the normalized script, one can hardly figure out what this character refers to. However, its earliest form, in the oracle-bone inscriptions, clearly depicted a bird. The dot in the center of the character in the normalized script is still believed to represent the eye of the bird.

Oracle	Bronze	Seal	Clerical	Regular	Normal-ized	Semi-cursive	Cursive

隹   The earliest form of this character in the oracle-bone inscriptions may not be clear, but from its form in the bronze inscriptions, we can see that it is a bird with its head, wings, and legs. The difference in meaning between this character and the previous one is that this character refers to birds with short tails. This character is seldom used by itself in modern Chinese. It is often seen as a component in other characters.

Oracle	Bronze	Seal	Clerical	Regular	Normal-ized	Semi-cursive	Cursive

贝 The earliest forms of this character in the oracle-bone and bronze inscriptions were drawings of an opening seashell. Therefore, this character means "shell" or "cowrie." Because cowries were often used as currency in ancient times, this character is often used as a semantic component in other characters, the meanings of which are related to money and wealth.

Oracle	Bronze	Seal	Clerical	Regular	Normal-ized	Semi-cursive	Cursive

虫 In the oracle-bone inscriptions, this character took the form of a worm. In the bronze inscriptions, the head and the two eyes were emphasized. In the seal script, the character was formed with three "worms" and meant "worm" and all creatures that look like a worm, including snakes. In the normalized form, the character is simplified with only one "worm," reverting to its earliest form in the oracle-bone and bronze inscriptions. In modern Chinese, this character refers not only to worms but also to insects in general.

Oracle	Bronze	Seal	Clerical	Regular	Normal-ized	Semi-cursive	Cursive

鱼 In the earliest forms of this character in the oracle-bone and bronze inscriptions, we can see a picture of a fish with scales and fins. In the normalized script, the fish body with scales is represented by a part that looks like the character 田 (farmland), but it has nothing to do with farmland. The tail becomes a horizontal stroke in the normalized script.

Oracle	Bronze	Seal	Clerical	Regular	Normal-ized	Semi-cursive	Cursive

角 In the oracle-bone inscriptions, this character was a picture of a horn. In the bronze inscriptions, the character is a picture of a horn with something attached to its top, perhaps the string tied to a horn that is used as a clarion. The character in the normalized script does not have the shape of a horn, and like many other characters, it is just a symbol representing "horn."

Oracle	Bronze	Seal	Clerical	Regular	Normal-ized	Semi-cursive	Cursive

爪 The earliest form of this character in the oracle-bone inscriptions looked like a hand, indicating the meaning "to grasp." The form of this character in the bronze inscriptions had nails added to two of the fingers. Beginning with the seal script, this character has maintained the shape of a claw and mostly refers to the claw of an animal when it is used alone. When used as a component in a character, it still represents a grasping hand.

Oracle	Bronze	Seal	Clerical	Regular	Normal-ized	Semi-cursive	Cursive

毛 The earliest form of this character has not been found in the oracle-bone inscriptions, but in the bronze inscriptions the character is a sketch of fur or hair. Therefore, the meaning of the character is "fur" or "hair."

Oracle	Bronze	Seal	Clerical	Regular	Normal-ized	Semi-cursive	Cursive

羽 The previous character, 毛, refers to hair that grows on the bodies of animals and human beings in general, whereas this character, 羽, specifically refers to the feathers of birds.

Oracle	Bronze	Seal	Clerical	Regular	Normal-ized	Semi-cursive	Cursive

皮 The earliest form of this character can be found in the bronze inscriptions. It showed a hand on the lower right peeling off the skin of a beast. This character, therefore, has as its primary meaning "hide" or "leather." The character is also commonly used to mean "skin."

Oracle	Bronze	Seal	Clerical	Regular	Normal-ized	Semi-cursive	Cursive

瓜 Although it looks like the character for "claw," this character means "melon." The earliest form of this character in the bronze inscriptions depicted a melon hanging from two branching vines. The part depicting the melon has been simplified, starting with the seal script.

Oracle	Bronze	Seal	Clerical	Regular	Normal-ized	Semi-cursive	Cursive

果 This character means "fruit." From its earliest form in the oracle-bone inscriptions, we can see that the character is a sketch of a tree bearing fruit. In the bronze inscriptions, the fruit on the tree was shown among leaves. Starting with the seal script, the top of the tree with fruit has been represented by a part that looks like the character for "farmland."

Oracle	Bronze	Seal	Clerical	Regular	Normal-ized	Semi-cursive	Cursive

巾 The form of this character has remained the same throughout history. It is a sketch of a piece of cloth hanging on a pole. The meaning of the character is "towel."

Oracle	Bronze	Seal	Clerical	Regular	Normal-ized	Semi-cursive	Cursive

丝 Thousands of years ago, people in China knew how to make silk fabric from the fibers produced by silkworm larvae to form cocoons. This character depicts two wisps of silk reeled from cocoons, and it means "silk."

Oracle	Bronze	Seal	Clerical	Regular	Normal-ized	Semi-cursive	Cursive

衣 This character means "garment." We can easily see, from its earliest forms in the oracle-bone and bronze inscriptions that the character is a sketch of an upper garment. The top part of the character indicates the collar, the two sides are the sleeves, and at the bottom is the front of the garment.

Oracle	Bronze	Seal	Clerical	Regular	Normal-ized	Semi-cursive	Cursive
衣	衣	衣	衣	衣	衣	衣	衣

C. Recognition Reinforcement 辨认巩固练习

1. Go back to the beginning of this chapter. Look at the drawings and the characters. Then cover the drawings and try to remember the meaning of each character.

2. Link each character on the first line with its corresponding meaning in English on the second line:

a.   牛   羊   马   犬   象

   horse   elephant   sheep   ox   dog

b.   鸟   隹   贝   虫   鱼

   fish   bird   shell   short-tailed bird   insect

c.   角   爪   毛   羽   皮

   claw   skin/leather   horn   fur/hair   feather

d.   瓜   果   巾   丝   衣

   melon   silk   fruit   garment   towel

3. There are ten characters on the left side and eleven words in English on the right side. Put the letter for each character in the blank next to the corresponding English word. In each group, there is an extra blank that should be left empty.

Group 1:

a. 犬

b. 贝

c. 鱼

d. 象

e. 虫

f. 牛

g. 隹

h. 马

i. 鸟

j. 羊

_____elephant

_____bird

_____horse

_____shell

_____ox

_____sheep

_____dog

_____horn

_____insect

_____ short-tailed bird

_____fish

Group 2:

a. 皮

b. 果

c. 毛

d. 巾

e. 丝

f. 瓜

g. 衣

h. 角

i. 羽

j. 爪

_____silk

_____fur/hair

_____ garment

_____melon

_____insect

_____leather/skin

_____claw

_____fruit

_____feather

_____towel

_____horn

4. Provide the meaning in English for each of the following characters:

牛_____ 羊_____ 马_____ 犬_____ 象_____

鸟＿＿＿＿＿   隹＿＿＿＿＿   贝＿＿＿＿＿   虫＿＿＿＿＿   鱼＿＿＿＿＿

角＿＿＿＿＿   爪＿＿＿＿＿   毛＿＿＿＿＿   羽＿＿＿＿＿   皮＿＿＿＿＿

瓜＿＿＿＿＿   果＿＿＿＿＿   巾＿＿＿＿＿   丝＿＿＿＿＿   衣＿＿＿＿＿

II. Challenge 1: Write the Characters 挑战一: 知义书形

A. Strokes in Characters 详说笔画

Two characters in this chapter contain a new complex stroke:

ㄅ *shùzhézhégōu* (a vertical stroke with two turns and a hook), as in 马 鸟

Write this stroke, paying attention to the direction of the stroke movement as indicated.

ㄅ					

Review the strokes you have learned by doing the following two exercises.

Exercise 1: What are the six basic strokes? Match them with their names in *pinyin*.

a) 一   b) ｜   c) ／   d) ＼   e) 丶   f) ✓

piě ＿＿＿＿＿＿   diǎn ＿＿＿＿＿＿   shù ＿＿＿＿＿＿

tí ＿＿＿＿＿＿   héng ＿＿＿＿＿＿   nà ＿＿＿＿＿＿

Exercise 2: These strokes end with a hook. Match them with their names in *pinyin*.

a) ㇆   b) ㇄   c) ㇠   d) ㇈   e) ｜   f) ）   g) ㇄   h) ㄅ

shùgōu ＿＿＿   wāngōu ＿＿＿   héngzhéwāngōu ＿＿＿   héngzhégōu ＿＿＿

shùwāngōu ＿＿＿   héngzhéxiégōu ＿＿＿   shùzhézhégōu ＿＿＿   wògōu ＿＿＿

B. *Stroke Order Analysis* 笔顺分析

Write a new character by applying your knowledge of the stroke order first, and then compare it with the standard stroke order for that character. The number of empty boxes provided indicates the number of strokes for the character in the first box.   Write one stroke after another in the empty boxes provided as the example given below shows. Try to determine the reason for any difference in the stroke order or the number of strokes.

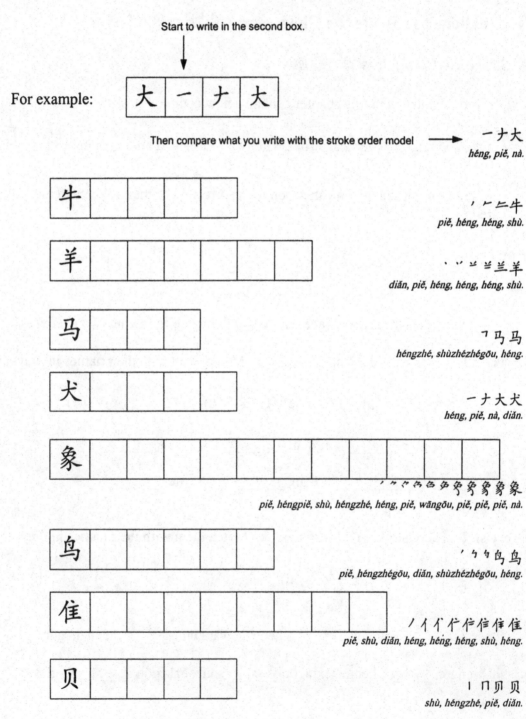

Start to write in the second box.

For example:

Then compare what you write with the stroke order model ⟶ 一 ナ 大
héng, piě, nà.

牛
, , ⺧ 牛
piě, héng, héng, shù.

羊
, ⺀ ⺨ 兰 兰 羊
diǎn, piě, héng, héng, héng, shù.

马
⁊ 马 马
héngzhé, shùzhézhégōu, héng.

犬
一 ナ 大 犬
héng, piě, nà, diǎn.

象
, ⺀ ⺈ 仱 仱 刍 刍 刍 象 象 象
piě, héngpiě, shù, héngzhé, héng, piě, wāngōu, piě, piě, nà.

鸟
, ⺈ ⺈ 鸟 鸟
piě, héngzhégōu, diǎn, shùzhézhégōu, héng.

隹
ノ 亻 亻 仁 仼 仼 住 隹
piě, shù, diǎn, héng, héng, héng, shù, héng.

贝
丨 冂 贝 贝
shù, héngzhé, piě, diǎn.

虫

丨 冂 口 中 虫 虫
shù, héngzhé, héng, shù, héng, diǎn.

鱼

丿 ⺈ ⺈ 鱼 鱼 鱼 鱼
piě, héngpiě, piě, héngzhé, héng, shù, héng, héng.

角

丿 ⺈ ⺈ 角 角 角 角
piě, héngpiě, shù, héngzhégōu, héng, héng, shù.

爪

丿 厂 爪 爪
piě, piě, shù, nà.

毛

丿 二 三 毛
piě, héng, héng, shùwāngōu.

羽

丨 丨 习 羽 羽 羽
héngzhégōu, diǎn, tí, héngzhégōu, diǎn, tí.

皮

一 厂 广 皮 皮
hénggōu, piě, shù, héngpiě, nà.

瓜

丿 厂 爪 瓜 瓜
piě, piě, shùtí, diǎn, nà.

果

丨 冂 曰 旦 旦 甲 里 果
shù, héngzhé, héng, héng, héng, shù, piě, nà.

巾

丨 冂 巾
shù, héngzhégōu, shù.

丝

丿 ⺱ ⺱ 丝 丝
piězhé, piězhé, piězhé, piězhé, héng.

衣

丶 一 ⼇ 亠 衣 衣
diǎn, héng, piě, shùtí, piě, nà.

C. Write with a Pencil 动手动笔

Now that you know the meaning as well as the standard stroke order for each of the characters, it is time to practice writing balanced and well-proportioned characters. Use the following "well" boxes to write each character. It is actually not enough just to write in the boxes provided in the book. You may want to practice writing each character on a piece of paper. While writing, you should take a good look at the model character and then try to write it by heart without referring to the model. Each time you finish writing the character, you can compare it with the model. Correct any mistakes and write until you do it correctly without looking at the model.

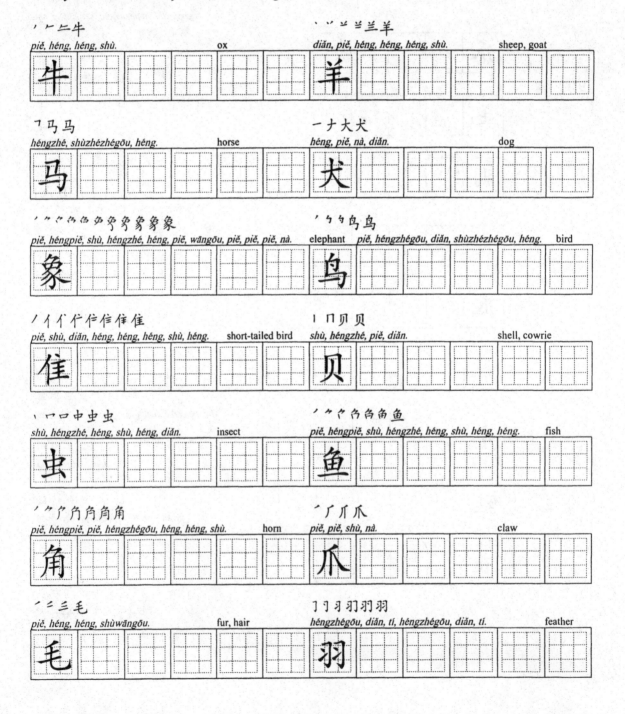

ノ 亻 二 牛
piě, héng, héng, shù.   ox

丶 丷 兰 羊
diǎn, piě, héng, héng, héng, shù.   sheep, goat

牛

羊

フ 马 马
héngzhé, shùzhézhégōu, héng.   horse

一 ナ 大 犬
héng, piě, nà, diǎn.   dog

马

犬

ノ 夕 夕 夕 冬 夸 夸 象 象 象
piě, héngpiě, shù, héngzhé, héng, piě, wāngōu, piě, piě, piě, nà.   elephant

ノ ク ク 乌 鸟
piě, héngzhégōu, diǎn, shùzhézhégōu, héng.   bird

象

鸟

ノ 亻 亻 亻 亻 仨 隹 隹 佳
piě, shù, diǎn, héng, héng, héng, shù, héng.   short-tailed bird

丨 冂 贝 贝
shù, héngzhé, piě, diǎn.   shell, cowrie

隹

贝

丨 冂 口 中 虫 虫
shù, héngzhé, héng, shù, héng, diǎn.   insect

ノ ク ク 鱼 鱼 角 鱼
piě, héngpiě, shù, héngzhé, héng, shù, héng, héng.   fish

虫

鱼

ノ 夕 广 角 角 角 角
piě, héngpiě, piě, héngzhégōu, héng, héng, shù.   horn

ノ 广 爪 爪
piě, piě, shù, nà.   claw

角

爪

ノ 二 三 毛
piě, héng, héng, shùwāngōu.   fur, hair

丁 丁 羽 羽 羽 羽
héngzhégōu, diǎn, tí, héngzhégōu, diǎn, tí.   feather

毛

羽

一 厂 广 皮 皮
hénggōu, piě, shù, héngpiě, nà.　　leather, skin

丿 厂 瓜 瓜 瓜
piě, piě, shùtí, diǎn, nà.　　melon

皮

瓜

丨 冂 曱 日 旦 早 果 果
shù, héngzhé, héng, héng, héng, shù, piě, nà.　　fruit

丨 冂 巾
shù, héngzhégōu, shù.　　towel

果

巾

乙 幺 幺 纟 纟 丝
piězhé, piězhé, piězhé, piězhé, héng.　　silk

丶 亠 亠 衣 衣 衣
diǎn, héng, piě, shùtí, piě, nà.　　garment

丝

衣

III. Challenge 2: Apply Your Knowledge　挑战二: 举一反三

A. Know Many Things by Learning One 闻一知十

1. You have learned the character 象, which means "elephant." Once you can recognize this character and know how to write it, you should be able to learn another two characters almost effortlessly: 豕 and 兔. The first one, 豕, resembles the lower part of 象, and the second one, 兔, takes after the upper part of 象. However, they have nothing to do with "elephant" except that they are also animals. 豕 means "pig," which looks like a small elephant without a trunk. 兔 means "rabbit," which has long ears but a very short tail.

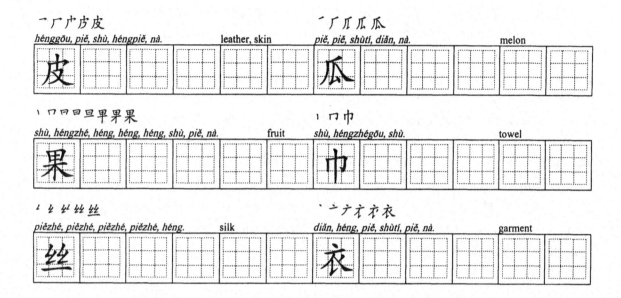

Oracle	Bronze	Seal	Clerical	Regular	Normalized	Semi-cursive	Cursive

2. The character 虫 means "worm" and all creatures that look like a worm, including snakes. There are another three characters that were originally used to mean "snake," and you can see that their earliest forms were in the shape of a snake. However, in modern Chinese, they are all used to mean something other than "snake."

One is 巴, which has several meanings now, but the major one is "to hope earnestly." It is pronounced as *bā*, and you will see it often as a phonetic component in forming other complex characters, such as 把 (hold), 爸 (dad), and 疤 (scar).

Another character is 它. A long time ago when people lived in thatched houses, they were often bitten by snakes and sometimes died. When people met, they would show concern for each other by asking, "There is no 它, right?" It then became a form of greeting each other. 它 then slowly began to be used as a pronoun, meaning "it" in modern Chinese.

The third character that used to refer to a snake is 也. However, in modern Chinese, it is used to mean "also." In addition, in modern Chinese, the pronouns "he" and "she" have 也 as a component: 他 (he) and 她 (she).

If in modern Chinese 虫 means "worm" or "insect," and none of the other three characters (i.e., 巴, 它, and 也) means "snake," then how is "snake" represented? The character that is used for "snake" in modern Chinese is a complex character that combines 虫 and 它: 蛇.

Original Meaning	Oracle	Bronze	Seal	Clerical	Regular	Normalized	Semi-cursive	Cursive	Modern Chinese Meaning
snake		己	弓	巴	巴	巴	巴	弓	to hope earnestly
snake	◇	它	它	它	它	它	它	它	it
snake	也	也	也	也	也	也	也	also
snake			蛇	蛇	蛇	蛇	蛇	蛇	snake

3. The characters 瓜 and 果 refer to "melon" and "fruit," which are common foods for humans. Beans are also a common food for humans; however, no character has ever been created for beans. Rather, a character originally used to refer to a food container with a stand and a cover was borrowed to mean "beans." This character is 豆.

Original Meaning	Oracle	Bronze	Seal	Clerical	Regular	Normalized	Semi-cursive	Cursive	Modern Chinese Meaning
food container	豆	豆	豆	豆	豆	豆	豆	豆	beans

Now, let's solve the problem of food for each of the following. Who or what eats which kind of food? Fill in the blanks with all the applicable choices:

米   艸(草)   瓜   果   肉   豆

人 _____ _____ _____ _____ _____ _____

牛 ___ ___ ___ ___ ___ ___

虫 ___ ___ ___ ___ ___ ___

鸟 ___ ___ ___ ___ ___ ___

象 ___ ___ ___ ___ ___ ___

蛇 ___ ___ ___ ___ ___ ___

Answers:
人：米瓜果
肉豆
牛：草
虫：米草瓜
果肉豆
鸟：米草瓜
果豆：草果
象：草果
蛇：肉

4. Here are some two-syllable words and phrases formed by some of the characters in this chapter and previous chapters. Can you figure out what they mean?

a. 牛肉 _____ fruit skin

b. 象牙 _____ woolen sweater

c. 羊角 _____ ivory

d. 羽毛 _____ ram's horn

e. 毛衣 _____ silk scarf

f. 果皮 _____ beef

g. 丝巾 _____ plume

Answers:
f. fruit skin
e. woolen sweater
b. ivory
c. ram's horn
g. silk scarf
a. beef
d. plume

B. Be Perceptive of the Slightest Differences 明察秋毫

1. Which character in each group have you not yet learned? Circle it.

a. Group 1
   i. 牛   ii. 犬   iii. 马   iv. 车

b. Group 2
   i. 刀   ii. 爪   iii. 贝   iv. 虫

c. Group 3
   i. 鸟   ii. 羽   iii. 井   iv. 皮

d. Group 4
     i. 果   ii. 斗   iii. 巾   iv. 衣

e. Group 5
     i. 丝   ii. 瓜   iii. 网   iv. 角

f. Group 6
     i. 象   ii. 穴   iii. 隹   iv. 毛

Answers: a. iv. b. i. c. iii. d. iii. e. ii. f. ii.

2. Which of the characters in each group is different?

a. Which character does not have a *héng* as the last stroke?
     i. 马   ii. 丝   iii. 羊   iv. 鱼

b. Which character does not have a *nà* as the last stroke?
     i. 犬   ii. 象   iii. 瓜   iv. 衣

c. Which character does not have a *piě* as the first stroke?
     i. 皮   ii. 牛   iii. 鸟   iv. 角

d. Which character does not have a *shù* as the first stroke?
     i. 贝   ii. 马   iii. 巾   iv. 虫

e. Which character does not have a *diǎn* as the first stroke?
     i. 羽   ii. 羊   iii. 衣   iv. 文

f. Which character does not have a *héngpiě* stroke?
     i. 角   ii. 象   iii. 鸟   iv. 鱼

g. Which character contains a *shùzhézhégōu* stroke?
     i. 毛   ii. 马   iii. 象   iv. 皮

h. Which character contains a *shùtí* stroke?
     i. 巾   ii. 虫   iii. 鸟   iv. 衣

Answers: a. iii. b. iv. c. i. d. iii. e. ii. f. iii. g. ii. h. iv.

3. How many strokes are there?

a. Which character has fewer than four strokes?

     i. 牛   ii. 犬   iii. 马   iv. 爪

b. Which character has more than four strokes?

     i. 贝   ii. 皮   iii. 巾   iv. 毛

c. Which character has only five strokes?

     i. 鸟   ii. 衣   iii. 羽   iv. 虫

e. Which character has only seven strokes?

     i. 羊   ii. 瓜   iii. 角   iv. 象

f. Which character does not have eight strokes?

     i. 隹   ii. 果   iii. 鱼   iv. 丝

Answers: a. iii. b. ii. c. i. d. e. iv. f. iv.

C. Be Aware of the Complex Counterpart 学简知繁

If you choose not to learn the complex forms now, at the beginning level, you may skip this section and go on to the next section for Challenge 3.

1. Comparison. In this chapter, there are six simplified characters. Look at the following table and compare the simplified forms of the characters with their complex counterparts:

	Simplified Form	Complex Form	Meaning
1	马	馬	horse
2	鸟	鳥	bird
3	贝	貝	shell
4	虫	蟲	insect
5	鱼	魚	fish
6	丝	絲	silk

2. Explanation.

馬. This is the traditional form of the character. The upper part has a vertical stroke across two horizontal strokes, indicating the eye and mane of a horse. The four dots in the lower part of the character represent the four legs.

鳥. The four dots in this traditional form of the character represent the two legs of a bird; the bird eye is also indicated with a short horizontal stroke in the upper part of the character. The left-falling stroke at the top of the character appears to indicate the crest of a bird.

貝. The traditional form of this character has three horizontal strokes for the shell, and the two strokes at the bottom indicate the mollusk coming from inside the shell.

蟲. The earliest forms of the character in the oracle-bone and bronze inscriptions had only one 虫. However, this character had three 虫 in its form in the seal script, clerical script, and regular script. The normalized form of the character has reassumed the original shape of the character with only one 虫.

魚. The four dots at the bottom of this character are not used to indicate legs but the tail of a fish.

絲. The traditional form of this character is a combination of two 糸 side by side. However, the lower part of 糸 on the left has been changed from 小 to three dots to accommodate 糸 on the right, melding the two components together as an integral whole.

For explanations of the simplified counterparts of these complex characters, please refer to Section B in Part I of this chapter.

3. Writing. Write these six characters in their traditional form.

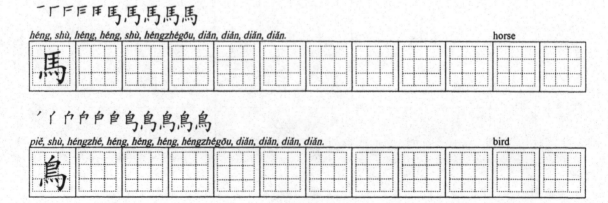

一丆厂FF馬馬馬馬馬

héng, shù, héng, héng, shù, héngzhégōu, diǎn, diǎn, diǎn, diǎn.   horse

馬										

´ ⺁ ⼾ ⼾ 自 鳥鳥鳥鳥鳥

piě, shù, héngzhé, héng, héng, héng, héngzhégōu, diǎn, diǎn, diǎn, diǎn.   bird

鳥										

丨 冂 冂 冃 目 貝 貝

shù, héngzhé, héng, héng, héng, piě, diǎn.　　　　　　　　　　　　　　shell

貝

丶 冂 口 中 虫 虫 虫 虫 蚩 ……

shù, héngzhé, héng, shù, tí, diǎn. (three times)　　　　　　　　　　insect

蟲

丿 ⺈ ⺈ 夂 夅 角 鱼 鱼 鱼 魚 魚

piě, héngpiě, shù, héngzhé, héng, shù, héng, diǎn, diǎn, diǎn, diǎn.　　fish

魚

乚 ⺋ ⺋ ⺋ 幺 幺 糸 紅 絲 絲 絲 絲

piězhé, piězhé, diǎn, diǎn, diǎn, diǎn, piězhé, piězhé, diǎn, shùgōu, diǎn, diǎn.　silk

絲

IV. Challenge 3: Pronounce the Characters 挑战三：见形发音

To establish the link between the shape of a character and its pronunciation is the purpose of Challenge 3. As the shape of a character does not provide a clue to the pronunciation of the character, it will be a real challenge for you. To take on the challenge successfully, you will need to listen to a recording of the verse written with the characters in this chapter. If you do not have a recording of the verse, then ask your instructor to make one for you. Only when you have repeatedly listened to the verse will you be ready to read it aloud. Read it aloud as accurately and as frequently as possible until you are able to memorize it. Memorization of the verse will help you remember the meaning, pronunciation, and shape of the characters in the verse.

If you are not ready for this challenge, you can skip this section and go to the next section to practice writing characters or go on to the next chapter to learn to recognize more Chinese characters. You can return to this section later.

1. Listen and read (choose the form you prefer):

(In the traditional form)　　　　　　　*(In the normalized form)*

Niú yáng mǎ quǎn xiàng,　　　　　　Niú yáng mǎ quǎn xiàng,
牛羊馬犬象，　　　　　　　　　　牛羊马犬象，

Niǎo zhuī bèi chóng yú,
鳥隹貝虫魚,

Jiǎo zhuǎ máo yǔ pí,
角爪毛羽皮,

Guā guǒ jīn sī yī.
瓜果巾絲衣。

Niǎo zhuī bèi chóng yú,
鸟隹贝虫鱼,

Jiǎo zhuǎ máo yǔ pí,
角爪毛羽皮,

Guā guǒ jīn sī yī.
瓜果巾丝衣。

2. Read aloud by looking only at the characters:

(In the traditional form)

牛羊馬犬象,

鳥隹貝虫魚,

角爪毛羽皮,

瓜果巾絲衣。

(In the normalized form)

牛羊马犬象,

鸟隹贝虫鱼,

角爪毛羽皮,

瓜果巾丝衣。

3. Guess the answers to the following riddles using the characters in the list. Answer the riddle in Chinese aloud to yourself or to someone who can help with your pronunciation, and write the character in the box and its *pinyin* transliteration outside the box after each riddle. Note that in each group there are nine riddles for nine of the ten characters in the list.

Group 1: 牛羊马犬象鸟隹贝虫鱼

a) It has no legs but has eyes, and it swims in the water.

b) It is big and runs fast; therefore, it is fun to watch in races.

c) It has wings but its tail is short.

d) It can be found at the beach and was once used as money.

e) It is the animal that has the longest nose of all.

f) It can help with the farm work and is good at producing milk.

g) It is famous for its hair, which people use to make clothing.

h) It can help people hunt and is often kept as a pet.

i) It is a generic term for small creatures that crawl or fly.

Group 2: 角爪毛羽皮瓜果巾丝衣

a) It usually grows on trees and is delicious to eat.

b) It is hard and pointed and grows on an ox's or a ram's head.

c) It comes from cocoons and makes elegant dresses.

d) It can be hard and pointed and is used to refer to the feet of a bird or an animal.

e) It is a long piece of cloth people use to dry themselves with.

f) It can be huge and delicious to eat and grows on a vine.

g) It grows on a bird's body and once was used as a writing instrument in Europe.

h) It is made by people to cover their bodies.

□

i) It refers to the surface of animals, fruits, and human
   beings.

□

V. Challenge 4: Dictation 挑战四: 听音书形知义

1. By now, you should be able to recite the character verse for this chapter. Write
the verse in Chinese characters and the meaning for each character in the spaces provided
below:

Niú	yáng	mǎ	quǎn	xiàng	,

Niǎo	zhuī	bèi	chóng	yú	,

Jiǎo	zhuǎ	máo	yǔ	pí	,

Guā	guǒ	jīn	sī	yī	.

2. Look at the *pinyin*, say it aloud, and write the character in the first box and the
meaning in English in the second.

pinyin	*character*	*meaning*	*pinyin*	*character*	*meaning*
yī			niǎo		

yǔ			quǎn		
bèi			pí		
yáng			chóng		
niú			mǎ		
zhuī			jiǎo		
máo			jīn		
sī			guǒ		
guā			xiàng		
zhuǎ			yú		

3. Have your instructor dictate the characters or words covered in Chapter 7.

Chapter 8 第八章
Basic Characters for Habitation, Household Utensils, Weapons, Means of Transportation, and Tools
表示住所、器皿、武器、交通工具及劳动工具的基本汉字

I. Fundamental Knowledge 基础知识

A. Shapes and Meanings 见形思义

	Drawing 图	Ancient Character Shape 古字形	Modern Character Shape 今字形	Meaning 字义
1.		門	门	door
2.		戶	户	one-leaf door/ household
3.		内	穴	cave
4.		廣	广	shelter/vast
5.		厰	厂	cliff/factory
6.		勺	勺	ladle
7.		皿	皿	utensil
8.		酉	酉	jar

9.		丼	井	well
10.		网	网	net
11.		刀	刀	knife
12.		戈	戈	dagger-axe
13.		弓	弓	bow
14.		車	车	vehicle
15.		舟	舟	boat
16.		个	丁	nail/person
17.		斤	斤	axe/500 Grams
18.		斗	斗	grain measure
19.		力	力	plow/strength

20.		工	工	tool/work

B. Trace the Roots and Understand with Reason 追根溯源，晓之以理

门　This character means "door" or "gate." The earliest forms of this character in the oracle-bone and bronze inscriptions depicted a door with two leaves. The normalized form derives from the cursive script, which has a frame and a dot on the upper left side of the frame indicating an opening.

Oracle	Bronze	Seal	Clerical	Regular	Normal-ized	Semi-cursive	Cursive
門	門	門	门	門	门	门	门

户　The earliest form of this character in the oracle-bone inscriptions was a sketch of a door with one leaf. A component indicating a tree was added to the form in the bronze inscriptions. This character may be used to refer to either a door or a window, but it is most commonly used in its extended meaning: "household."

Oracle	Bronze	Seal	Clerical	Regular	Normal-ized	Semi-cursive	Cursive
户	户	户	户	户	户	户	户

穴　The earliest form of this character, which means "cave," can be found in the seal script. It is believed that it depicted a semi-underground residence with a thatched roof from ancient times.

Oracle	Bronze	Seal	Clerical	Regular	Normal-ized	Semi-cursive	Cursive
		穴	穴	穴	穴	穴	穴

广　The earliest form of this character found in the oracle-bone inscriptions depicted a shelter with a cliff as its back wall. Therefore, its original meaning was "shelter" or "a house built against a mountain slope." In the normalized script, this character replaced the character 廣, which has the meaning "vast."

Therefore, 广 is now most commonly used to mean "vast" rather than "shelter."

Oracle	Bronze	Seal	Clerical	Regular	Normal-ized	Semi-cursive	Cursive
厂	廣	廣	廣	廣	广	广	广

厂 This character looks very similar to the previous character, 广. The only difference is that it does not have the dot on top. The earliest forms of this character in the oracle-bone and bronze inscriptions depicted a cliff, and its original meaning was "cliff." The place beneath a cliff could be a favorite place for people to dwell. In the normalized script, this character replaced the character 廠, which means "factory," and is most commonly used to refer to "factory" now.

Oracle	Bronze	Seal	Clerical	Regular	Normal-ized	Semi-cursive	Cursive
厂	厂	厰	廠	廠	厂	厂	厂

勺 This character means "ladle." In the seal script, we can still see the shape of a ladle depicted vertically. The lower part is the handle, attached to the part that looks like a bowl, and the dot in the bowl-shaped part appears to indicate something the ladle holds.

Oracle	Bronze	Seal	Clerical	Regular	Normal-ized	Semi-cursive	Cursive
		勺	勺	勺	勺	勺	勺

皿 This character means "utensil." Its earliest form in the oracle-bone inscriptions looks like a goblet or a vessel with a stand. After the clerical change, the goblet disappeared from the character.

Oracle	Bronze	Seal	Clerical	Regular	Normal-ized	Semi-cursive	Cursive
皿	皿	皿	皿	皿	皿	皿	皿

酉 From the earliest forms of this character in the oracle-bone and bronze inscriptions, we can see that the character is a sketch of a jar. As jars were commonly used to keep rice wine in the old days, this character was also used referred to "rice wine" until another character (酒) for rice wine was created.

Oracle	Bronze	Seal	Clerical	Regular	Normal-ized	Semi-cursive	Cursive
酉	酉	酉	酉	酉	酉	酉	丞

井 This character means "well." To protect a well from damage and make it safe for people to fetch water, edges and railings of some kind are often built as part of the well. Therefore, the earliest form of the character in the oracle-bone inscriptions had four strokes indicating railings of some kind. In the bronze inscriptions and the seal script, a dot was added in the center of the character to indicate water in the well. After the clerical change, the dot stroke was dropped.

Oracle	Bronze	Seal	Clerical	Regular	Normal-ized	Semi-cursive	Cursive
井	井	井	井	井	井	井	井

网 The earliest forms of this character in the oracle-bone and bronze inscriptions depicted a net. However, this character in the seal script began to have two forms. One of the forms became very complicated (see Seal [2] below). It has three components: 网, 糸, and 亡. 网 stands for "net," 糸 for "thread," which is what is used to make a net, and 亡 for the pronunciation of the character. The complex form of the character did not cease to be used in mainland China until the normalized form was introduced, which takes after the simple seal script form (see Seal [1]) below.

Oracle	Bronze	Seal (1)	Seal (2)	Clerical	Regular	Normal-ized	Semi-cursive	Cursive
网	网	网	網	網	網	网	网	网

刀 The earliest form of this character in the oracle-bone inscriptions was a sketch of a knife with its handle at the top. However, the handle has not been indicated in any form of the character since the clerical change.

Oracle	Bronze	Seal	Clerical	Regular	Normal-ized	Semi-cursive	Cursive
刀		刀	刀	刀	刀	刀	刀

戈 This character refers to a type of weapon similar to a spear. While a spear has a long handle with a pointed, vertical blade at its head, 戈 is a dagger-axe with a horizontal blade at its head and a long handle.

Oracle	Bronze	Seal	Clerical	Regular	Normal-ized	Semi-cursive	Cursive

弓 The meaning of this character is "bow"(the weapon). The earliest form of this character in the oracle-bone inscriptions was a picture of a complete bow with its back and string. However, we can see, from the form of the character in the bronze inscriptions, that the string was omitted with the back of the bow left to represent "bow." All the forms of the character after the bronze inscriptions have followed suit. This character, therefore, has no stroke to indicate the string of a bow.

Oracle	Bronze	Seal	Clerical	Regular	Normal-ized	Semi-cursive	Cursive

车 The earliest form of the character in the oracle-bone inscriptions was a picture of a cart with yokes at the top and a shaft linking it with a carriage at the bottom. We can also see that the carriage has an axle with two wheels. In the bronze inscriptions, there were two major forms for the character. One kept the yoke and the shaft and emphasized the two wheels while omitting the carriage in between them (Bronze [1]). The other emphasized a carriage with an axle and wheels at each end (Bronze [2]). As this second form kept the most important features of a cart (i.e., carriage, axle, and wheels), its shape was retained in the seal script, the clerical script, and the regular script. The form in the normalized script, however, has been further simplified, as it has in the cursive script. This character has long been used as a generic representation of vehicles.

Oracle	Bronze (1)	Bronze (2)	Seal	Clerical	Regular	Normal-ized	Semi-cursive	Cursive

舟　This character refers to another important means of transportation: a boat. Although it is hard to see that the character refers to "boat" from its various forms after the clerical change, it is relatively easy to understand and remember that it is a boat from its depiction in the oracle-bone and bronze inscriptions.

Oracle	Bronze	Seal	Clerical	Regular	Normal-ized	Semi-cursive	Cursive

丁　This character originally represented "nail." Its earliest form in the oracle-bone inscriptions is a tiny square, so the character has also been used to mean "small cubes." Since the character in the bronze inscriptions and the seal script also looked like an upright person, another meaning this character has represented is "sturdy person." To avoid confusion between its original meaning and its other extended meanings, the component 钅, meaning "metal" (which you will learn in Chapter 12), was added to the left side of 丁, and 钉 instead of 丁 is commonly used now to refer to a nail.

Oracle	Bronze	Seal	Clerical	Regular	Normal-ized	Semi-cursive	Cursive

斤　The original meaning of this character is "axe." The earliest form in the oracle-bone inscriptions depicted an axe with a handle and a sharp head. In the bronze inscriptions, the character appeared to have an axe on the left and a broken tree branch on the right. As the "axe" was once used as a measuring weight, this character has most commonly been used as a unit of weight equal to 500 grams.

Oracle	Bronze	Seal	Clerical	Regular	Normal-ized	Semi-cursive	Cursive

斗　The earliest form of this character in the bronze inscriptions was a sketch of a ladle, which is an instrument for measuring grain in China. It is also used as a unit of measure equal to one liter. In addition, the same form of the character in the normalized script also means "to fight." From the earliest form of the character that means "to fight" in the oracle-bone inscriptions, we can see that it is a picture of two people fighting with fists. However, in the normalized script, the character 斗 (with the tone changing from the dipping to the falling:

dŏu → dòu) is used in place of the character 鬥 to convey the meaning: "to fight."

Oracle	Bronze	Seal	Clerical	Regular	Normal-ized	Semi-cursive	Cursive
🦅	🦅	斗	斗	斗	斗	斗
🦅		🦅	鬥	鬥			

力 The original meaning of this character was "plow." We can see the shape of a plow in the earliest forms of this character in the oracle-bone and bronze inscriptions. Plows are powerful farming tools, and to use them well requires a lot of strength. Therefore, this character has been most commonly used for its extended meaning: "strength."

Oracle	Bronze	Seal	Clerical	Regular	Normal-ized	Semi-cursive	Cursive
⼒	⼒	肵	力	力	力	力	力

工 The original meaning of this character was "tool." As a sketch of a tool, the lower part represented a blade, and the upper horizontal and vertical strokes indicated the handle of the tool. The shape of the character has remained the same throughout history. People work with a tool to be more productive, and thus the character 工 has been most commonly used for its extended meaning: "work."

Oracle	Bronze	Seal	Clerical	Regular	Normal-ized	Semi-cursive	Cursive
吂	工	工	工	工	工	乙

C. Recognition Reinforcement 辨认巩固练习

1. Go back to the beginning of this chapter. Look at the drawings and the characters. Then cover the drawings and try to remember the meaning of each character.

2. Link each character on the first line with its corresponding meaning in English on the second line:

a. 门　户　穴　广　厂

shelter/vast　door　cliff/factory　one leaf of a door/household　cave

b. 勺　皿　酉　井　网

jar　well　utensil　net　ladle

c. 刀　戈　弓　车　舟

bow　boat　knife　vehicle　spear

d. 丁　斤　斗　力　工

axe/weight measure　strength　tool/work　nail/person　grain measure/fight

3．There are ten characters on the left side and eleven words in English on the right side.　Put the letter for each character in the blank next to the corresponding English word.　In each group, there is an extra blank that should be left empty.

Group 1:

a. 井

b. 勺
　　　　　　　　　　　　_____cave

c. 门
　　　　　　　　　　　　_____jar

d. 穴
　　　　　　　　　　　　_____net

e. 网
　　　　　　　　　　　　_____cliff/factory

f. 皿
　　　　　　　　　　　　_____ladle

g. 广
　　　　　　　　　　　　_____well

h. 酉
　　　　　　　　　　　　_____household

i. 户
　　　　　　　　　　　　_____knife

j. 厂
　　　　　　　　　　　　_____door

　　　　　　　　　　　　_____shelter/vast

　　　　　　　　　　　　_____ utensil

Group 2:

a. 弓   _____spear

b. 斤   _____nail

c. 工   _____boat

d. 刀   _____strength

e. 舟   _____grain measure/fight

f. 丁   _____bow

g. 力   _____vehicle

h. 斗   _____utensil

i. 戈   _____knife

j. 车   _____tool/work

_____axe/weight measure

4. Provide the meaning in English for each of the following characters:

门_____ 户_____ 穴_____ 广_____ 厂_____

勺_____ 皿_____ 酉_____ 井_____ 网_____

刀_____ 戈_____ 弓_____ 车_____ 舟_____

丁_____ 斤_____ 斗_____ 力_____ 工_____

II. Challenge 1: Write the Characters 挑战一: 知义书形

A. Strokes in Characters: The Dot 详说笔画: 点

1. *Different dots.* Among all the characters you have learned so far, each of the following characters contains at least one dot stroke (*diǎn*):

六 火 玉 米 雨 母 立 父 文 言 交 页

首 歹 肉 羊 犬 羽 鸟 瓜 衣 隹 贝 虫

These dots can be called right dots as they are written from left to right.   Another four characters you have learned also contain one or two right dots:

小 心 示 穴

They also contain a left dot, which is written from right to left:

小 心 示 穴

2. *The left dot stroke vs. the small left-falling stroke*. The left dot stroke should not be confused with the small left-falling stroke (*piě*) because they are different. The left dot stroke starts by putting the pen on the paper lightly, moving the pen towards the lower left side with some pressure and ending the stroke with a pause and the most pressure on the pen. However, the small left-falling stroke starts by pressing the pen on the paper and moving the pen quickly to the lower left side while lifting it up. If a brush pen is used, the differences in the thickness at both ends of these two different strokes can be seen clearly:

Stroke Names	Strokes	Examples
Left dot stroke	丶	小 心 示 穴
Small left-falling stroke	丿	小 心 示 穴

3. *The stroke order for the dot strokes*. For all the dot strokes in characters, the stroke order rules you have learned are applicable. However, when a dot stroke is over a horizontal stroke and on the right side of a left-falling stroke or of a right-falling stroke (i.e., in the upper right corner of a character), it should be the last stroke written. 犬 (dog), one of the characters you have learned, is a good example.

一 ナ 大 犬

How should the character 戋 in this chapter be written? Write the character one stroke after another cumulatively in the boxes provided below and compare with the answer provided below upside-down. By the way, 乀 in 戋 is *xiégōu* (a slanting stroke with a hook). Because it is a part of the stroke, 乚 *héngzhéxiégōu*, in 气 (air), which you learned in Chapter 4, you are expected to be able to write it.

戈 | | | |

弌 弌 弋 一

B. Stroke Order Analysis 笔顺分析

Write a new character by applying your knowledge of the stroke order first, and then compare it with the standard stroke order for that character. The number of empty boxes provided indicates the number of strokes for the character in the first box. Write one stroke after another in the empty boxes, as indicated in the example below. Try to determine the reason for any difference in the stroke order or the number of strokes.

Start to write in the second box.

For example: 大 | 一 | 大 | 大

Then compare what you write with the stroke order model ⟶ 一 ナ 大
héng, piě, nà.

门 | | |

`丶 冂 门`
diǎn, shù, héngzhégōu.

户 | | | |

`丶 ㇕ ㇇ 户`
diǎn, héngzhé, héng, piě.

穴 | | | | |

`丶 丷 宀 宀 穴`
diǎn, diǎn, hénggōu, piě, nà.

广 | | |

`丶 亠 广`
diǎn, héng, piě.

厂 | |

`一 厂`
héng, piě.

勺 | | |

`丿 勹 勺`
piě, héngzhégōu, diǎn.

皿

丶 冂 冂 皿 皿
shù, héngzhé, shù, shù, héng.

酉

一 丆 冂 丙 丙 西 酉
héng, shù, héngzhé, piě, shùwān, héng, héng.

井

一 二 扌 井
héng, héng, piě, shù.

网

丨 冂 冈 冈 网 网
shù, héngzhégōu, piě, diǎn, piě, diǎn.

刀

𠃌 刀
héngzhégōu, piě.

戈

一 弋 戈 戈
héng, xiégōu, piě, diǎn.

弓

𠃌 𠃍 弓
héngzhé, héng, shùzhézhégōu.

车

一 𠂇 � 车
héng, piězhé, héng, shù.

舟

丿 丿 刀 月 舟 舟
piě, piě, héngzhégōu, diǎn, héng, diǎn.

丁

一 丁
héng, shùgōu.

斤

丿 丆 厂 斤
piě, piě, héng, shù.

斗

丶 丷 三 斗
diǎn, diǎn, héng, shù.

力 □ □

フ力
héngzhégōu, piě.

工 □ □

一 丁 工
héng, shù, héng.

C. Write with a Pencil 动手动笔

Now that you know the meaning and the standard stroke order for each of the characters, it is time to practice writing balanced and well-proportioned characters. Use the following "well" boxes to write each character. It is actually not enough just to write in the boxes provided in the book. You may want to practice writing each character on a piece of paper. While writing, you should take a good look at the model character and then try to write it by heart without referring to the model. Each time you finish writing the character, you can compare it with the model. Correct any mistakes and write until you do it correctly without looking at the model.

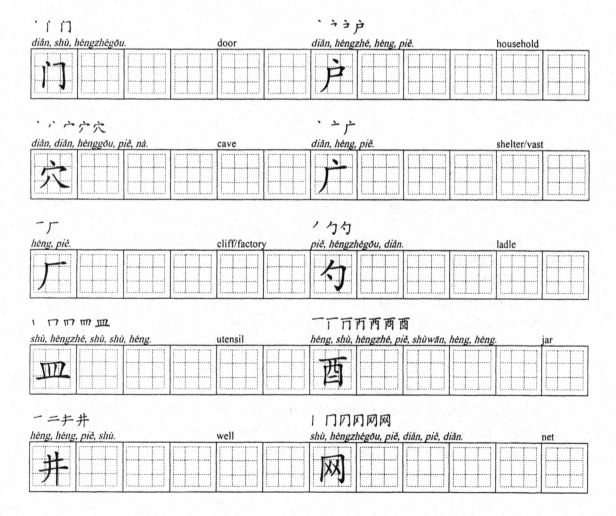

`丶 亻 门`
diǎn, shù, héngzhégōu. — door

门

`丶 ⺈ ⼎ 户`
diǎn, héngzhé, héng, piě. — household

户

`丶 丷 宀 宀 穴`
diǎn, diǎn, hénggōu, piě, nà. — cave

穴

`丶 亠 广`
diǎn, héng, piě. — shelter/vast

广

`一 厂`
héng, piě. — cliff/factory

厂

`丿 勹 勺`
piě, héngzhégōu, diǎn. — ladle

勺

`丨 冂 冂 皿 皿`
shù, héngzhé, shù, shù, héng. — utensil

皿

`一 丁 丙 丙 西 丙 酉`
héng, shù, héngzhé, piě, shùwān, héng, héng. — jar

酉

`一 二 丰 井`
héng, héng, piě, shù. — well

井

`丨 冂 冂 网 网 网`
shù, héngzhégōu, piě, diǎn, piě, diǎn. — net

网

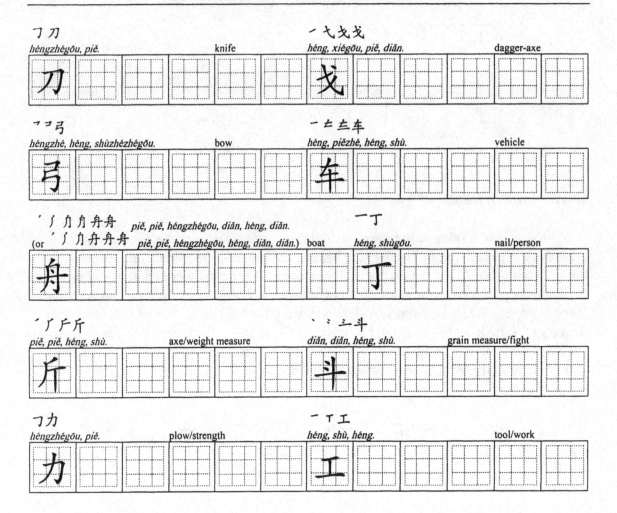

III. Challenge 2: Apply Your Knowledge 挑战二：举一反三

A. Know Many Things by Learning One 闻一知十

1. In this chapter, you have learned some of the characters related to tools. Here are five more that may be paired with five of those you have just learned in the previous sections in this chapter: 瓦, 缶, 臼, 矢, 干.

Let's look at each in detail.

瓦 means "tile"; it is a piece of pottery used for covering the roof of a house.

缶 means "container"; it has a large body and a small opening with a cover.

臼 means "mortar"; it is a stone or hard wood bowl in which something, such as rice, can be pounded with a pestle.

矢 means "arrow"; it has a pointed and sharp head mounted on a slender shaft at one end and feathers at the other end and can be shot from a bow.

干 means "shield"; it was a fork-like defensive weapon used to block the charge of a wild animal or the attack of an enemy in ancient times.

Oracle	Bronze	Seal	Clerical	Regular	Normal-ized	Semi-cursive	Cursive	Meaning
		瓦	瓦	瓦	瓦	瓦	瓦	tile
			缶	缶	缶	缶	缶	container
			臼	臼	臼	臼	臼	mortar
			矢	矢	矢	矢		arrow
			干	干	干	干		shield

2. Can you explain the difference in meaning between the characters in each of following five pairs?

    a. 瓦 vs. 穴

    b. 缶 vs. 酉

    c. 臼 vs. 皿

    d. 矢 vs. 弓

    e. 干 vs. 戈

3. Please regroup the following characters according to the categories to which they belong.

门户穴广厂勺皿酉井网刀戈弓车舟丁斤斗力工瓦缶臼矢干

    a. Habitation facilities: _____

    b. Household utensils: _____

    c. Working tools: _____

    d. Weapons: _____

e. Means of transportation: _____

Answers:
a. 门户穴广厂
井瓦
b. 勺皿酉刀斗
缶臼
c. 网丁斤刀工
刀
d. 刀戈弓夫干
e. 车舟

4. Here are some two-syllable words and phrases formed by some of the characters in this chapter and previous chapters. Can you figure out what they mean?

a.	火车	_____	man-made
b.	鱼网	_____	female worker
c.	工人	_____	saber
d.	马刀	_____	incisor, front tooth
e.	人工	_____	train
f.	女工	_____	fishnet
g.	车门	_____	worker
h.	门牙	_____	vehicle door

Answers:
e. man-made
f. female worker
d. saber
h. front tooth
a. train
b. fishnet
c. worker
g. vehicle door

5. Here are some two-syllable words and phrases that end in 力. Can you figure out what they mean?

a.	人力	_____	eyesight
b.	马力	_____	electric power
c.	火力	_____	wind power
d.	水力	_____	hearing ability
e.	风力	_____	firepower
f.	电力	_____	mental efforts
g.	目力	_____	manpower

h. 耳力 _____waterpower

i. 心力 _____horsepower

Answers:
g. eyesight
f. electric power
e. wind power
h. hearing ability
c. firepower
i. mental efforts
a. manpower
d. waterpower
b. horsepower

B. Be Perceptive of the Slightest Differences 明察秋毫

1. Which character in each group have you not yet learned? Circle it.
   a. Group 1
      i. 门   ii. 本   iii. 穴   iv. 戈

   b. Group 2
      i. 皿   ii. 井   iii. 网   iv. 血

   c. Group 3
      i. 刀   ii. 力   iii. 刃   iv. 勺

   d. Group 4
      i. 广   ii. 尺   iii. 厂   iv. 户

   e. Group 5
      i. 太   ii. 酉   iii. 工   iv. 车

   f. Group 6
      i. 斤   ii. 斗   iii. 弓   iv. 甘

Answers:
a. ii.
b. iv.
c. iii.
d. ii.
e. i.
f. iii.

2. Which of the characters in each group is different?
   a. Which character does not have a *héng* as its last stroke?
      i. 车   ii. 皿   iii. 酉   iv. 工

   b. Which character does not have a *shù* as its last stroke?
      i. 井   ii. 斤   iii. 丁   iv. 斗

   c. Which character does not have a *diǎn* as its last stroke?
      i. 勺   ii. 网   iii. 戈   iv. 穴

   d. Which character does not have a *piě* as its last stroke?

i. 广 ii. 戈 iii. 力 iv. 户

e. Which character does not have a *piě* as its first stroke?
i. 井 ii. 舟 iii. 斤 iv. 刀

f. Which character does not have a *héngzhégōu* stroke?
i. 酉 ii. 勺 iii. 网 iv. 舟

g. Which character contains a *hénggōu* stroke?
i. 门 ii. 弓 iii. 穴 iv. 力

h. Which character contains a *shùzhézhégōu* stroke?
i. 戈 ii. 勺 iii. 网 iv. 弓

Answers:
a. i. b. iii. c. iv. d. ii. e. ii. f. i. g. iii. h. iv.

3. How many strokes are there?
a. Which character does not have three strokes?
i. 门 ii. 力 iii. 勺 iv. 广

b. Which character has fewer than four strokes?
i. 弓 ii. 戈 iii. 户 iv. 车

c. Which character has more than four strokes?
i. 井 ii. 斤 iii. 斗 iv. 穴

d. Which character has fewer than six strokes?
i. 舟 ii. 网 iii. 皿 iv. 酉

e. Which character has seven strokes?
i. 穴 ii. 酉 iii. 网 iv. 舟

Answers:
a. ii. b. i. c. iv. d. iii. e. ii.

C. Be Aware of the Complex Counterpart 学简知繁

You may skip this section and go on to the next section for Challenge 3 if you do not wish to learn the complex forms for some of the characters in this chapter.

1. Comparison. In this chapter, there are five simplified characters. Look at the following table and compare the simplified forms of the characters with their complex counterparts:

	Simplified Form	Complex Form	Meaning
1	门	門	door
2	广	廣	vast
3	厂	廠	factory
4	网	網	net
5	车	車	vehicle

2. Explanation.

門. This is the traditional form of 门, depicting a door with two leaves and meaning "door."

廣. This traditional form of the character has two components: 广 and 黃. The component 黃 indicates the pronunciation of the character.

廠. The traditional form of this character also has two major components: 广 and 敞. The component 敞 indicates the pronunciation of the character.

網. This is the traditional form of the character 网, although the form 网 is a lot older. The form 網 did not come into being until the clerical change. It has three parts. On the left, 糸 indicates the materials used to make a net. On the right is the component 罔, which can be further separated into two parts: a reduced form of 网 as a top down frame and 亡 underneath and inside the frame indicating the pronunciation of the whole character.

車. Before the normalized script adopted 车, a regulated cursive script form, 车, had been the officially recognized form for a long time. Although 車 is more of a logo representing a cart than a sketch depicting a cart, we can still see the 田 in the center indicating the carriage, the vertical stroke representing the axle, and the two horizontal strokes indicate two wheels.

For explanations of their simplified counterparts, refer to Section B in Part I of this chapter.

3. Writing. Write these six characters in their traditional form.

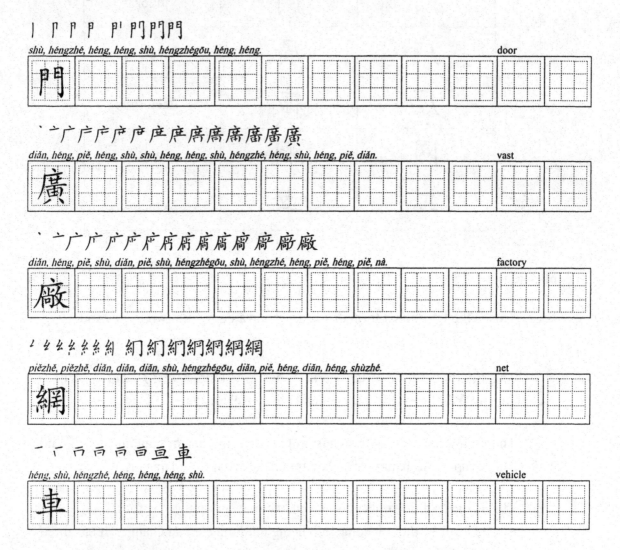

丨 冂 冃 冃 冃丨 門 門丨 門

shù, héngzhé, héng, héng, shù, héngzhégōu, héng, héng.   door

門

丶 亠 广 广 广 庐 庐 庐 庐 庐 庐 庐 廣

diǎn, héng, piě, héng, shù, shù, héng, héng, shù, héngzhé, héng, shù, héng, piě, diǎn.   vast

廣

丶 亠 广 广 广 庐 庐 府 府 庽 庽 庽 庽 廠

diǎn, héng, piě, shù, diǎn, piě, shù, héngzhégōu, shù, héngzhé, héng, piě, héng, piě, nà.   factory

廠

幺 幺 幺 幺 幺 糹 紀 紀 紀 網 網 網 網

piězhě, piězhě, diǎn, diǎn, diǎn, shù, héngzhégōu, diǎn, piě, héng, diǎn, héng, shùzhě.   net

網

一 厂 厅 厅 两 百 亘 車

héng, shù, héngzhé, héng, héng, héng, shù.   vehicle

車

IV. Challenge 3: Pronounce the Characters 挑战三：见形发音

It is time now to establish the link between the shapes of the characters and their pronunciations. To establish the link efficiently, you must learn the following verse so thoroughly that eventually you will be able to recite it. If you do not have a recording of the verse, ask your instructor to make one for you. Only when you have repeatedly listened to the verse will you be ready to read it aloud. Read it aloud as accurately and as frequently as possible until you are able to memorize it. Memorize the verse as a whole to help you recall the meaning, pronunciation, and shape of the characters.

If you are not ready for this challenge, skip this section and go to the next section to practice writing characters, or go on to the next chapter to learn to recognize more Chinese characters. After you learn to speak some Chinese, you can return to this section later.

1. Listen and read (choose the form you prefer):

(In the traditional form)   *(In the normalized form)*

Mén hù xué guǎng chǎng,   Mén hù xué guǎng chǎng,
門戶穴廣廠,   门户穴广厂,

Shǎo mǐn yǒu jǐng wǎng,   Shǎo mǐn yǒu jǐng wǎng,
勺皿酉井網,   勺皿酉井网,

Dāo gē gōng chē zhōu,   Dāo gē gōng chē zhōu,
刀戈弓車舟,   刀戈弓车舟,

Dīng jīn dǒu lì gōng.   Dīng jīn dǒu lì gōng.
丁斤斗力工。   丁斤斗力工。

2. Read aloud by looking only at the characters:

(In the traditional form)   *(In the normalized form)*

門戶穴廣廠,   门户穴广厂,

勺皿酉井網,   勺皿酉井网,

刀戈弓車舟,   刀戈弓车舟,

丁斤斗力工。   丁斤斗力工。

3. Guess the answers to the following riddles using the characters in the list. Answer the riddle in Chinese aloud to yourself or to someone who can help with pronunciation, and write the character in the box and its *pinyin* transliteration outside the box after each riddle. Note that in each group there are nine riddles for nine of the ten characters in the list.

Group 1: 门户穴广厂勺皿酉井网

a) It is where people can get water with a pail.

b) It has a lot of holes, but it catches fish.

c) It used to be a wall-less house, but now it means "vast."

d) It is a container usually used for keeping rice wine.

e) It is a bowl-shaped object with a handle.

f) It is a vessel usually used for holding food.

g) It is a one-leaf door and can also be a window.

h) It is a place where things are manufactured.

i) It is an entrance for people to get in and out.

Group 2: 刀戈弓车舟丁斤斗力工

a) It floats over the water.

b) It looks like a spear but has a horizontal blade.

c) It does not shoot arrows without a sturdy string.

d) It is a tool that people used to cut down trees before the invention of the saw.

e) It goes fast because it has wheels.

f) It is a unit of measure for weight and is equal to 500 grams.

g) It is a cutting tool with a sharp blade and a short
handle.

☐

h) It is equal to one liter, and it does not really fight as
another meaning of this character suggests.

☐

i) You may lose it if you are seriously sick. You regain
it if you rest and eat well.

☐

V. Challenge 4: Dictation 挑战四: 听音书形知义

1. By now, you should be able to recite the character verse for this chapter. Write
the verse in Chinese characters and the meaning of each character in the spaces provided
below:

Mén	hù	xué	guǎng	chǎng	,

Shǎo	mǐn	yǒu	jǐng	wǎng	,

Dāo	gē	gōng	chē	zhōu	,

Dīng	jīn	dǒu	lì	gōng	.

2. Look at the *pinyin*, say it aloud, and write out the cooresponding character in
the first box and the meaning in English in the second. If two characters have the same
pronunciation, a clue in the English meaning is given.

pinyin	character	meaning	pinyin	character	meaning
dīng			sháo		
gē			hù		
yǒu			mǐn		
guǎng			gōng		b____
gōng		w____	zhōu		
chē			wǎng		
jǐng			dāo		
xué			dǒu		
chǎng			lì		
mén			jīn		

3. Have your instructor dictate the characters or words covered in Chapter 8.

Chapter 9 第九章
Characters with Indicative Strokes: Indicative Characters 带有象征意义笔画的汉字: 指事字

I. Fundamental Knowledge 基础知识

In Chapters 4-8, you learned one hundred pictographic characters, or the kind of characters that were first created by drawing sketches to depict things. In this chapter, you will look at characters that were created by changing or adding strokes to existing pictographic characters in order to express concepts that would have been very difficult without making use of existing pictographic characters.

A. Shapes and Meanings 见形思义

	Drawing 图	Ancient Character Shape 古字形	Modern Character Shape 今字形	Formation 构形	Meaning 字义
1.		白	白	日 plus 丿	white
2.		血	血	皿 plus 丿	blood
3.		曰	曰	口 plus 一	say
4.		太	太	大 plus 、	excessively
5.		甘	甘	口 plus 一	delicious
6.		本	本	木 plus 一	root

7.			术	末	木 plus 一	tip/end
8.			尺	尺	尸 plus 丶	foot/ruler
9.			彐	寸	彐 (又) plus 丶	Inch
10.			片	片	Left side of 木	slice/piece
11.			丗	世	Three 十 linked together	generation
12.			少	少	小 plus 丿	few
13.			彐	叉	又 plus 丶	fork
14.			由	由	田 plus 丨	through
15.			刃	刃	刀 plus 丶	blade
16.			旦	旦	日 plus 一	dawn
17.			鸟	乌	鸟 minus 丶	crow

18.			夕	 (月) minus 丶	dusk
19.			入	Prolong ㇏	enter
20.			天	大 plus 一	sky

B. Trace the Roots and Understand with Reason 追根溯源，晓之以理

白 The meaning of this character is "white"; however, there are three explanations for its meaning. The first explanation is that the earliest form of the character in the oracle-bone inscriptions resembled a grain of unhusked rice, which is white. The second is that it looks like a candle emitting bright light in the darkness. The third is that the lower part of the character is the sun. Early in the morning when the sun is about to appear at the horizon, the light of the sun is already apparent. Although there is no agreement on what sends out the light, what is not disputed is that the stroke on top of the character in its later forms indicates brightness. It is, therefore, easier to understand and remember that over the character 日 (sun), a stroke is added to indicate brightness.

Oracle	Bronze	Seal	Clerical	Regular	Normal-ized	Semi-cursive	Cursive
			白	白	白	白	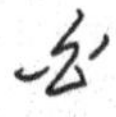

血 This is the character 皿 (utensil) with a left-falling stroke added to its top. The earliest forms of this character in the oracle-bone and bronze inscriptions, as well as in the seal script, shown that there is something in the utensil. It is the blood of animals put in the utensil as a sacrificial offering by people in ancient times. Therefore, the character 血 now means "blood."

Oracle	Bronze	Seal	Clerical	Regular	Normal-ized	Semi-cursive	Cursive
			血	血	血	血	

曰　This character looks like 日 (sun), but the shape is wider. We can see, from the earliest forms of this character in the oracle-bone and bronze inscriptions, as well as in the seal script, that it is a sketch of a mouth with a short stroke above the mouth, indicating speech. The meaning of this character, therefore, is "say." Although it is not commonly used nowadays, frequently this character appears in Chinese classical works such as the *Analects*, a collection of Confucius' sayings recalled by his students.

Oracle	Bronze	Seal	Clerical	Regular	Normal-ized	Semi-cursive	Cursive
𠙵	𠙵	𠙵	曰	曰	曰	曰	曰

太　This character is formed by adding a stroke under the character 大 (big), suggesting something even bigger. The meaning of this character, therefore, is "extremely" or "excessively."

Oracle	Bronze	Seal	Clerical	Regular	Normal-ized	Semi-cursive	Cursive
	太	太	太	太	太	太	太

甘　The earliest form of this character in the oracle-bone inscriptions is a sketch of a mouth with a horizontal stroke in it. This horizontal stroke indicates delicious food in the mouth. Although the mouth shape changed after the clerical change, the character still means "pleasant, sweet taste."

Oracle	Bronze	Seal	Clerical	Regular	Normal-ized	Semi-cursive	Cursive
甘		甘	甘	甘	甘	甘	甘

本　This character is formed by the character 木 (tree) and a horizontal stroke at the bottom, indicating its root. The whole character, therefore, means "root" or "basis."

Oracle	Bronze	Seal	Clerical	Regular	Normal-ized	Semi-cursive	Cursive
	本	本	本	本	本	本	本

末   This character is formed by the character 木 (tree) and a horizontal stroke at the top, indicating the top of the tree. The meaning of the character is "tip" or "end."

Oracle	Bronze	Seal	Clerical	Regular	Normal-ized	Semi-cursive	Cursive
	朱	朱	末	末	末	末	赤

尺   The character 尺 refers to a Chinese unit of measure for length. One 尺 is equal to 1.09 feet or 0.33 meters. It is formed by 尸 (person or dead body) with a right-falling stroke indicating the shinbone, which is about the length of one Chinese foot. Another belief is that this right-falling stroke indicates the forearm, and the length of the ulna is the length of 尺. Despite the different explanations for the root of this character, we know that this stroke indicates a part of a human limb that is about the length of a Chinese foot. This character is, therefore, also commonly used to refer to the instrument for measuring length: a ruler.

Oracle	Bronze	Seal	Clerical	Regular	Normal-ized	Semi-cursive	Cursive
		尺	尺	尺	尺	尺	又

寸   In the seal script, this character is formed by 㝱 (the right hand) and a stroke indicating a position below the palm of the hand where traditional Chinese medicine doctors feel the pulse of a patient (㝱). The character originally stood for the name of this important position in traditional Chinese medicine. As the distance from the edge of the palm to this position is about one Chinese inch, the character 寸 is also used as a unit of measurement for one Chinese inch, which equals 1.3 English inches. Ten 寸 (Chinese inch) equals one 尺 (Chinese foot).

Oracle	Bronze	Seal	Clerical	Regular	Normal-ized	Semi-cursive	Cursive
		㝱	寸	寸	寸	寸	寸

片   The form of this character in the seal script is 片. If you compare it with the character 木 (tree) in its form in the seal script (朱), you can see that 片 is actually the right half of 朱. After the clerical change, it was difficult to see that 片 is a half of 木. As 片 is a piece of 木, it means "a piece of" or "a slice of."

Oracle	Bronze	Seal	Clerical	Regular	Normalized	Semi-cursive	Cursive
乚		片	片	片	片	片	片

世 This character is formed by linking three characters for 十 (ten), meaning "thirty years." As thirty years are considered to be the time duration for one generation, the character also means "generation." Other extended meanings are "lifetime" or "world."

Oracle	Bronze	Seal	Clerical	Regular	Normalized	Semi-cursive	Cursive
	业	世	世	世	世	世	乡

少 This character is similar to the character 小 (small) in shape and meaning. The earliest form in the oracle-bone inscriptions is a sketch of four grains of sand rather than three as in the earliest form of the character 小. The form in the regular script is 小 with a left-falling stroke added at the bottom, indicating that it is not completely the same as 小. While the character 小 means "small in size," the character 少 is used to mean "small in number," that is, "few" or "little."

Oracle	Bronze	Seal	Clerical	Regular	Normalized	Semi-cursive	Cursive
小	小	少	少	少	少	少	少

叉 This character is formed by the character 又 (right hand) with a dot stroke in the middle, indicating that there is something between the fingers or that the fingers are pinching something. The character is commonly used to mean "fork," the utensil used for eating or a tool for picking or stabbing something.

Oracle	Bronze	Seal	Clerical	Regular	Normalized	Semi-cursive	Cursive
		叉	叉	叉	叉	叉	叉

由　This is the character 田 (farmland) with the vertical stroke in the middle prolonged.　This prolonged stroke indicates the road used to enter the farmland. This character, therefore, means "by way of" or "through."

Oracle	Bronze	Seal	Clerical	Regular	Normal-ized	Semi-cursive	Cursive
		曲	由	由	由	由	由

刃　This character is formed with the character 刀 (knife) and a dot stroke emphasizing one particular part of the knife: the blade.　This character is, therefore, used to refer to the blade of a knife.

Oracle	Bronze	Seal	Clerical	Regular	Normal-ized	Semi-cursive	Cursive
ヒ		彡	刃	刃	刃	刃	刃

旦　The earliest forms of this character in the oracle-bone and bronze inscriptions depicted early morning when the sun rises.　In the seal script, a horizontal stroke was added under the character 日 (sun), indicating the horizon.　The meaning of this character, therefore, is "dawn."

Oracle	Bronze	Seal	Clerical	Regular	Normal-ized	Semi-cursive	Cursive
⊖	♀	旦	旦	旦	旦	旦	旦

乌　In the normalized script, this character does not have the dot stroke as does the character 鸟 (bird).　When we also compare these two characters in the other forms (鳥 vs. 鳥 ，鳥 vs. 鳥 ，and 乌 vs. 鸟), we see that the horizontal stroke indicating the eye of the bird is missing in all of them.　The missing stroke does not mean the bird has no eye but rather that the bird is black in color, making its eyes invisible to human eyes.　The black bird this character refers to is the crow, and the character also means "black."

Oracle	Bronze	Seal	Clerical	Regular	Normal-ized	Semi-cursive	Cursive
		鳥	烏	烏	乌	乌	乌

夕　If the form of this character in the seal script, ♪, is compared with the character ♪ (moon) in its seal script form, we can see that the two differ by just one short stroke. The stroke missing from the character 月 (moon) indicates that the moon is not very bright, as it often is early in the evening when the sky is not yet dark. Therefore, this character means "evening."

Oracle	Bronze	Seal	Clerical	Regular	Normal-ized	Semi-cursive	Cursive
⟨	⟩	♪	夕	夕	夕	夕	夕

入　The earliest forms of this character in the oracle-bone and bronze inscriptions as well as in the seal script are a pointed shape, indicating that it is easy for a pointed object to get into another object. The meaning of the character, therefore, is "get into" or "enter." Since the clerical change, the character has been written in such a way that the right-falling stroke goes over the top of the left-falling stroke to distinguish it from the character 人 (person), in which the left-falling stroke goes over the top of the right-falling stroke.

Oracle	Bronze	Seal	Clerical	Regular	Normal-ized	Semi-cursive	Cursive
∧	人	入	入	入	入	入	入

天　This character in the oracle-bone and bronze inscriptions is a view of a person with a prominent head. In the seal script, the head was changed to a horizontal stroke that no longer indicates a head but rather the sky above one's head. The character now means "sky."

Oracle	Bronze	Seal	Clerical	Regular	Normal-ized	Semi-cursive	Cursive
天	夫	天	天	天	天	天	天

C. Recognition Reinforcement 辨认巩固练习

1. Go back to the beginning of this chapter. Look at the drawings and the characters. Then cover the drawings and try to remember the meaning of each character.

2. Link each character on the first line with its corresponding meaning in English on the second line:

a. 白　　血　　日　　太　　甘

　　say　white　sweet　blood　extremely

b. 本　　末　　尺　　寸　　片

　　ruler　root　inch　slice　tip

c. 世　　少　　叉　　由　　刃

　　little　blade　through　fork　generation

d. 旦　　烏　　夕　　入　　天

　　crow　dawn　sky　evening　enter

3. There are ten characters on the left side and eleven words in English on the right side. Put the letter for each character in the blank next to the corresponding English word. In each group, there is an extra blank that should be left empty.

Group 1:

a. 太

b. 日

c. 尺

d. 片

e. 白

f. 末

g. 本

h. 血

i. 寸

j. 甘

_____root

_____sweet

_____white

_____blood

_____inch

_____ruler

_____extremely

_____say

_____tip

_____enter

_____slice

Group 2:

a. 入   _____fork

b. 少   _____dawn

c. 乌   _____sky

d. 刃   _____through

e. 天   _____little

f. 叉   _____blade

g. 世   _____enter

h. 夕   _____inch

i. 由   _____generation

j. 旦   _____crow

_____evening

4. Provide the meaning in English for each of the following characters:

白_____ 血_____ 日_____ 太_____ 甘_____

本_____ 末_____ 尺_____ 寸_____ 片_____

世_____ 少_____ 叉_____ 由_____ 刃_____

旦_____ 乌_____ 夕_____ 入_____ 天_____

II. Challenge 1: Write the Characters 挑战一: 知义书形

A. Strokes in Characters: The Left-Falling Stroke 详说笔画: 撇

1. *Different left-falling strokes*. Among all the characters you have learned so far, each of the following characters contains at least one left-falling stroke (*piě*). Regroup the following characters according to the four major types of left-falling strokes listed in the table.

百石艸气儿长自立舌牙面文艮见元尸牛羊犬鸟
贝鱼毛果穴勺广酉井刀白血太本末片尺少入天

#	Stroke Name	Shape	Examples	Other Characters from the List
1	*Regular left-falling (piě)*	丿	人 万 木	
2	*Vertical left-falling (shùpiě)*	丿	月 川 大	
3	*Small left-falling (xiǎopiě)*	丿	六 父 首	
4	*Leveled left-falling (píngpiě)*	一	千 手 爪	

1) 石牙丈 元果刀木 禾少入 2) 神儿见 尸夫贝广 酉井太片 尺夭 3) 百气长 自立面艮 牛羊鸟鱼 穴白血 4) 舌毛

2. *Complex strokes that contain a left-falling stroke.* The left-falling strokes listed above are all simple strokes. There are also complex strokes that contain a left-falling stroke, as found in these characters learned in previous chapters:

#	Stroke Name	Example
1	A horizontal stroke linked with a left-falling stroke (*héngpiě*):	水
2	A left-falling stroke linked with a turn (*piězhé*):	云
3	A left-falling stroke linked with a dot (*piědiǎn*):	女

Which character has one of the three types of complex strokes that contain a left-falling stroke? Examine the following six characters, and fill in the blanks accordingly.

歹 鬼 女 皮 车 叉

1. *héngpiě:* _____ _____ _____

2. *piězhé:* _____ _____ _____

3. *piědiǎn:* _____ _____ _____

1. 鬼车 2. 歹皮叉 3. 女

3. *The common feature that the different left-falling strokes share.* Although left-falling strokes may have differences in their shapes, all left-falling strokes share one common feature: they all start by pressing the pen on the paper and then moving the pen to the lower left side while lifting it up and forming a pointed ending. Because of this common feature, we simply use the general term *piě* to refer to them.

Regroup the following characters according to the number of left-falling strokes each contains:

八九火禾角舟斤衣瓜页交象金欠米肉网身亿
隹戈竹足力厂户白血太本末片尺少刃乌入天

No.	Category	Characters from the list
1	Characters with one *piě*	
2	Characters with two *piě*	
3	Characters with more than two *piě*	

1) 八九亿隹戈足力厂户白血太本末片尺少刃乌入天　2) 火禾角舟斤衣瓜页交金欠米肉网身竹　3) 象

B. Stroke Order Analysis 笔顺分析

Write a new character by applying your knowledge of the stroke order first, and then compare it with the standard stroke order for that character. The number of empty boxes provided indicates the number of strokes for the character in the first box. Write one stroke after another in the empty boxes as indicated in the example below. Try to discover the reason for any difference in the stroke order or the number of strokes.

Start to write in the second box.

For example:　| 大 | 一 | 大 | 大 |

Then compare what you write with the stroke order model ⟶ 一ナ大
héng, piě, nà.

白
'ⁱ白白白
piě, shù, héngzhé, héng, héng.

血
'ⁱ白白血血
piě, shù, héngzhé, shù, shù, héng.

日
丨冂日日
shù, héngzhé, héng, héng.

太
一ナ大太
héng, piě, nà, diǎn.

甘
一十廿廿甘
héng, shù, shù, héng, héng.

本
一十才木本
héng, shù, piě, nà, héng.

末
一二丰末末
héng, héng, shù, piě, nà.

尺
'ⁱ尸尺
héngzhé, héng, piě, nà.

寸
一寸寸
héng, shùgōu, diǎn.

片
'ⁱ片片
shù, héng, piě, héngzhé.

世
一十廿廿世
héng, shù, shù, héng, shùzhé.

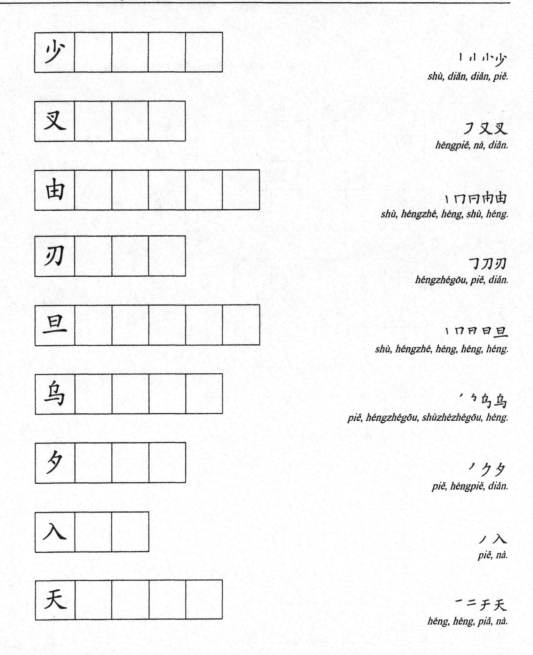

少   丨 小 小 少
shù, diǎn, diǎn, piě.

叉   フ 又 叉
héngpiě, nà, diǎn.

由   丨 冂 冋 由 由
shù, héngzhé, héng, shù, héng.

刃   フ 刀 刃
héngzhégōu, piě, diǎn.

旦   丨 冂 冃 日 旦
shù, héngzhé, héng, héng, héng.

乌   ノ ㇆ 乌 乌
piě, héngzhégōu, shùzhézhégōu, héng.

夕   ノ ㇆ 夕
piě, héngpiě, diǎn.

入   ノ 入
piě, nà.

天   一 二 チ 天
héng, héng, piě, nà.

C. Write with a Pencil 动手动笔

Now that you know the meaning and the standard stroke order for each of the characters, it is time to practice writing balanced and well-proportioned characters. Use the following "well" boxes to write each character. It is actually not enough just to write in the boxes provided in the book. You may want to practice writing each character on a piece of paper. While writing, you should take a good look at the model character and then try to write it by heart without referring to the model. Each time you finish writing the character, you can compare it with the model. Correct any mistakes and write until you do it correctly without looking at the model.

丿亻白白白
piě, shù, héngzhé, héng, héng.   white

白

丿亻白白血血
piě, shù, héngzhé, shù, shù, héng.   blood

血

丨冂冃日
shù, héngzhé, héng, héng.   say

日

一ナ大太
héng, piě, nà, diǎn.   excessively/too

太

一十廿甘甘
héng, shù, shù, héng, héng.   sweet

甘

一十才木本
héng, shù, piě, nà, héng.   root

本

一二十才末
héng, héng, shù, piě, nà.   tip/end

末

フコ尸尺
héngzhé, héng, piě, nà.   ruler

尺

一寸寸
héng, shùgōu, diǎn.   Chinese inch

寸

丿丿尸片
shù, héng, piě, héngzhé.   piece/slice

片

一十廿世世
héng, shù, shù, héng, shùzhé.   generation

世

丨小小少
shù, diǎn, diǎn, piě.   few/little

少

フ又叉
héngpiě, nà, diǎn.   fork

叉

丨冂冃由由
shù, héngzhé, héng, shù, héng.   through

由

フ刀刃
héngzhégōu, piě, diǎn.   blade

刃

丨冂冃日旦
shù, héngzhé, héng, héng, héng.   dawn

旦

丿𠂉乌乌
piě, héngzhégōu, shùzhézhégōu, héng.   crow/black

乌

丿勹夕
piě, héngpiě, diǎn.   evening

夕

丿入
piě, nà.   enter   一二于天   sky
                                                hēng, hēng, piǎ, nà.

| 入 | | | | | | 天 | | | | | |

III. Challenge 2: Apply Your Knowledge 挑战二: 举一反三

A. Know Many Things by Learning One 闻一知十

1. All the characters you have learned in this chapter are considered indicative characters because they either add or discard or change a stroke as an indicating sign to convey a specific meaning. These characters are often related to ones you have learned in previous chapters. Here are ten of them. Do you still remember what they mean?

日_____   月_____   木_____   人_____   口_____

手_____   田_____   鸟_____   刀_____   十_____

> **Answers:**
> 日: sun
> 月: moon
> 木: tree
> 人: person
> 口: mouth
> 手: hand
> 田: farmland
> 鸟: bird
> 刀: knife
> 十: ten

Write each of the following characters after the character it is related to:

白日太甘本末尺寸片世由叉刃旦乌夕天

日_____   _____   _____

月_____   _____

木_____   _____   _____

人_____   _____   _____

口_____   _____   _____

手_____   _____   _____

田_____   _____   _____

鸟_____   _____

刀＿＿＿＿＿＿　＿＿＿＿＿＿　＿＿＿＿＿＿

十＿＿＿＿＿＿　＿＿＿＿＿＿　＿＿＿＿＿＿

Answers:
日：白旦
月：夕
木：本末未片
人：太尺天
口：日甘
手：寸叉
田：由
鸟：刃
刀：刃
十：世

2. Here are some two-syllable words and phrases formed by some of the characters in this chapter and previous chapters. Can you figure out what they mean?

a.　白天　　＿＿＿＿＿＿ stanch

b.　乌云　　＿＿＿＿＿＿ fillet

c.　交叉　　＿＿＿＿＿＿ entrance

d.　入口　　＿＿＿＿＿＿ daytime

e.　元旦　　＿＿＿＿＿＿ dark cloud

f.　尺寸　　＿＿＿＿＿＿ crisscross

g.　止血　　＿＿＿＿＿＿ New Year's Day

h.　鱼叉　　＿＿＿＿＿＿ measurements

i.　肉片　　＿＿＿＿＿＿ harpoon

Answers:
g. stanch
i. fillet
d. entrance
a. daytime
b. dark cloud
c. crisscross
e. New Year's Day
f. measurement
h. harpoon

B. Be Perceptive of the Slightest Differences 明察秋毫

1. Which character in each group have you not yet learned? Circle it.
    a. Group 1
        i. 右　　ii. 白　　iii. 乌　　iv. 尺

    b. Group 2
        i. 血　　ii. 世　　iii. 甘　　iv. 南

    c. Group 3
        i. 日　　ii. 本　　iii. 里　　iv. 寸

    d. Group 4
        i. 末　　ii. 前　　iii. 片　　iv. 少

e. Group 5
    i. 旦   ii. 东   iii. 夕   iv. 入

f. Group 6
    i. 外   ii. 叉   iii. 由   iv. 刃

Answers:
a. i.   b. iv.   c. iii.   d. ii.   e. ii.   f. i.

2. Which of the characters in each group is different?
    a. Which character does not have a *héng* as its last stroke?
        i. 皿   ii. 甘   iii. 末   iv. 本

    b. Which character does not have a *nà* as its last stroke?
        i. 入   ii. 天   iii. 尺   iv. 太

    c. Which character does not have a *diǎn* as its last stroke?
        i. 叉   ii. 刃   iii. 夕   iv. 寸

    d. Which character does not have a *piě* as its first stroke?
        i. 夕   ii. 尺   iii. 白   iv. 血

    e. Which character does not have a *shù* as its first stroke?
        i. 片   ii. 本   iii. 少   iv. 由

    f. Which character does not have a *héngzhé* stroke?
        i. 甘   ii. 由   iii. 片   iv. 血

    g. Which character contains a *shùgōu* stroke?
        i. 少   ii. 寸   iii. 刃   iv. 乌

    h. Which character contains a *héngzhégōu* stroke?
        i. 夕   ii. 旦   iii. 世   iv. 乌

Answers:
a. iii.   b. iv.   c. i.   d. iii.   e. ii.   f. i.   g. ii.   h. iv.

3. How many strokes are there?
    a. Which character does not have three strokes?
        i. 寸   ii. 入   iii. 刃   iv. 叉

    b. Which character has fewer than four strokes?

    i. 夕   ii. 太   iii. 少   iv. 天

c. Which character has more than four strokes?
    i. 乌   ii. 片   iii. 尺   iv. 甘

d. Which character has fewer than five strokes?
    i. 由   ii. 本   iii. 曰   iv. 末

e. Which character has six strokes?
    i. 世   ii. 旦   iii. 白   iv. 血

Answers:
a. ii.
b. i.
c. iv.
d. iii.
e. iv.

C. Be Aware of the Complex Counterpart 学简知繁

If you do not wish to learn the complex forms now at the beginning level, you may skip this section and go to the next section for Challenge 3.

1. Comparison. In this chapter, there is one simplified character. Look at the following table and compare the simplified form of the character with its complex counterpart:

	Simplified Form	Complex Form	Meaning
1	乌	烏	crow

2. Explanation.

烏. This character is similar to the character 鳥 (bird). The only difference is that the horizontal stroke in the upper part of the character 鳥 is omitted in the character 烏, indicating that the eye of a crow is invisible because of its black color.

3. Writing. Write this character in its traditional form.

ノ 亻 亇 亽 兦 烏 烏 烏 烏 烏

piě, shù, héngzhé, héng, héng, héngzhégōu, diǎn, diǎn, diǎn, diǎn.   crow

烏

D. Simplification Method (1): Keep the Contour 简化方法 (一): 保持轮廓

In the normalized script, some characters were simplified by reducing the strokes inside and keeping the contour of their complex counterparts. A good example is the character 乌, which is the simplified form of 烏. In previous chapters, you have also learned 鸟 and 马.

	Keep the	
Traditional	contour	Simplified
烏	⟶	乌
鳥	⟶	鸟
馬	⟶	马

IV. Challenge 3: Pronounce the Characters 挑战三: 见形发音

After you have established the link between the shape and the meaning of each of the characters introduced in this chapter, you are ready to establish the link between the shape and the pronunciation of each of these characters. Because the shape of a character does not provide a clue to its pronunciation, it will be a real challenge.

Again, if you are not ready for this challenge, you can skip this section and go to the next section to practice writing characters or go on to the next chapter to learn to recognize more Chinese characters. After you learn to speak some Chinese, you can return to this section later.

1. Listen and read (choose the form you prefer):

(In the traditional form)	*(In the normalized form)*
Bái xuè yuē tài gān,	Bái xuè yuē tài gān,
白血曰太甘,	白血曰太甘,
Běn mò chǐ cùn piàn,	Běn mò chǐ cùn piàn,
本末尺寸片,	本末尺寸片,
Shì shǎo chā yóu rèn,	Shì shǎo chā yóu rèn,
世少叉由刃,	世少叉由刃,
Dàn wū xī rù tiān.	Dàn wū xī rù tiān.
旦乌夕入天。	旦乌夕入天。

2. Read aloud by looking only at the characters:

(In the traditional form)   *(In the normalized form)*

白血日太甘，   白血日太甘，

本末尺寸片，   本末尺寸片，

世少叉由刃，   世少叉由刃，

旦烏夕入天。   旦乌夕入天。

3. Guess the answers to following riddles using the characters in the list. Answer the riddle in Chinese aloud to yourself or to someone who can help with pronunciation, and write the character in the box and its *pinyin* transliteration outside the box after each riddle. Note that in each group there are nine riddles for nine of the ten characters in the list.

Group 1: 白血日太甘本末尺寸片

a) It is part of a tree and is used to mean "slice."

b) It is the color of milk.

c) It is something people use to get measurements.

d) It is a pleasant taste people experience from eating candy.

e) It is the part of a tree that gets water from soil.

f) It is the action people take to utter words.

g) It is red and flows to all parts of one's body.

h) It is the equivalent of 3.33 centimeters.

i) It looks like the character for "big," but its meaning is "excessive." ☐

Group 2: 世少叉由刃旦乌夕入天

a) It is bigger than the world. ☐

b) It is the time of day when it starts to become dark. ☐

c) It is a utensil often used at dinner. ☐

d) It is something that people usually want sharp. ☐

e) It is the opposite of "exit." ☐

f) It is the time the sun rises in the east. ☐

g) It looks like the character for "small," but it is "small in number." ☐

h) It is a black bird. ☐

i) It is a time span of thirty years but is often used to refer to the "world." ☐

V. Challenge 4: Dictation 挑战四：听音书形知义

1. By now you should be able to recite the character verse for this chapter. Write the verse in Chinese characters and the meaning for each character in the spaces provided below:

Bái	xuè	yuē	tài	gān	,

Běn	mò	chǐ	cùn	piàn	,

Shì	shǎo	chā	yóu	rèn	,

Dàn	wū	xī	rù	tiān	.

2. Look at the *pinyin*, say it aloud, and write the appropriate character in the first box and the meaning in English in the second.

pinyin	*character*	*meaning*	*pinyin*	*character*	*meaning*
shì			xuè		
gān			bái		
wū			mò		
dàn			yóu		
shǎo			rù		

chǐ		
tài		
tiān		
chā		
chǐ		

běn		
xī		
rèn		
piàn		
cùn		

3. Have your instructor dictate the characters or words covered in Chapter 9.

Chapter 10 第十章
Characters for Directions and Positions 表示位置方向的汉字

I. Fundamental Knowledge 基础知识

A. Shapes and Meanings 见形思义

	Drawing 图	Ancient Character Shape 古字形	Modern Character Shape 今字形	Meaning 字义
1.		上	上	upper, above, over, on
2.		下	下	lower, beneath, below, under
3.		左	左	left
4.		右	右	right
5.		正	正	straight
6.		前	前	front
7.		后	后	back

8.		裏	里	inside
9.		外	外	outside
10.		旁	旁	beside
11.		東	东	east
12.		西	西	west
13.		南	南	south
14.		北	北	north
15.		中	中	central

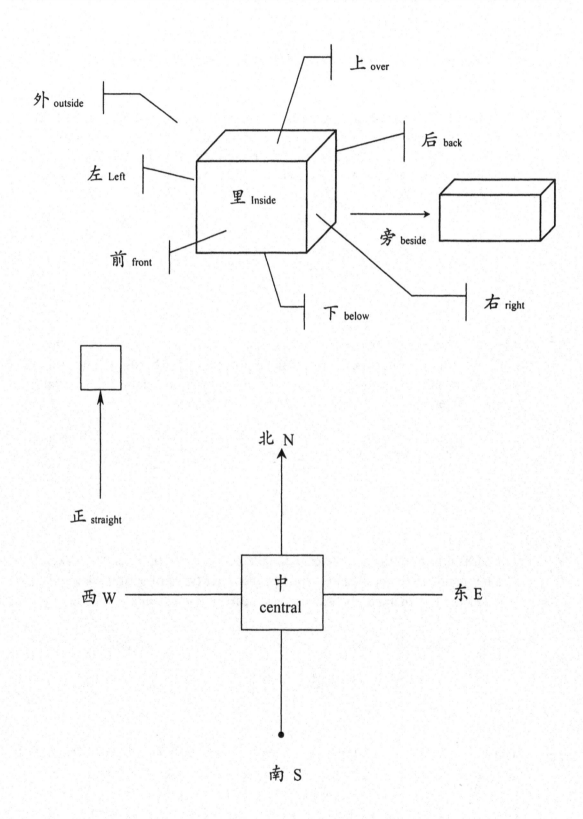

B. Trace the Roots and Understand with Reason 追根溯源，晓之以理

上　The forms of this character in the oracle-bone and bronze inscriptions had two strokes: the longer one represented the baseline and the shorter horizontal stroke above it indicated the upper position. In the seal script and other scripts, a vertical stroke was added. This character, therefore, means "upper position," "on," "over," or "above."

Oracle	Bronze	Seal	Clerical	Regular	Normal-ized	Semi-cursive	Cursive
⌣	=	上	上	上	上	上	⌣

下　This character is just the opposite of the character 上 (upper position). The horizontal stroke under the longer stroke representing the baseline in the oracle-bone and bronze inscriptions signified the lower position. Hence, the character means "lower position," "under," "beneath," or "below."

Oracle	Bronze	Seal	Clerical	Regular	Normal-ized	Semi-cursive	Cursive
⌢	=	下	下	下	下	下	下

左　The earliest form of this character in the oracle-bone inscriptions was a sketch of a left hand. In the bronze inscriptions and other types of scripts, 工 (tool) was added. The character is now used to mean "left-hand side."

Oracle	Bronze	Seal	Clerical	Regular	Normal-ized	Semi-cursive	Cursive
K	左	左	左	左	左	左	左

右　This character means the opposite of the character 左 (left). It means "right." The earliest form of this character in the oracle-bone inscriptions showed a right hand, and in the bronze inscriptions and the seal script, 口 (mouth) was added. Since the clerical change, the part representing "right hand" has been moved to the left side of 口. However, the character still means "right-hand side."

Oracle	Bronze	Seal	Clerical	Regular	Normal-ized	Semi-cursive	Cursive
⼽	⼿	司	右	右	右	右	右

正 In the oracle-bone and bronze inscriptions, the meaning of this character, "straight," was indicated by a foot pointing to the destination represented by a dot. In later scripts, the dot became a horizontal stroke.

Oracle	Bronze	Seal	Clerical	Regular	Normal-ized	Semi-cursive	Cursive
⼭	⼟	疋	正	正	正	正	正

前 The earliest forms of this character in the oracle-bone and bronze inscriptions as well as in the seal script had a foot at the top and a boat at the bottom, signifying that a foot is in the front of the boat, going forward without walking. The seal script has another form that has "knife" added to the lower right: 歬. The forms of the character in the various scripts later on have kept the part for "knife." The character means not only "to go forward, " but is also commonly used to mean "front."

Oracle	Bronze	Seal (1)	Seal (2)	Clerical	Regular	Normal-ized	Semi-cursive	Cursive
肖	肖	肯	歬	前	前	前	前	前

后 The earliest form of this character in the oracle-bone inscriptions was a sketch of a person and a baby. In the bronze inscriptions as well as in later scripts, a "mouth" was substituted for "baby," perhaps to indicate the importance of the mother. It makes sense that this character is also used to mean "female king" or "queen." The normalized script substitutes this character for the character 後. The earliest form of the character 後 in the oracle-bone inscriptions has three components: 彳, 8, and 夊. 彳 indicates a small step, 8 indicates a rope that is tied to the foot "夊", preventing forward motion. The character 後, thus, has the meaning "be left behind," and it also means "back." A good reason for the normalized script to substitute 后 for 後 to mean "back" is that 后 was used to mean "back" as early as the oracle-bone inscriptions more than 3,000 years ago, while 後 has never been used in place of 后 to mean "queen."

Oracle	Bronze	Seal	Clerical	Regular	Normal-ized	Semi-cursive	Cursive
季	后	后	后	后	后	后	后
後	後	後	後	後			

里   This character is formed by 田 (farmland) and 土 (soil) and means "village." It is also used for the Chinese unit of measure that is equal to 500 meters. The normalized script, however, also substitutes this character for 裏, which means "inside." From the structure of the character, we can see that the character 衣 (coat) is separated with the character 里 inserted in between. Therefore, 裏 means "inside the coat" or just "inside." One good reason for the character 里 to substitute for the character 裏 to mean "inside" is that both characters in the bronze inscriptions once shared an identical form. Also 里 has had a long history (more than 2,000 years) of being used in place of 裏 to mean "inside." After all, soil is in the farmland, and the farmland is formed in soil.

Oracle	Bronze (1)	Bronze (2)	Seal	Clerical	Regular	Normal-ized	Semi-cursive	Cursive
	里	里	里	里	里	里	里	里
	里	裏	裏	裏	裏			

外   This character is formed by two components. One is the character 夕 (evening) and the other is the character 卜 (divination). You have learned that 夕 represents a less bright moon that is seen early in the evening; hence it also means "evening." The character 卜 depicts the crack on a tortoise shell that was read by people in ancient times to foretell the future. Divination would usually take place during the daytime before an important decision had to be made. Putting 卜 beside 夕 suggests that divination often could not wait until the daytime and had to be done in the evening, perhaps before a battle far from home when quick decisions had to be made. As 外 is associated with making a decision for external war affairs, it is used to mean "external" or "outside."

Oracle	Bronze	Seal	Clerical	Regular	Normal-ized	Semi-cursive	Cursive
	外	外	外	外	外	外	外

旁   The earliest form of this character in the oracle-bone inscriptions had two components. The upper one was the ancient form of the character 凡, indicating ridges in the fields, and the lower part was the ancient form of the character 方, depicting a fork-like farming tool. The combination of these two components suggests that a farming tool forms ridges next to it in the fields; thus, the meaning "beside" is derived. The form of the upper component later changed to 亠.

Oracle	Bronze	Seal	Clerical	Regular	Normal-ized	Semi-cursive	Cursive
旁	旁	旁	旁	旁	旁	旁	旁

东   This character means "east" because, according to one popular explanation, the meaning of "east" is suggested by the structure of the character in the seal script: the θ (sun) is in a 木 (tree), as is frequently seen in the east in the morning. However, this explanation is not applicable to the earlier forms of the character in the oracle-bone and bronze inscriptions. Their configuration is just a sketch of something wrapped up with both ends tied. Therefore, it originally meant "something," and, it has been borrowed as a phonetic loan character to mean "east." The form of the character in the normalized script came from the cursive script.

Oracle	Bronze	Seal	Clerical	Regular	Normal-ized	Semi-cursive	Cursive
東	東	東	東	東	东	东	东

西   This character means "west." One explanation is that the character comes from the form of the character (鹵) in the seal script. The upper part is believed to be a bird, and the lower a nest. When the sun goes down in the west, it is the time for birds to get back to their nests; therefore, the character implies "west." This explanation, however, does not work well for the earlier forms of the character in the oracle-bone and bronze inscriptions because there is no part indicating a bird there. The alternative explanation is that like the character 东, 西 is also a phonetic loan character that originally meant "nest" but has been borrowed to refer to "west."

Oracle	Bronze	Seal	Clerical	Regular	Normal-ized	Semi-cursive	Cursive
西	西	西	西	西	西	西	西

南 The earliest forms of this character in the oracle-bone and bronze inscriptions as well as in the seal script show that it is the shape of a bell used as a musical instrument. It has been borrowed and used to mean "south."

Oracle	Bronze	Seal	Clerical	Regular	Normal-ized	Semi-cursive	Cursive
㕑	湳	湳	南	南	南	南	甬

北 In the earliest forms of this character, we can see two people sitting back to back. Although it originally meant "back of one's body," it has been borrowed to mean "north." For the meaning "back of one's body," another character, 背, had to be created.

Oracle	Bronze	Seal	Clerical	Regular	Normal-ized	Semi-cursive	Cursive
夶	夶	川	北	北	北	北	北

中 The forms of this character in the oracle-bone and bronze inscriptions are sketches of a flagpole with streamers or decorative bands on both ends. An indicating sign placed in the middle of the flagpole suggests that it is the middle point of the flagpole. The streamers or decorative bands were omitted in later forms of the character. Therefore, the character 中 means "middle" or "central."

Oracle	Bronze	Seal	Clerical	Regular	Normal-ized	Semi-cursive	Cursive
㐀	㑇	中	中	中	中	中	中

C. Recognition Reinforcement 辨认巩固练习

1. Go back to the beginning of this chapter. Look at the drawings and the characters. Try to memorize the shape and the meaning of each character.

2. Link each character on the first line with its corresponding meaning in English on the second line:

a. 上   下   左   右   正

    right   left   below   above   straight

b. 前　　后　　里　　外　　旁

back　　outside　　beside　　front　　inside

c. 东　　西　　南　　北　　中

central　　south　　west　　east　　north

3. There are ten characters on the left side and eleven words in English on the right side. Put the letter for each character in the blank next to the corresponding English word. In each group, there is an extra blank that should be left empty.

Group 1:

a. 北

b. 西　　　　　　　　　　　　　_____left

　　　　　　　　　　　　　　　_____central

c. 前　　　　　　　　　　　　_____beside

d. 东　　　　　　　　　　　　_____west

e. 左　　　　　　　　　　　　_____above

f. 后　　　　　　　　　　　　_____right

g. 旁　　　　　　　　　　　　_____south

　　　　　　　　　　　　　　　_____north

h. 右　　　　　　　　　　　　_____back

i. 南　　　　　　　　　　　　_____ east

j. 中　　　　　　　　　　　　_____ front

Group 2:

a. 左

b. 里　　　　　　　　　　　　_____west

c. 下　　　　　　　　　　　　_____front

　　　　　　　　　　　　　　　_____outside

d. 右　　　　　　　　　　　　_____left

e. 外　　　　　　　　　　　　_____east

f. 上   _____below

g. 西   _____north

h. 南   _____south

i. 后   _____ back

j. 北   _____right

                                    _____above

4. Provide the meaning in English for each of the following characters:

上_____ 下_____ 左_____ 右_____ 正_____

前_____ 后_____ 里_____ 外_____ 旁_____

东_____ 西_____ 南_____ 北_____ 中_____

II. Challenge 1: Write the Characters 挑战一: 知义书形

A. Strokes in Characters: The Horizontal Stroke with a Turn 详说笔画: 横折

1. The horizontal stroke with a turn *(héngzhé).* We know that the horizontal stroke with a turn is in fact a horizontal stroke that is linked with a vertical stroke. Because a turn that starts with a horizontal stroke can only go downward rather than upward, there is no need to specify in which direction the turn will be. Among all the characters learned in the previous chapters, each of the following characters contains at least one horizontal stroke with a turn *(héngzhé).*

1) 日 白 曰 四 田 由 百 目 自 首 面 酉

2) 口 足 舌 言 艮 贝 页 见 户 尸 尺 虫 马 电 鱼 果 鬼 皿 血 旦 骨 象

2. *Héngzhé* written as *héngzhégōu.* If you look closely at the characters listed above, each of which is supposed to contain a horizontal stroke with a turn *(héngzhé),* you may notice that all the characters in the first row actually have a horizontal stroke with a turn and a hook, which is a *héngzhégōu* stroke rather than a *héngzhé* stroke. Have we mistakenly viewed and included these characters in the first row as containing a *héngzhé* stroke? No, we have not. It has been a custom for calligraphers to end a *héngzhé* stroke with a hook to make it a *héngzhégōu* stroke. However, when naming strokes in the stroke order for these characters, we still do not call them *héngzhégōu.* You may have also noticed that the *héngzhé* stroke in each of the characters in the second

row has not been written as *héngzhégōu.* Is there a reason? There are three. First, there is no stroke in the enclosed frame; second, the frame is relatively small; and third, there is no horizontal stroke to enclose the frame.

From these three reasons, you can figure out the rule for writing a *héngzhégōu* stroke in place of a *héngzhé* stroke in a character: A *héngzhé* stroke can be written as a *héngzhégōu* stroke when the frame it forms is relatively big, includes other strokes, and is to be enclosed with a horizontal stroke. Of course, since this is a rule for an optional way of writing, even when these three conditions are present, you do not have to write the *héngzhé* stroke as a *héngzhégōu* stroke.

Each of the following five characters contains a *héngzhé* stroke. Which character is most likely to have its *héngzhé* stroke written as a *héngzhégōu* stroke?

右　后　里　西　中
目　白　由　见　足

Answers:
由
目
西
白

3. *Héngzhé* vs. *héngzhégōu.* A *héngzhé* stroke may be written as a *héngzhégōu* stroke under certain circumstances; however, under no circumstances should a *héngzhégōu* stroke be written as a *héngzhé* stroke. The following characters learned in the previous chapters contain at least one *héngzhégōu* stroke.

月 雨 肉 角 羽 巾 门 勺 网 刀 舟 力 刃 鸟 乌

Look at the following characters learned in this chapter, which ones contain a genuine *héngzhégōu* stroke?

右 前 后 里 旁 东 西 南 北 中

Answers:
旁
前
南

B. Stroke Order Analysis 笔顺分析

Write a new character by applying your knowledge of the stroke order first, and then compare it with the standard stroke order for that character. The number of empty boxes provided indicates the number of strokes for the character in the first box. Write one stroke after another in the empty boxes, as indicated in the example below. Try to discover the reason for any difference in the stroke order or the number of strokes.

Start to write in the second box.

For example:

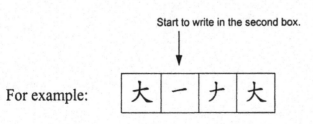

Then compare what you write with the stroke order model ——→   一ナ大

héng, piě, nà.

上

丨卜上

shù, héng, héng.

下

一丅下

héng, shù, diǎn.

左

一ナ左左左

héng, piě, héng, shù, héng.

右

一ナ才右右

héng, piě, shù, héngzhé, héng.

正

一丅下正正

héng, shù, héng, shù, héng.

前

丷丷广前前前前前前

diǎn, piě, héng, shù, héngzhégōu, héng, héng, shù, shùgōu.

后

一厂厂斤后后

piě, piě, héng, shù, héngzhé, héng.

里

丨口日日甲里里

shù, héngzhé, héng, héng, shù, héng, héng.

外

ノ夕夕外外

piě, héngpiě, diǎn, shù, diǎn.

旁

丶丷广广立立立旁旁

diǎn, héng, diǎn, piě, diǎn, hénggōu, diǎn, héng, héngzhégōu, piě.

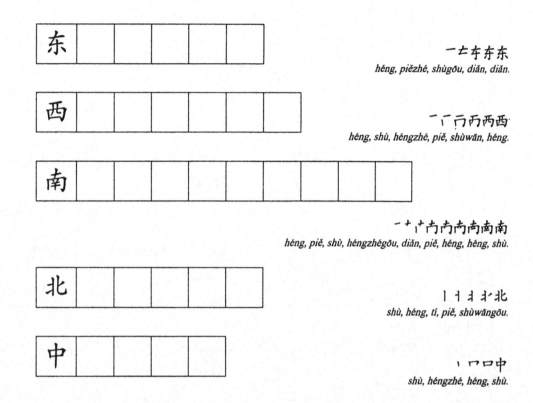

一 t 左 车 东 东
héng, piězhé, shùgōu, diǎn, diǎn.

一 丆 两 西 西
héng, shù, héngzhé, piě, shùwān, héng.

一 十 广 内 内 南 南 南 南
héng, piě, shù, héngzhégōu, diǎn, piě, héng, héng, shù.

丨 十 丬 北
shù, héng, tí, piě, shùwāngōu.

丨 冂 口 中
shù, héngzhé, héng, shù.

C. Write with a Pencil *动手动笔*

Now that you know the meaning and the standard stroke order for each of the characters, it is time to practice writing balanced and well-proportioned characters. Use the following "well" boxes to write each character. It is actually not enough just to write in the boxes provided in the book. You may want to practice writing each character on a piece of paper. While writing, you should take a good look at the model character and then try to write it by heart without referring to the model. Each time you finish writing the character, you can compare it with the model. Correct any mistakes and write until you do it correctly without looking at the model.

丨 卜 上
shù, héng, héng.　　　　　　　　　upper, on

一 丁 下
héng, shù, diǎn.　　　　　　　　lower, under

一 ナ 左 左 左
héng, piě, héng, shù, héng.　　　left

一 ナ 右 右 右
héng, piě, shù, héngzhé, héng.　right

一 丁 下 正 正
héng, shù, héng, shù, héng.　　　straight

丷 丷 广 肖 肖 前 前 前
diǎn, piě, héng, shù, héngzhégōu, héng, héng, shù, shùgōu. front

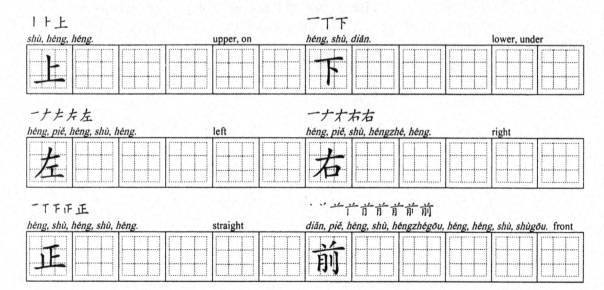

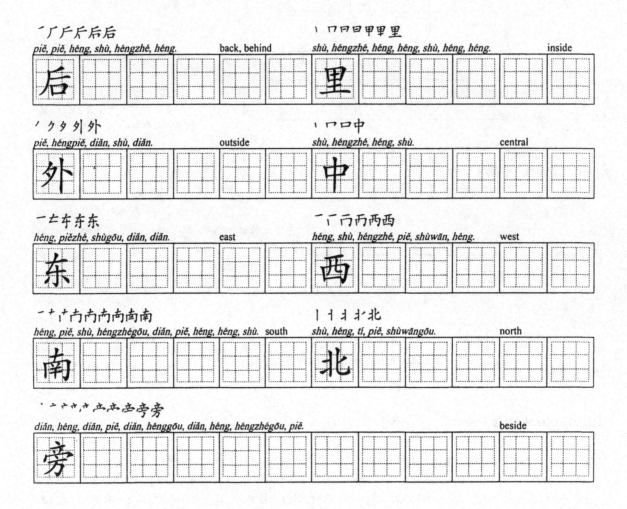

丿厂厂户后后
piě, piě, héng, shù, héngzhé, héng.   back, behind

后

丿夕夕外外
piě, héngpiě, diǎn, shù, diǎn.   outside

外

一七七车东东
héng, piězhé, shùgōu, diǎn, diǎn.   east

东

一十十广内内内内南南
héng, piě, shù, héngzhégōu, diǎn, piě, héng, héng, shù.   south

南

丶一一十一丁立立立育旁
diǎn, héng, diǎn, piě, diǎn, hénggōu, diǎn, héng, héngzhégōu, piě.   beside

旁

丨口曰日甲甲里
shù, héngzhé, héng, héng, shù, héng, héng.   inside

里

丨口口中
shù, héngzhé, héng, shù.   central

中

一丆丆两两西
héng, shù, héngzhé, piě, shùwān, héng.   west

西

丨丬丬十北
shù, héng, tí, piě, shùwāngōu.   north

北

III. Challenge 2: Apply Your Knowledge 挑战二: 举一反三

A. Know Many Things by Learning One 闻一知十

1. All the characters you have learned in this chapter indicate positions or directions. They can be used together with other characters to form phrases. For example:

门(door) + 前(front) => 门前 (in front of the door)
前(front) + 门(door) => 前门 (front door)

Can you figure out what these phrases mean?

a. 门后   _____the back mountain

b. 后门   _____behind the mountain

c. 门旁   _____in front of the mountain

d. 旁门   _____at the top of the mountain

e. 山前 _____the back door

f. 山后 _____behind the door

g. 后山 _____outside the vehicle

h. 山上 _____inside the vehicle

i. 车里 _____beside the door

j. 车外 _____the side door

Answers:
g. the back mountain
f. behind the mountain
e. in front of the mountain
h. at the top of the mountain
b. the back door
a. behind the door
j. outside the vehicle
i. inside the vehicle
c. beside the door
d. the side door

2. The characters 上 and 下 can also be used to refer to actions before an object. For example:

上 + 车 => get on the vehicle
下 + 车 => get off the vehicle

Can you figure out what these mean?

a. 上山 _____get into the water

b. 下山 _____get off the horse

c. 上门 _____go up the mountain

d. 下水 _____get on the horse

e. 上马 _____go up to the door of a house

f. 下马 _____go down the mountain

Answers:
d. get into the water
f. get off the horse
a. go up the mountain
e. get on the horse
c. go up to the door of a house
b. go down the mountain

3. Here are some two-syllable words formed by the characters for directions. Can you figure out what they mean?

a. 东北 _____ southwest

b. 西北 _____ midmost

c. 东南 _____ northeast

d. 西南   _____ Middle East

e. 正中   _____ northwest

f. 中东   _____ southeast

Answers:
d. southwest
e. midmost
a. northeast
f. Middle East
b. northwest
c. southeast

4. You have learned four characters 东, 西, 南, and 北 for the four major directions. They all happen to be phonetic loan characters, that is, characters that were originally borrowed to indicate the directions because they are pronounced the same as the spoken words for those directions. There is, however, a character that really does indicate a direction by its shape rather than its sound. This character is 向, and it is related to "north" and pronounced *xiàng*. The earliest form of this character in the oracle-bone inscriptions is a sketch of a house with a simple window. China is in the northern hemisphere, and it has long been a tradition that Chinese people build their houses with doors and fancy windows facing south, the side from which they get the most sunshine. The side of the house depicted in the character is not the side with doors and fancy windows; on the contrary, it is the northern side of the house. However, it has never been used to mean "north." Instead, one common meaning is "towards."

Oracle	Bronze	Seal	Clerical	Regular	Normal-ized	Semi-cursive	Cursive
向	向	向	向	向	向	向	向

If 向东 means "towards east" or "eastwards," then what does each of the following mean?

向西_____   向南_____   向北_____

向前_____   向后_____   向左_____

Can you translate the following into Chinese?

rightward _____   downward_____

upward_____   inward _____

outward_____

Answers:
向西: westward
向南: southward
向北: northward
向前: forward
向后: backward
向左: leftward
rightward: 向右
downward: 向下
upward: 向上
inward: 向里
outward: 向外

5. The character 旁 (beside), which you learned in this chapter, has a component 方. It is actually also a character that can be used independently and is pronounced *fāng*. Based on the forms of the character in the oracle-bone and the bronze inscriptions, especially those shown in Oracle (1) and Bronze (1), it is believed that 方 was a fork-like farming tool in ancient times. However, based on other forms of the character, it is also believed that the character depicted two boats that are tied together side by side. When two boats are tied together, they would go either nowhere or anywhere together. Therefore, one meaning of 方 is "side."

Oracle (1)	Oracle (2)	Bronze (1)	Bronze (2)	Seal	Clerical	Regular	Normal-ized	Semi-cursive	Cursive
才	才	才	少	方	方	方	方	方	方

If 东方 means "east side" or "orient," what does each of the following mean?

西方_____   南方_____

左方_____   东方人_____

Can you translate the following into Chinese?

front side_____   back side _____

westerner_____   northerner_____

Answers:
西方: occident
南方: south side
左方: left side
东方人: oriental, easterner

front side: 前方
back side: 后方
westerner: 西方人
northerner: 北方人

B. Be Perceptive of the Slightest Differences 明察秋毫

1. Which character in each group have you not yet learned? Circle it.
   a. Group 1
      i. 右   ii. 左   iii. 旁   iv. 多

   b. Group 2
      i. 尖   ii. 上   iii. 下   iv. 前

   c. Group 3
      i. 后   ii. 外   iii. 从   iv. 里

d. Group 4
    i. 正   ii. 好   iii. 东   iv. 西

e. Group 5
    i. 中   ii. 北   iii. 时   iv. 南

Answers:
a. iv. b. i. c. iii. d. ii. e. iii

2. Which character in each group is different?

a. Which character does not have a *héng* as its last stroke?
    i. 上   ii. 中   iii. 左   iv. 后

b. Which character does not have a *diǎn* as its last stroke?
    i. 前   ii. 外   iii. 东   iv. 下

c. Which character does not have a *héng* as its first stroke?
    i. 右   ii. 南   iii. 东   iv. 后

d. Which character does not have a *shù* as its first stroke?
    i. 中   ii. 正   iii. 北   iv. 里

e. Which character does not have a *piě* as its second stroke?
    i. 右   ii. 前   iii. 南   iv. 西

f. Which character does not have a *héngzhé* stroke?
    i. 前   ii. 西   iii. 右   iv. 中

g. Which character contains a *shùgōu* stroke?
    i. 外   ii. 南   iii. 东   iv. 北

h. Which character contains a *héngzhégōu* stroke?
    i. 西   ii. 东   iii. 北   iv. 旁

Answers:
a. ii. b. i. c. iv. d. ii. e. iv. f. i. g. iii. h. iv.

3. How many strokes are there?

a. Which character has more than four strokes?
    i. 中   ii. 北   iii. 上   iv. 下

    b.   Which character has more than five strokes?
           i. 后   ii. 左   iii. 右   iv. 正

    c.   Which character has fewer than five strokes?
           i. 东   ii. 外   iii. 北   iv. 中

    d.   Which character has fewer than six strokes?
           i. 西   ii. 后   iii. 正   iv. 里

    e.   Which character has ten strokes?
           i. 前   ii. 南   iii. 里   iv. 旁

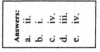

Answers:
a. ii. b. i. c. iv. d. iii. e. iv.

C. Be Aware of the Complex Counterpart 学简知繁

    If you do not wish to learn the complex forms now, at the beginning level, you may skip this section and go on to the next section for Challenge 3.

1. Comparison. In this chapter, there are three simplified characters. Please look at the following table and compare the simplified forms of the three characters with their complex counterparts:

	Simplified Form	Complex Form	Meaning
1	后	後	back
2	里	裏	inside
3	东	東	east

2. Explanation.

    後. This character has three components: 彳, 幺, and 夂. As explained earlier, 彳 stands for "small step," 幺 stands for "rope," and 夂 stands for "foot." The idea is that when a rope is tied to the foot, one can hardly walk and is, therefore, left behind or at the back.

    裏. This character is formed by inserting the character 里 into the character 衣, indicating the idea of "inside." The character 里 also indicates the pronunciation of the whole character: *lǐ*.

東. The most cited explanation for this character is that the sun (日) is in the tree (木), indicating "east," the place from which the sun rises. However, the various forms of this character in the oracle-bone inscriptions suggest that it is the shape of something wrapped up and tied on both ends. Therefore, it originally referred to "something" and was later borrowed as a phonetic loan character to mean "east."

3. Writing. Write this character in its traditional form.

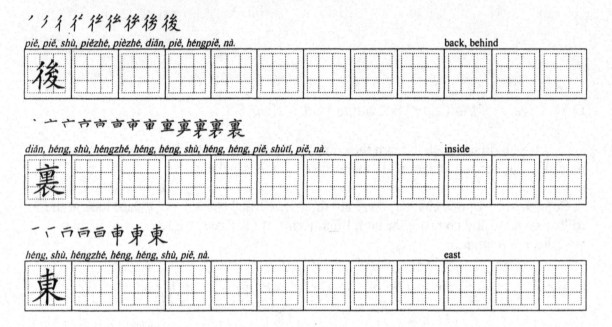

ノ ⺅ 彳 彳 彳 彳 彳 彳 後

piě, piě, shù, piězhé, pièzhé, diǎn, piě, héngpiě, nà.   back, behind

後

丶 亠 广 亩 高 亩 审 审 审 重 裏 裏 裏

diǎn, héng, shù, héngzhé, héng, héng, shù, héng, héng, piě, shùtí, piě, nà.   inside

裏

一 ⺈ 一 一 白 車 東 東

héng, shù, héngzhé, héng, héng, shù, piě, nà.   east

東

D. Simplification Method (2): Homophonic Substitution 简化方法 (二): 同音替代

In the normalized script, some characters were simplified by using other characters that are simpler in structure or have fewer strokes but share the same pronunciation.

Traditional	Homophonic Substitution	Simplified
後	⟶	后
裏	⟶	里
鬥	⟶	斗

IV. Challenge 3: Pronounce the Characters 挑战三：见形发音

After you have established the link between the shape and the meaning of each of the characters introduced in this chapter, you are ready to establish the link between the shape and the pronunciation of each of these characters. Because the shape of a character does not provide a clue to its pronunciation, it will be a real challenge. To succeed in this challenge, you must learn the following verse so thoroughly that eventually you will be able to recite it. If you do not have a recording of the verse, ask your instructor to make one for you. Only when you have repeatedly listened to the verse will you be ready to read it aloud. Read it aloud as accurately and as frequently as possible until you are able to memorize it. Memorization of the verse will help you remember the meaning, pronunciation, and shape of the characters in the verse more efficiently.

Again, if you are not ready for this challenge, you can skip this section and go to the next section to practice writing characters or go on to the next chapter to learn to recognize more Chinese characters. After you learn to speak some Chinese, you can return to this section later.

1. Listen and read (choose the form you prefer):

(In the traditional form)	*(In the normalized form)*
Shàng xià zuǒ yòu zhèng, 上下左右正，	Shàng xià zuǒ yòu zhèng, 上下左右正，
Qián hòu lǐ wài páng, 前後里外旁，	Qián hòu lǐ wài páng, 前后里外旁，
Dōng xī nán běi zhōng. 東西南北中。	Dōng xī nán běi zhōng. 东西南北中。

2. Read aloud by looking only at the characters:

(In the traditional form)	*(In the normalized form)*
上下左右正，	上下左右正，
前後里外旁，	前后里外旁，
東西南北中。	东西南北中。

3. Guess the answers to following riddles using the characters in the list. Answer the riddle in Chinese aloud to yourself or to someone who can help with pronunciation, and write the character in the box and its *pinyin* transliteration outside the box after each riddle. Note that there are 14 riddles for the 15 characters in the list.

上下左右正前后东西南北中里外旁

a) It is the side on which you drive a car in China and the US.

b) It is the position where the stars are.

c) If you go east and then turn right, what direction would you be facing?

d) If you look at a map, what is usually the direction of the upper side of the map?

e) If you go west and then turn right, what direction would you be facing?

f) What character would you use to refer to a situation in which someone goes to a destination without straying?

g) What is the position of the mouth in reference to that of the nose in the face?

h) What is the direction that runners should dash to during a competition?

i) What is the direction that drivers check when they look into their rearview mirrors?

j) It is the direction that the sun goes toward to have a rest (as believed by many people in the old days).

k) What turn should you make if you are going south but need to change the direction to east?

l) What is the position of all matter in reference to the universe?

m) What was the position, with reference to the universe, that people before Copernicus believed the earth was in?

n) What is the position that is always close to you?

☐

V. Challenge 4: Dictation 挑战四: 听音书形知义

1. By now, you should be able to recite the character verse for this chapter. Write the verse in Chinese characters and the meaning for each character in the spaces provided below:

Shàng	xià	zuǒ	yòu	zhèng	,

Qián	hòu	lǐ	wài	páng	,

Dōng	xī	nán	běi	zhōng	.

2. Look at the *pinyin*, say it aloud, and write the appropriate character in the first box and the meaning in English in the second.

pinyin	*character*	*meaning*	*pinyin*	*character*	*meaning*
zuǒ			nán		
wài			shàng		
xī			lǐ		

xià		
yòu		
zhōng		
hòu		
zhèng		

qián		
dōng		
páng		
běi		

3. Have your instructor dictate the characters or words covered in Chapter 10.

Chapter 11 第十一章
Characters Formed by Two or More Basic Characters:
Associative Characters 由基本汉字合成的汉字: 会意字

I. Fundamental Knowledge 基础知识

In the previous eight chapters, you have learned 14 characters for numbers, 15 characters for positions and directions, 20 indicative characters, and 100 basic characters, plus 12 supplementary basic characters. That is 161 characters in total. Knowing these characters well will help you continue with ease to learn the new characters in this chapter and the next three chapters. One common feature you are about to learn is that they are all formed with one of the 161 characters that have already been covered. In this chapter, you will look at 20 new characters that are formed by two or more basic characters you have learned. These new characters are called "associative characters," as the meaning of each new character comes from the combination of the two or more component characters.

A. Character Formation 组字方式

1.	田 *farmland*	+ 力 *plow/strength*	=>	男 male
2.	日 *sun*	+ 月 *moon*	=>	明 bright
3.	穴 *cave*	+ 牙 *tooth*	=>	穿 penetrate/wear
4.	禾 *standing grain*	+ 日 *sun*	=>	香 fragrant
5.	日 *sun*	+ 寸 *Chinese inch*	=>	时 time
6.	夕 *evening*	+ 夕 *evening*	=>	多 many

7.	口	+	口	+	犬	=>	哭
	mouth		*mouth*		*dog*		cry

8.	八	+	刀	=>	分
	eight/separate		*knife*		divide

9.	角	+	刀	+	牛	=>	解
	horn		*knife*		*ox*		dissect

10.	门	+	日	=>	间
	door		*sun*		space

11.	木	+	目	=>	相
	tree		*eye*		observe/mutually

12.	人	+	人	=>	从
	person		*person*		follow/from

13.	又	+	又	=>	双
	hand/again		*hand/again*		double

14.	禾	+	火	=>	秋
	standing grain		*fire*		autumn

15.	女	+	子	=>	好
	female		*baby*		good

16.	火	+	页	=>	烦
	fire		*head*		annoyed

17.	耳	+	又	=>	取
	ear		*hand*		fetch

18.	鱼	+	羊	=>	鲜
	fish		*sheep*		fresh/delicious
19.	雨	+	田	=>	雷
	rain		*farmland*		thunder
20.	小	+	大	=>	尖
	small		*big*		pointed

B. Forms and Meanings 知形会意

男 This character is formed with the character 田 (farmland) at the top and the character 力 (plow) at the bottom. Because in ancient times men usually did the hard work in the fields such as plowing, this character was created to mean "men" or "male."

Oracle	Bronze	Seal	Clerical	Regular	Normal-ized	Semi-cursive	Cursive
田丿	甼	眀	男	男	男	男	男

明 This character is formed by the character 日 (sun) and the character 月 (moon). Because the sun and the moon are the brightest objects in the sky, this character with "sun" and "moon" combined means "bright."

Oracle	Bronze	Seal	Clerical	Regular	Normal-ized	Semi-cursive	Cursive
☉𝈩	𝈙𝈩	眀	明	明	明	明	明

穿 Formed with the characters 穴 (cave) and 牙 (tooth), this character suggests that something as hard and sharp as teeth can make a hole, implying the idea of getting through something. When we put on our clothes, we put our arms through the sleeves and our legs through the pants. In Chinese, the character 穿 means not only "to get through" but also "to wear."

Oracle	Bronze	Seal	Clerical	Regular	Normal-ized	Semi-cursive	Cursive
窅	㝢	穿	穿	穿	穿	穿

香   From the earliest form of this character in the seal script, we can see that this character was first formed with 黍 (millet) and 甘 (delicious). However, after the clerical change, the character became a combination of 禾 (standing grain) and 日 (sun), suggesting that standing grains send out a good smell because of the sun. This character is now used to mean "fragrant."

Oracle	Bronze	Seal	Clerical	Regular	Normal-ized	Semi-cursive	Cursive
		薔	香	香	香	香	𣌣

时   The earliest form of this character in the oracle-bone and the bronze inscriptions was formed with 止 (stop) at the top and 日 (sun) at the bottom. 止 indicates the pronunciation of the character, and 日 is the object of reference in telling the time of day. In the seal script, 寺 (temple) instead of 止 was used to indicate the pronunciation. In the normalized script, in place of 寺, 寸 (inch) is used. Thus the character combines 寸, a unit of measurement, with 日, a point of reference in telling the time of day, to mean "time."

Oracle	Bronze	Seal	Clerical	Regular	Normal-ized	Semi-cursive	Cursive
峕	峕	嗜	時	時	时	时	时

多   This character is formed by piling up the character 夕 (evening), suggesting the accumulation of past time, one evening after another. Accumulation implies "many." Therefore, the character 多 means "many" or "a lot."

Oracle	Bronze	Seal	Clerical	Regular	Normal-ized	Semi-cursive	Cursive
吕	DD	多	多	多	多	多	多

哭   No form of this character can be found in the oracle-bone and bronze inscriptions. Therefore, the form of this character in the seal script is the oldest. The character is formed with two 口 (mouth) characters side by side at the top and 犬 (dog) at the bottom, suggesting the howling noise made by a dog. As the crying sound of a human being sounds somewhat similar to the howl of a dog, the character 哭 is used to mean "to cry."

Oracle	Bronze	Seal	Clerical	Regular	Normal-ized	Semi-cursive	Cursive
		哭	哭	哭	哭	哭	哭

分   This character is formed with the character 八 (separate), which also means "eight," as a phonetic loan character, and the character 刀 (knife). The combination of these two characters presents a picture of using a knife to cut something apart, indicating the idea of "divide."

Oracle	Bronze	Seal	Clerical	Regular	Normal-ized	Semi-cursive	Cursive
小	小	分	分	分	分	分	分

解   This character is formed by combining three characters: 角 (horn), 刀 (knife), and 牛 (ox). It presents a picture of using a knife to cut the horn off of an ox. The meaning conveyed by the character, therefore, is "dissect" or "take apart."

Oracle	Bronze	Seal	Clerical	Regular	Normal-ized	Semi-cursive	Cursive
解	解	解	解	解	解	解	解

间   This character means "space." The earliest form of this character in the bronze inscriptions was the character 月 (moon) over 門 (door). In the seal script, 月 was between 門, indicating that a door has a gap that the moonlight can go through. As the character 閒 once was often used to mean "idle," another character with 日 placed inside 門 was then created. Thus sunshine instead of moonlight goes through the space between the door panels. As we mentioned previously, in the normalized script, 門 is simplified as 门 as result of regularization of the form in the cursive script. Therefore, we now use 间 to refer to "space."

Oracle	Bronze	Seal	Clerical	Regular	Normal-ized	Semi-cursive	Cursive
𦥑	𨳍	間	間	间	间	旬

相

In the earliest forms of this character in the oracle-bone and bronze inscriptions, we can see a sketch of a big eye looking at a tree. It indicates the idea of taking a closer look or observing. This character now is often used for its extended meaning: "each other."

Oracle	Bronze	Seal	Clerical	Regular	Normal-ized	Semi-cursive	Cursive
相	相	相	相	相	相	相	お

从

The earliest forms of this character in the oracle-bone and bronze inscriptions have two persons, one behind the other. Therefore, the meaning of the character is "to follow."

Oracle	Bronze	Seal	Clerical	Regular	Normal-ized	Semi-cursive	Cursive
𠃊	𠂉	從	從	從	从	从	从

双

The earliest form of this character can be found in the seal script. It had a 又 (hand) at the bottom and two 隹 (short-tailed bird) at the top, indicating that one hand gets two birds. The normalized script, however, has two 又 (hand) side by side, indicating the idea of "pair" or "double."

Oracle	Bronze	Seal	Clerical	Regular	Normal-ized	Semi-cursive	Cursive
		雙	雙	雙	双	双	双

秋

Several forms of this character can be found in the oracle-bone inscriptions. One form, which is also the oldest form that has been found, looked like a cricket, suggesting the season of fall, with the kinds of insects that thrive at that time. Another form had a "fire" component added at the bottom, indicating autumn by the seasonal practice of setting straw and stalks left in the field on fire to kill insects. No form of this character is available from the bronze inscriptions. However, in the seal script, the form was simplified by replacing the part representing an insect with 禾 (standing grain). All the later forms of the character use this combination of 禾 (standing grain) and 火 (fire) to refer to autumn.

Oracle (1)	Oracle (2)	Bronze	Seal	Clerical	Regular	Normal-ized	Semi-cursive	Cursive
				秋	秋	秋	秋	

好 This character is formed with 女 (woman) and 子 (baby). The earliest form of this character in the oracle-bone inscriptions showed a sketch of a kneeling woman holding a baby. Having babies assures the continuation of human existence on the earth; therefore, it is good. In ancient China, the foremost requirement of a good woman was to be able to bear and raise children. Thus, a woman and a baby together have the meaning of "good."

Oracle	Bronze	Seal	Clerical	Regular	Normal-ized	Semi-cursive	Cursive
			好	好	好	好	

烦 This character is formed with 火 (fire) and 頁 (head). Originally, it meant "headache caused by a fever" (in this case 火 indicates "fever"). However, this character now commonly has the extended meaning: "to be annoyed."

Oracle	Bronze	Seal	Clerical	Regular	Normal-ized	Semi-cursive	Cursive
			煩	煩	烦	烦	

取 The meaning of this character is "fetch" or "get," and it is formed with 耳 (ear) and 又 (hand). How did the form and the meaning come to be associated in the first place? This character in fact records a cruel practice in ancient war times. A soldier's ability to fight was judged by how many enemies he could kill, the proof being the number of left ears he cut off. The earliest form of this character in the oracle-bone inscriptions showed a hand taking an ear. Now, this character is commonly used for its extended meaning, "to fetch or get," and people have forgotten how its original meaning was derived.

Oracle	Bronze	Seal	Clerical	Regular	Normal-ized	Semi-cursive	Cursive
			取	取	取	取	

鲜　The earliest form of this character in the bronze inscriptions has 羊 (sheep) on top of 鱼 (fish). This top-bottom structure was later changed to a left-right structure in the seal script and later scripts. This character was originally used to refer to a special kind fish, so 鱼 (fish) is used as one part of the character. This fish was considered delicious, as was the meat of 羊 (sheep), which forms the other part in this character. It no longer means that special kind fish, but retains the meaning "delicious."

Oracle	Bronze	Seal	Clerical	Regular	Normal-ized	Semi-cursive	Cursive
	羴	鮮	鮮	鮮	鲜	鲜	鲜

雷　This character means "thunder." Its form in the bronze inscriptions was quite a complicated sketch to indicate "thunder." As thunder is a loud drum-like sound, usually accompanied by lightning and rain, we see, in the form in the bronze inscriptions, "rain" at the top and a zigzag curvy line that represents "lightning" surrounded by four circles with crossed lines representing drums. In the seal script, "lightning" was omitted and the number of drums was reduced to three. After the clerical change, the number of drums was reduced to one, and the shape of the "drum" component became identical with the shape of "farmland."

Oracle	Bronze	Seal	Clerical	Regular	Normal-ized	Semi-cursive	Cursive
	靁	靁	雷	雷	雷	雷	雷

尖　This character is formed with 小 (small) on top of 大 (big), suggesting a pointed shape that is bigger on one side and gets smaller and smaller on the other. 尖 is a relatively new character. Before this character came to mean pointed, the complicated character 鑯 (sharp ironware) in the seal script had been used to refer to concept of "pointed."

Oracle	Bronze	Seal	Clerical	Regular	Normal-ized	Semi-cursive	Cursive
		鑯	尖	尖	尖	尖	尖

C. Recognition Reinforcement 辨认巩固练习

1. Go back to the beginning of this chapter. Look at the structure of each character and think about the meaning that each character commonly has now. Try to memorize the shape of each character by analyzing its components, and try to deduce the meaning for yourself from the combination of the components.

2. Link each character on the first line with its corresponding meaning in English on the second line:

a.　男　　明　　穿　　香　　时

　　bright　fragrant　male　time　penetrate

b.　多　　哭　　分　　解　　间

　　divide　dissect　many　space　cry

c.　相　　从　　双　　秋　　好

　　mutually　double　good　follow　fall

d.　烦　　取　　鲜　　雷　　尖

　　fetch　delicious　pointed　annoyed　thunder

3. There are ten characters on the left side and eleven words in English on the right side. Put the letter for each character in the blank next to the corresponding English word. In each group, there is an extra blank that should be left empty.

Group 1:

a. 哭

b. 解　　　　　　　　　_____ divide

c. 香　　　　　　　　　_____ space

　　　　　　　　　　　　_____ penetrate

d. 时　　　　　　　　　_____ many

e. 间　　　　　　　　　_____ cry

f. 多   _____ time

g. 男   _____ bright

h. 穿   _____ dissect

                                        _____ fetch

i. 分   _____ fragrant

j. 明   _____ male

Group 2:

a. 取

b. 秋   _____ pointed

c. 双   _____ double

d. 从   _____ annoyed

e. 相   _____ good

f. 尖   _____ fetch

g. 烦   _____ many

h. 雷   _____ delicious

                                        _____ thunder

i. 好   _____ autumn

                                        _____ mutually

j. 鲜   _____ follow

4. Provide the meaning in English for each of the following characters:

男_____ 明_____ 穿_____ 香_____ 时_____

多_____ 哭_____ 分_____ 解_____ 间_____

相_____ 从_____ 双_____ 秋_____ 好_____

烦_____ 取_____ 鲜_____ 雷_____ 尖_____

II. Challenge 1: Write the Characters 挑战一: 知义书形

A. Strokes in Characters: Changes of Stroke Shapes 详说笔画: 笔画变形

    1. When two or more basic Chinese characters are put together to form a new character, the new character does not occupy more space than the basic character. In the Chinese writing system, one character occupies only one square box regardless of how many strokes it has and how many characters or components have been used to form it. Look at the following characters: when the first two are put together to form the third, you can see that the size of the first two, the component characters, is considerably reduced in the newly formed character. By shrinking the size of the component characters, the newly formed character can be written in the square box of the same size as the other characters.

1	2	3		1	2	3		1	2	3
田	力	男		日	月	明		禾	日	香

    Look at the following characters: the first three component characters are put together to form the fourth character. Again, the first three characters are components squeezed together into one square box. When you write, you must learn to put all the components together so as to keep the whole character balanced.

1	2	3	4		1	2	3	4
口	口	犬	哭		角	刀	牛	解

    2. However, when two or more characters are "squeezed together" and put into the space of one square box, some component characters must be reduced in size, and also the shape of some of their strokes must be changed. Very often, this change is in the last stroke of the component character on the left or on the top.

1.	穴	=>	宀 穿	The last stroke in the component character 穴, which is at the top of the character 穿, changes from *nà* to *diǎn*.
2.	木	=>	朩 相	The last stroke in the component character 木, which is on the left in the character 相, changes from *nà* to *diǎn*.
3.	人	=>	亻 从	The last stroke in the component character 人, which is on the left in the character 从, changes from *nà* to *diǎn*.

4.	又	=>	又　双	The last stroke in the component character 又, which is on the left in the character 双, changes from *nà* to *diǎn*.
5.	禾	=>	禾　秋	The last stroke in the component character 禾, which is on the left in the character 秋, changes from *nà* to *diǎn*.
6.	女	=>	女　好	The last stroke in the component character 女, which is on the left in the character 好, changes from *héng* to a leveled *tí*.
7.	耳	=>	耳　取	The last stroke in the component character 耳, which is on the left of the character 取, changes from *héng* to *tí*.

With your knowledge of stroke changes, combine the two given characters into a new one. Write the new character and compare it with the answer on the right.

1. 火 + 页　=>

火　烦

2. 鱼 + 羊　=>

鱼　鲜

3. If the component character on top has a *shùgōu* stroke or *shùzhégōu* stroke, they will also change.

1.	小	=>	小　尖	The *shùgōu* stroke in the component character on top changes to *shù*.
2.	雨	=>	雨　雷	The *héngzhégōu* stroke in the component character on top changes to *hénggōu*.

B. Character Structures 汉字结构

Because associative characters are formed by two or more component characters, their structures are determined by the way their component characters are put together. The numbers in the boxes below indicate the writing sequence.

1. The Top-Bottom (T-B) Structure: 男穿香分雷尖多

1
2

The T-B Structure imbedded with an L-R on top (T$_{(L-R)}$-B): 哭

2. The Left-Right (L-R) Structure: 明相从双秋好烦取鲜

The L-R Structure imbedded with a T-B on the right (L-R$_{(T-B)}$): 解

3. The Top-Wrap (T-Wrap) Structure: 间

C. *Stroke Order Analysis* 笔顺分析

The five types of character structures listed in the previous section also show the order, as indicated by the numbers, in which these component characters should be written. As you can see, they actually follow the basic rules for stroke order: from top to bottom, from left to right, and from outside to inside. Therefore, if you have learned all the basic characters in previous chapters, it is easy to form an associate character simply by writing it in compliance with the basic rules for stroke order. Can you separate the following associative characters into their component characters in the sequence in which they should be written?

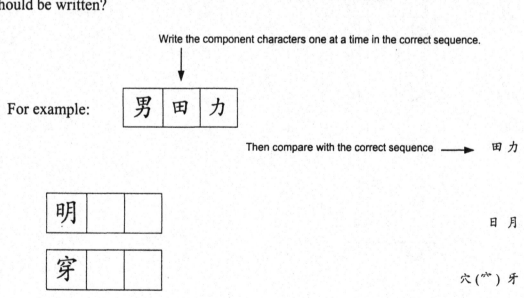

Write the component characters one at a time in the correct sequence.

For example: | 男 | 田 | 力 |

Then compare with the correct sequence ⟶ 田 力

| 明 | | |

日 月

| 穿 | | |

穴 (穴) 牙

香			禾 (禾) 日

时			日 寸

多			夕 夕

哭			口 口 犬

分			八 刀

解			角 刀 牛

间			门 日

相			木 (木) 目

从			人 (亻) 人

双			又 (又) 又

秋			禾 (禾) 火

好			女 (女) 子

烦			火 (火) 页

取			耳 (耳) 又

鲜			鱼 (鱼) 羊

雨 (⻗) 田

小 (⺌) 大

D. *Write with a Pencil* 动手动笔

Now that you know the meaning and the standard stroke order for each of the associative characters, it is time to practice writing them. Use the following "well" boxes to write each character. While writing, carefully observe the model character and keep the component characters in mind. Try to write without referring to the model again. Pay attention to the changes in some strokes in order to keep the balance of each character within the box. Each time you finish writing the character, you can compare it with the model. Correct any mistakes and write until you can form the character correctly without looking at the model. It is actually not enough just to write in the boxes provided in the book. You should also practice writing each character on a piece of paper.

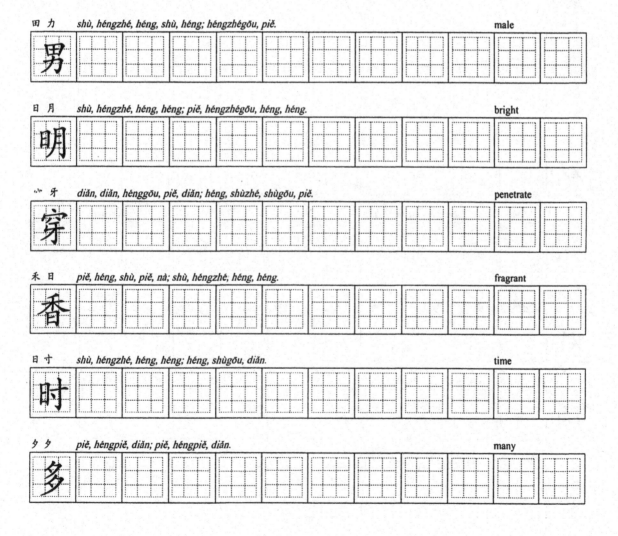

口 口 犬　shù, héngzhé, héng; shù, héngzhé, héng; héng, piě, nà, diǎn.　　　cry

哭

八 刀　piě, nà, héngzhégōu, piě.　　　divide

分

角 刀 牛　piě, héngpiě, piě, héngzhégōu, héng, héng, shù; héngzhégōu, piě; piě, héng, héng, shù.　　　dissect

解

门 日　diǎn, shù, héngzhégōu; shù, héngzhé, héng, héng.　　　space

间

木 目　héng, shù, piě, diǎn; shù, héngzhé, héng, héng, héng.　　　observe/mutually

相

亻 人　piě, diǎn; piě, nà.　　　follow/from

从

又 又　héngpiě, diǎn; héngpiě, nà.　　　double

双

禾 火　piě, héng, shù, piě, diǎn; diǎn, piě, piě, nà.　　　autumn

秋

女 子　piědiǎn, piě, héng; héngpiě, wāngōu, héng.　　　good

好

火 页　diǎn, piě, piě, diǎn; héng, piě, shù, héngzhé, piě, diǎn.　　　annoyed

烦

耳 又　héng, shù, shù, héng, héng, tí; héngpiě, nà.　　　fetch

取

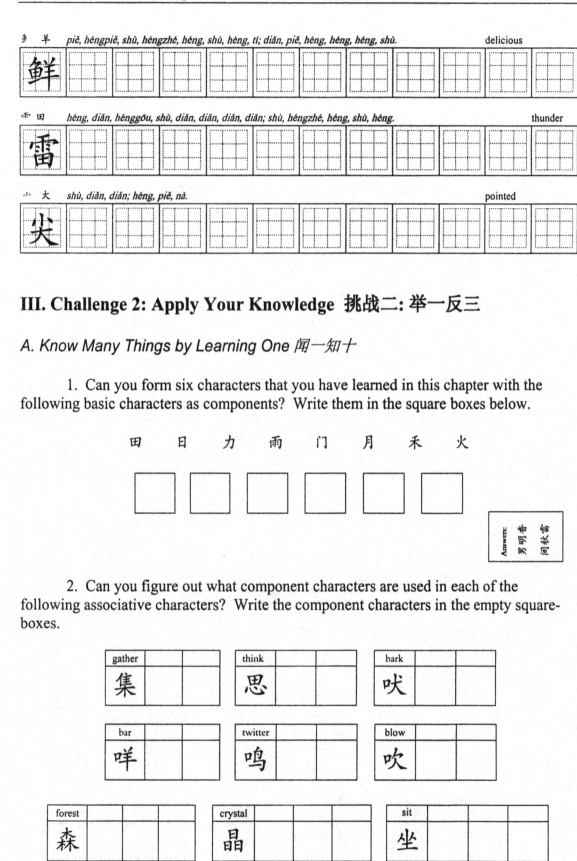

鱼 羊 *piě, héngpiě, shù, héngzhé, héng, shù, héng, tí; diǎn, piě, héng, héng, héng, shù.*   delicious

鲜

雨 田 *héng, diǎn, hénggōu, shù, diǎn, diǎn, diǎn, diǎn; shù, héngzhé, héng, shù, héng.*   thunder

雷

小 大 *shù, diǎn, diǎn; héng, piě, nà.*   pointed

尖

III. Challenge 2: Apply Your Knowledge 挑战二: 举一反三

A. Know Many Things by Learning One 闻一知十

1. Can you form six characters that you have learned in this chapter with the following basic characters as components? Write them in the square boxes below.

田   日   力   雨   门   月   禾   火

Answers:
男 明 香
闷 秋 雷

2. Can you figure out what component characters are used in each of the following associative characters? Write the component characters in the empty square-boxes.

gather
集

think
思

bark
吠

bar
咩

twitter
鸣

blow
吹

forest
森

crystal
晶

sit
坐

Answers:
集 隹木
思 田心
吠 口犬
哞 口牛
鸣 口鸟
吹 口欠
森 木木木
晶 日日日
坐 人人土

3. Write in the empty square box the character that is formed with the two preceding component characters. Pay extra attention to the change of the shape in the last stroke in the component character on the left, at the top, or inside.

(left)	(right)	woods
木	木	

(left)	(right)	correct
又	寸	

(left)	(right)	oven
火	土	

(top)	(bottom)	dust
小	土	

(top)	(bottom)	suddenly
穴	犬	

(outside)	(inside)	flash
门	人	

Answers:
林 woods
对 correct
灶 oven
尘 dust
突 suddenly
闪 f flash

4. The following two-syllable words and phrases are formed with the characters you have learned in this chapter and previous chapters. Can you figure out what they mean?

Group 1:

明天_____　　　　1. decompose

分解_____　　　　2. mid-autumn

时间_____　　　　3. thunder storm

中秋_____　　　　4. human world

好多_____　　　　5. tomorrow

香水_____　　　　6. dagger

尖刀_____　　　　7. a good many

人间_____　　　　8. time

雷雨_____　　　　9. perfume

Answers:
明天 5
分解 1
时间 8
中秋 2
好多 7
香水 9
尖刀 6
人间 4
雷雨 3

Group 2:

文明_____   1. lilac

明白_____   2. good intention

正好_____   3. torpedo

鱼雷_____   4. once upon a time

小时_____   5. civilization

丁香_____   6. clear about

从前_____   7. from among

好心_____   8. just right

从中_____   9. hour

Answers: 文明 5 明白 6 正好 8 鱼雷 3 小时 9 丁香 1 从前 4 好心 2 从中 7

Group 3:

入时_____   1. from childhood

分心_____   2. molecule

分子_____   3. lifeblood

中间_____   4. ever since

瓜分_____   5. trendy

鲜血_____   6. distracted

从小_____   7. temporarily

自从_____   8. carve up

一时_____   9. between

Answers: 入时 5 分心 6 分子 2 中间 9 瓜分 8 鲜血 3 从小 1 自从 4 一时 7

B. Be Perceptive of the Slightest Differences 明察秋毫

1. Which character in each group have you not yet learned? Circle it.
   a. Group 1
      i. 取   ii. 从   iii. 分   iv. 休

b. Group 2

　　　i. 香　　　ii. 针　　　iii. 好　　　iv. 雷

c. Group 3

　　　i. 笔　　　ii. 尖　　　iii. 秋　　　iv. 哭

d. Group 4

　　　i. 多　　　ii. 穿　　　iii. 打　　　iv. 相

e. Group 5

　　　i. 烦　　　ii. 饮　　　iii. 鲜　　　iv. 明

f. Group 6

　　　i. 时　　　ii. 间　　　iii. 酒　　　iv. 男

Answers: a. iv. b. ii. c. i. d. i. e. ii. f. iii.

2. Which of the characters in each group is different?

a. Which character does not have the L-R Structure?

　　　i. 明　　　ii. 多　　　iii. 从　　　iv. 双

b. Which character does not have the T-B Structure?

　　　i. 鲜　　　ii. 穿　　　iii. 雷　　　iv. 香

c. Which character has the T-Wrap Structure?

　　　i. 男　　　ii. 烦　　　iii. 秋　　　iv. 间

d. Which character has a slightly different structure from that of the others?

　　　i. 相　　　ii. 解　　　iii. 取　　　iv. 时

e. Which character does not have a change for any of its strokes?

　　　i. 尖　　　ii. 相　　　iii. 好　　　iv. 分

f. Which character contains a stroke whose shape has been changed to accommodate the other part of the character?

　　　i. 雷　　　ii. 男　　　iii. 间　　　iv. 明

Answers: a. i. b. i. c. iv. d. ii. e. iv. f. i.

3. Which stroke is that?

a. Which stroke in 穿 has changed its shape? It is the _____ stroke.

　　　i. 1ˢᵗ　　　ii. 3ʳᵈ　　　iii. 5ᵗʰ　　　iv. 7ᵗʰ

b. Which stroke in 相 has changed its shape? It is the _____ stroke.
    i. 2nd ii. 4th iii. 6th iv. 8th

c. Which stroke in 尖 has changed its shape? It is the _____ stroke.
    i. 1st ii. 3rd iii. 5th iv. 7th

d. Which stroke in 双 has changed its shape? It is the _____ stroke.
    i. 3rd ii. 4th iii. 1st iv. 2nd

e. Which stroke in 鲜 has changed its shape? It is the _____ stroke.
    i. 10th ii. 8th iii. 6th iv. 4th

f. Which stroke in 好 has changed its shape? It is the _____ stroke.
    i. 2nd ii. 4th iii. 1st iv. 3rd

Answers:
a. iii. b. ii. c. i. d. iv. e. ii. f. iv.

C. Be Aware of the Complex Counterpart 学简知繁

If you do not wish to learn the complex forms now, at the beginning level, you may skip this section and go on to the next section for Challenge 3.

1. Comparison. In this chapter, there are six simplified characters. Look at the following table and compare the simplified forms of these characters with their complex counterparts:

	Simplified Form	Complex Form	Meaning
1	时	時	Time
2	间	間	Space
3	从	從	Follow/From
4	双	雙	Double/Pair
5	烦	煩	Annoyed
6	鲜	鮮	Delicious/Fresh

2. Explanation.

時. The traditional form (時) is not the oldest form of this character. The earlier forms, in the oracle-bone and bronze inscriptions, had 止 at the top and 日 at the bottom. 時 first appeared in the seal script. 日 indicates the meaning, and 寺, the pronunciation. The traditional form of the character, therefore, is in fact a picto-phonetic character, a type to be introduced in Chapter 14.

間. This is the traditional form of the character, although it is not the oldest form. It is formed with 門, which is a two-leafed door and 日 (sun). If it is closed tight, without any crack, the sunshine will be blocked. However, if there is a space or gap between the two leaves of the door, the sunshine will get in. The character 間 obviously indicates the latter situation.

從. The oldest form of this character is 从, which is a sketch of one person following another. To emphasize the idea of "following by walking," 辵 (walking) was added using the components 彳 and 止. 止 is put underneath 从, and 彳 is placed on the left side of the combination of 从 and 止.

雙. This traditional form of the character for "pair" is formed with two 隹 (short-tailed bird) characters side by side over a 又 (hand).

3. Writing. Write this character in its traditional form.

日 寺   *shù, héngzhé, héng, héng; héng, shù, héng; héng, shùgōu, diǎn.*   time

時

門 日   *shù, héngzhé, héng, héng, shù, héngzhégōu, héng, héng; shù, héngzhé, héng, héng.*   space

間

彳 从 止   *piě, piě, shù; piě, diǎn, piě, diǎn; shù, héng, piě, nà.*   follow/from

從

隹 隹 又   *piě, shù, diǎn, héng, héng, héng, shù, héng; piě, shù, diǎn, héng, héng, héng, shù, héng; héngpiě, nà.*   double/pair

雙

火 頁   *diǎn, piě, piě, diǎn; héng, piě, shù, héngzhé, héng, héng, héng, piě, diǎn.*   annoyed

煩

魚 羊	*piě, héngpiě, shù, héngzhé, héng, shù, héng, diǎn, diǎn, diǎn, diǎn; diǎn, piě, héng, héng, héng, shù.*										delicious
鲜											

D. Simplification Method (3): Use the Original Ancient Form 简化方法 (三): 古字今用

In the normalized script, some characters were simplified by using the original ancient forms. No matter how traditional a complex form was, if it had an even older form that was simpler, it was restored to replace the relatively newer traditional form.

Traditional	Use the ancient form	Simplified
從	⟶	从
電	⟶	电
雲	⟶	云
氣	⟶	气
網	⟶	网
屍	⟶	尸

IV. Challenge 3: Pronounce the Characters 挑战三: 见形发音

After you have established the link between the shape and the meaning of each of the characters introduced in this chapter, you are ready to establish the link between the shape and the pronunciation of each of these characters. Because the shape of a character does not offer a clue to its pronunciation, it will be a real challenge.

Again, if you are not ready for this challenge, you can skip this section and go to the next section to practice writing characters or go on to the next chapter to learn to recognize more Chinese characters. After you learn to speak some Chinese, you can return to this section.

1. Listen and read (choose the form you prefer):

(In the traditional form)

Nán míng chuān xiāng shí,
男明穿香時,

Duō kū fēn jiě jiān,
多哭分解間,

(In the normalized form)

Nán míng chuān xiāng shí,
男明穿香时,

Duō kū fēn jiě jiān,
多哭分解间,

Xiāng cóng shuāng qiū hǎo,
相從雙秋好，

Xiāng cóng shuāng qiū hǎo,
相从双秋好，

Fán qǔ xiān léi jiān.
煩取鮮雷尖。

Fán qǔ xiān léi jiān.
烦取鲜雷尖。

2. Read aloud by looking only at the characters:

(In the traditional form)

(In the normalized form)

男明穿香時，

男明穿香时，

多哭分解間，

多哭分解间，

相從雙秋好，

相从双秋好，

煩取鮮雷尖。

烦取鲜雷尖。

3. Guess the answers to the following riddles using the characters in the list. Answer the riddle in Chinese aloud to yourself or to someone who can help with pronunciation, and write the character in the box and its *pinyin* transliteration outside the box after each riddle. Note that in each group there are nine riddles for nine of the ten characters in the list provided at the beginning.

Group 1: 男明穿香时多哭分解间

a) It is the scent emanating from cereal crops in the sunshine.

b) A cave can be created by the strength of teeth.

c) It records the changes in the position of the sun.

d) The sunshine can go through if there is a gap between the two leaves of a door.

e) Take the horn off an ox with a knife.

f) The easiest way to cut something apart is to use a knife.

g) One evening after another.

h) It sounds like a dog howling.

i) Who was expected to work in the fields with a plow in the old days?

Group 2: 相从双秋好烦取鲜雷尖

a) It feels like your head is on fire.

b) One person follows another.

c) A woman with a baby.

d) It is the taste associated with cooked fish and mutton.

e) It is the time when the stalks of cereal crops are burned.

f) It is the loud noise that is sometimes heard when it rains.

g) If an eye stares at a tree, the tree also stares at the eye.

h) It gets increasingly small at one end.

i) Two hands side by side.

V. Challenge 4: Dictation 挑战四：听音书形知义

1. By now, you should be able to recite the character verse for this chapter. Write the verse in Chinese characters and the meaning for each character in the spaces provided below:

Nán	míng	chuān	xiāng	shí	,

Duō	kū	fēn	jiě	jiān	,

Xiāng	cóng	shuāng	qiū	hǎo	,

Fán	qǔ	xiān	léi	jiān	.

2. Look at the meaning, write its character in the first box, and say it aloud in Chinese before putting its *pinyin* transliteration in the second.

meaning	character	pinyin	meaning	character	pinyin
double			penetrate		

fetch			bright		
delicious			follow		
pointed			good		
many			cry		
male			divide		
time			autumn		
mutually			fragrant		
annoyed			dissect		
thunder			space		

3. Have your instructor dictate the characters or words covered in Chapter 11.

Chapter 12 第十二章
Reduced Forms of Basic Characters as Semantic Components
由基本汉字简化而来的形旁

I. Fundamental Knowledge 基础知识

In the previous chapter you learned that associate characters are formed with two or more basic characters, and that when putting these basic characters as components into a new integral character in one square box, some strokes, often the last stroke in the component character on top or on the left, will change their shapes in order to keep the proportion and balance of the newly formed character. In this chapter, you will look at some of the basic characters that have been used so frequently as components that their overall shapes have changed. As a result of the changes, they are no longer characters that can be used independently but components representing meanings in the characters they have helped to form.

A. Shapes and Meanings 见形思义

First, let's look at how 20 of the most frequently used basic characters have been reduced into components in multicomponent characters. The 20 reduced forms are usually the components on the left side of the character unless indicated otherwise.

	Character		Reduced Form
1.	人 *person*	=>	亻
2.	手 *hand*	=>	扌
3.	心 *heart*	=>	忄
4.	辵/走 *walk*	=>	辶
5.	足 *foot*	=>	𧾷
6.	言 *speech*	=>	讠

7.	食 *food*	=>	饣
8.	示 *altar/reveal*	=>	礻
9.	衣 *garment*	=>	衤
10.	丝 *silk*	=>	纟
11.	水 *water*	=>	氵
12.	火 *fire*	=>	灬 (at the bottom)
13.	金 *metal*	=>	钅
14.	艸 *grass*	=>	艹
15.	竹 *bamboo*	=>	⺮
16.	邑 *town*	=>	阝 (on the right side)
17.	阜 *mound*	=>	阝 (on the left side)
18.	犬 *dog*	=>	犭
19.	刀 *knife*	=>	刂 (on the right side)
20.	网 *net*	=>	罒

B. Character Formation 组字方式

Now, look at how these reduced forms are used together with other basic characters to form multicomponent characters.

1.	(人) 亻 *person*	+	木 *tree*	=>	休 rest	
2.	(手) 扌 *hand*	+	戈 *dagger-axe*	=>	找 seek	
3.	(心) 忄 *heart*	+	兑 *person with a happy face*	=>	悦 pleased	
4.	(辵) 辶 *walk*	+	首 *head*	=>	道 way	
5.	(足) 𧾷 *foot (from knee to toes)*	+	止 *foot (sole and toes)*	=>	趾 toe	
6.	(言) 讠 *speech*	+	殳 *weapon in hand*	=>	设 display/set up	
7.	(食) 饣 *food*	+	欠 *person with an open mouth*	=>	饮 to drink	
8.	(示) 礻 *reveal*	+	兄 *person with a big mouth*	=>	祝 to wish	
9.	(衣) 衤 *garment*	+	刀 *knife*	=>	初 beginning	
10.	(丝) 纟 *silk*	+	少 *few*	=>	纱 gauze	

11.	(水) 氵 water	+	酉 jar	=>	酒 liquor	
12.	(火) 灬 fire	+	隹 short-tail bird	=>	焦 burned	
13.	(金) 钅 metal	+	十 ten	=>	针 needle	
14.	(艸) 艹 grass	+	田 farmland	=>	苗 seedling	
15.	(竹) 𥫗 bamboo	+	毛 fur	=>	笔 pen	
16.	(舟) 刕 steadily	+	(邑) 阝 town	=>	那 that	
17.	(阜) 阝 mound	+	月 moon	=>	阴 shade	
18.	(犬) 犭 dog	+ (言) 讠 speech	+ 犬 dog	=>	狱 lawsuit/jail	
19.	禾 standing grain	+	(刀) 刂 knife	=>	利 benefit/sharp	
20.	(网) 罒 net	+ (言) 讠 speech	+ (刀) 刂 knife	=>	罚 penalize	

C. Forms and Meanings 知形会意

休 In the old days, when out in the open, a common way to rest would be to sit under or lean against a tree that would provide shade. Nowadays, in rural areas in China, this scene of people resting under a tree can often still be seen. The idea represented by this character, which is formed with "person" and "tree," is, therefore, "to rest." 亻 on the left side is a reduced form of the character 人 and is a commonly used semantic component in forming many other multicomponent characters. The characters that have 亻 as a component are all related to human beings in one way or another.

Oracle	Bronze	Seal	Clerical	Regular	Normal-ized	Semi-cursive	Cursive
休	休	休	休	休	休	休	休

找 This character is formed with "hand" on the left and "dagger-axe" on the right. In the old days, weapons were usually stored somewhere in the house when not needed. When a war broke out, people had to locate the weapons. This character indicates the action of looking for something. Its meaning is "seek." The semantic component 扌 used in this character is a reduced form of the character 手. It is also commonly used to form many other characters, all of which are related to "hand."

Oracle	Bronze	Seal	Clerical	Regular	Normal-ized	Semi-cursive	Cursive
		找	找	找	找	找	找

悦 In the seal script, the old form of this character, 说, had the component character 言 (speech) on the left and four different pronunciations and meanings. One of the meanings was "pleased." After the clerical change, the "speech" component on the left was changed into 忄, the reduced form of the 心 (heart) component, indicating that the whole character is related to some kind of feeling in the heart. On the right is a component character that is a person with a big mouth and extended eyebrows, indicating "a happy face." When the two component characters are put together, the resulting character means "pleased." The semantic component 忄 is also used to form other characters. Any character that has 忄 as a component represents a state of the mind or a feeling of some kind.

Oracle	Bronze	Seal	Clerical	Regular	Normal-ized	Semi-cursive	Cursive
		說	悦	悦	悦	悦	悦

道 The earliest form of this character in the bronze script showed a head in the middle of the character 行, which represents a path and means "to go." The forms in the various scripts after the clerical change all have 辶, which is a reduced form of the character 辵, meaning "walking," and 首, meaning "head." The whole character suggests a person heading somewhere on foot: the way. 辶 is a commonly used semantic component. The characters that have 辶 as a component often have something to do with walking.

Oracle	Bronze	Seal	Clerical	Regular	Normal-ized	Semi-cursive	Cursive
	省	邋	道	道	道	道	道

趾 This character means "toe." Its old form is 止, which depicts a foot with its sole and toes. However, 止 took on the meaning of "stop," so the character 足, which is a representation of a foot from the knee to the toes, was added on the left side of 止 and formed a new character, 趾, to mean "toe" exclusively. Notice that 足 is reduced to 𧾷 when used as a component in other characters. The meaning of any character that has 𧾷 as a component is related to "foot."

Oracle	Bronze	Seal	Clerical	Regular	Normal-ized	Semi-cursive	Cursive
屮	止	止	趾	趾	趾	趾	趾

设 This character is formed with 言 (speech) on the left and 殳 on the right. 殳 is an ancient hitting weapon held in the hand as indicated in the earliest form of the character in the oracle-bone inscriptions. When a memorial ceremony was held after a victorious battle in ancient times, weapons were displayed, and a speech was also given. The combination of these two components, therefore, means "to display" or "to set up." Note that in the normalized script, the component 言 on the left is reduced to 讠. All characters that have 讠 as a component are related to "speech" in one way or another.

Oracle	Bronze	Seal	Clerical	Regular	Normal-ized	Semi-cursive	Cursive
𠂤		殼	設	設	设	设	设

饮　This character has two components, 饣 on the left and 欠 on the right. 饣 is the reduced form of 食, which is a food container with a cover, as depicted in its old form in the seal script. However, it is used to mean "food and beverage." 欠 is a person with an open mouth. The combination of these two parts means "to drink." The semantic component 饣 can be seen in many other characters. Any character that has 饣 has something to do with eating and drinking.

Oracle	Bronze	Seal	Clerical	Regular	Normal-ized	Semi-cursive	Cursive
		龡	飲	飲	饮	饮	饮

祝　This character consists of two parts. On the left is 示, which is an altar table used in a sacrificial ceremony; on the right is 兄, a person with a big mouth. The character 祝, formed by these two component characters, means "to wish." The component 示 was reduced to 礻 after the clerical change. If a character has 礻 as a component, it is usually related to sacrificial ceremonies or superhuman beings.

Oracle	Bronze	Seal	Clerical	Regular	Normal-ized	Semi-cursive	Cursive
祝	祝	祝	祝	祝	祝	祝	祝

初　This character means "beginning." It was derived from the idea that anybody who wants to tailor a garment must start with a cutter. Thus 衣 (garment) is on the left and 刀 (knife) on the right. After the clerical change, 衣 was reduced to 衤. Be careful not to confuse 衤 with 礻; the only difference between the two shapes is that 衤 has one extra small left-falling stroke. Characters with 衤 as a component are all somehow related to garments, whereas characters containing 礻 have nothing to do with garments.

Oracle	Bronze	Seal	Clerical	Regular	Normal-ized	Semi-cursive	Cursive
衱	衱	初	初	初	初	初	初

纱   On the left side of this character is 纟, the reduced form of the character 丝 (silk). Any character with 纟 as a component is related to fabric of some kind if not silk. On the right side of this character is 少 (few). The combination of these two components indicates something made of a few shreds of fabric, or yarn.

Oracle	Bronze	Seal	Clerical	Regular	Normal-ized	Semi-cursive	Cursive
		紗	紗	紗	纱	纱	纱

酒   The meaning of this character, "liquor," is derived from its two components: 水 (water) on the left and 酉 (jar) on the right. In the old days, liquid in a jar had to be liquor. The component 水 on the left was reduced to 氵 after the clerical change. Characters that have 氵 as a component are related to water or liquid.

Oracle	Bronze	Seal	Clerical	Regular	Normal-ized	Semi-cursive	Cursive
酒	酉	酒	酒	酒	酒	酒	酒

焦   This character had four components in its old form in the seal script. There are three 隹 (short-tail bird) characters at the top and the component 火 (fire) at the bottom. After the clerical change, the character was simplified by having only one 隹 at the top and 灬, which is the reduced form of 火, at the bottom. The meaning of this character is "burned," probably suggesting the result if birds cannot escape fire by flying away. All the characters in the normalized script that have 灬 are related to fire, except a few characters such as 燕 (swallow), in which 灬 does not represent "fire," but the swallow's tail.

Oracle	Bronze	Seal	Clerical	Regular	Normal-ized	Semi-cursive	Cursive
焦	焦	焦	焦	焦	焦	焦	焦

针　This character means "needle." On the left is the reduced form of the character 金 (metal); on the right is a component in the shape of the character 十 (ten), but originally it was in fact a depiction of a thread going through the eye of a needle. In the older form of the character in the seal script, the component character 咸 on the right indicated the pronunciation of the character rather than the meaning. This older form of the character is no longer used in modern Chinese. The semantic component 钅, which is the reduced form of 金 in the normalized script, is used in many other characters to refer to something related to metal.

Oracle	Bronze	Seal	Clerical	Regular	Normal-ized	Semi-cursive	Cursive
		鍼	針	針	针	针	针

苗　This character is formed with 艸 (grass) at the top and 田 (farmland) at the bottom. The combination of these two component characters indicates "seedling" or "young plant." The reduced form of the character 艸 in the normalized script is ⺾. It is commonly used as a component at the top of many characters that are related to plants and flowers.

Oracle	Bronze	Seal	Clerical	Regular	Normal-ized	Semi-cursive	Cursive
		苗	苗	苗	苗	苗

笔　This character refers to the writing instrument that Chinese people have used for more than two thousand years: the brush pen. The top part of the character is a reduced form of the character 竹 (bamboo), and the bottom part is 毛 (fur or hair). These are the materials needed to make a brush pen, with a bamboo shaft at one end and fur or hair from a sheep or wolf at the other, forming a pointed brush that can be dipped in ink to write characters. This form was used about 1,500 years ago, but it was not officially recognized as a standard form until the 1950's. It is now used as a generic term for pens of all kinds, even though they may have no fur or hair. The oldest form of the character is 聿, which is a hand grabbing the shaft of a brush pen. Later on, when 聿 was used to mean something other than a brush pen, "bamboo" was added to its top as 筆 to indicate the meaning "pen."

Oracle	Bronze	Seal	Clerical	Regular	Normal-ized	Semi-cursive	Cursive
		筆	筆	筆	笔	笔	笔

那 This character originally referred to a place, but it is now used as the demonstrative pronoun meaning "that." The character has two components. The component on the left depicts dropping hair or tree branches and means "tenderly" or "steadily." However, this component in fact does not contribute to the meaning of the whole character; instead, it indicates the pronunciation of the whole character. (Phonetic components in characters will be dealt with in depth in Chapter 14.) The component 阝 on the right is a reduced form of the character 邑 (town), indicating that the character it partially forms refers to a place.

Oracle	Bronze	Seal	Clerical	Regular	Normal-ized	Semi-cursive	Cursive
		那	那	那	那	那	那

阴 The component 阝 on the left side of this character has exactly the same shape as that used on the right side of the character 那, which you have just seen. However, its meaning differs depending on where it is placed. When it is placed on the right side of a character, it is the reduced form of the character 邑 (town); when it is placed on the left side of a character, it is the reduced form of the character 阜 (earth mound). In this character, the component 阝 represents "earth mound," and the component on the right is 月 (moon), indicating that the side of the earth mound does not get sunshine. Therefore, the basic meaning of this character is "shady" and "gloomy."

Oracle	Bronze	Seal	Clerical	Regular	Normal-ized	Semi-cursive	Cursive
陰	陰	陰	陰	阴	阴	阴	

狱 This character has three components. The component in the middle is the reduced form of the character 言 (speech). The component on the right side is 犬 (dog), and the one on the left is a reduced form of the character 犬. "Speech" between two "dogs" indicates an argument. This character means "lawsuit" or "jail," the place someone might end up at as the result of a lawsuit. As a reduced form of the character 犬, 犭 is used as a component in many other characters. Characters having 犭 as a component are all related to animals.

Oracle	Bronze	Seal	Clerical	Regular	Normal-ized	Semi-cursive	Cursive
	獄	獄	獄	獄	獄	獄	獄

利   This character is composed of two components. On the left is 禾 (standing grain) with its last stroke changed from a right-falling stroke to a dot to accommodate the component on the right-hand side. 刂 on the right is the reduced form of the character 刀 (knife). The combination of the two components depicts the idea of reaping for profit. The meaning of the character is, therefore, "profit" or "benefit." Sometimes it is also used to mean "sharp." 刂 is a component that is always used on the right side of a character. Any character with 刂 is related to "knife" in one way or another.

Oracle	Bronze	Seal	Clerical	Regular	Normal-ized	Semi-cursive	Cursive
利	利	利	利	利	利	利	利

罚   This character consists of three parts. At the top, 罒 is the reduced form of the character 网 (net), which is a metaphor for "law" in Chinese. The component 讠 on the lower left stands for "conviction," and the component 刂 on the lower right stands for "instrument of torture." The meaning of the whole character is "penalize." Characters with 罒 often have something to do with "net" or its figurative meaning—"law."

Oracle	Bronze	Seal	Clerical	Regular	Normal-ized	Semi-cursive	Cursive
		罰	罰	罰	罚	罚	罚

D. Recognition Reinforcement 辨认巩固练习

1. Reduced forms originated from characters, but they cannot stand alone nor can they be used as whole characters. They can only be parts of characters and suggest the meaning of those characters. Link each reduced form with the character it originated from:

a. 亻　　扌　　忄　　辶　　⻊

　　心　　足　　手　　人　　走

b. 讠　　饣　　礻　　衤　　纟

　　食　　衣　　丝　　言　　示

c. 氵　　灬　　钅　　艹　　竹

　　艸　　水　　竹　　金　　火

d. 阝(left)　　阝(right)　　犭　　刂　　罒

　　犬　　邑　　网　　阜　　刀

2. Link each reduced form with the meaning it represents:

a. 亻　　扌　　忄　　辶　　⻊

　　hand　heart　foot　person　walk

b. 讠　　饣　　礻　　衤　　纟

　　silk　speech　altar　food　garment

c. 氵　　灬　　钅　　艹　　竹

　　metal　grass　water　fire　bamboo

d. 阝(left)　　阝(right)　　犭　　刂　　罒

　　mound　net　knife　town　dog

3. Link each character on the first line with its corresponding meaning in English on the second line:

a. 休　　找　　悦　　道　　趾

toe　　seek　　way　　rest　　pleased

b. 设　　饮　　祝　　初　　纱

wish　　beginning　　set up　　yarn　　drink

c. 酒　　焦　　针　　苗　　笔

liquor　　seedling　　burned　　pen　　needle

d. 那　　阴　　狱　　利　　罚

jail　　that　　penalize　　shade　　benefit

4. There are ten characters on the left side and eleven words in English on the right side. Put the letter for each character in the blank next to the corresponding English word. In each group, there is an extra blank that should be left empty.

Group 1:

a. 趾

b. 设　　　　　　　　_____ way

c. 纱　　　　　　　　_____ drink

d. 休　　　　　　　　_____ wish

e. 饮　　　　　　　　_____ seek

f. 悦　　　　　　　　_____ rest

g. 道　　　　　　　　_____ toe

h. 初　　　　　　　　_____ set up

i. 找　　　　　　　　_____ beginning

j. 祝　　　　　　　　_____ benefit

　　　　　　　　　　　_____ pleased

　　　　　　　　　　　_____ yarn

Group 2:

a. 利

b. 笔   _____ needle

c. 那   _____ shade

       _____ liquor

d. 苗   _____ seek

e. 酒   _____ burned

f. 狱   _____ pen

g. 罚   _____ penalize

       _____ seedling

h. 阴   _____ that

i. 针   _____ benefit

j. 焦   _____ lawsuit/jail

5. Provide the meaning in English for each of the following characters:

休_____ 找_____ 悦_____ 道_____ 趾_____

设_____ 饮_____ 祝_____ 初_____ 纱_____

酒_____ 焦_____ 针_____ 苗_____ 笔_____

那_____ 阴_____ 狱_____ 利_____ 罚_____

II. Challenge 1: Write the Characters 挑战一：知义书形

A. Strokes in Characters 详说笔画: ㇆ ㇜ ㇚ ㇓ ㇛

In the reduced forms you have learned in this chapter, there are four new strokes:

㇆   *héngpiěwān* (a horizontal stroke with a left-falling stroke connected with a curve),

as in 辶

⟍   *píngnà* (leveled right-falling stroke), as in 辶

乁   *píngnà* (leveled right-falling stroke), as in 辶

阝   *héngpiěwāngōu* (a horizontal stroke with a left-falling stroke connected with a curved stroke and a hook), as in 阝

乙   *héngzhéwān* (a horizontal stroke with a turn and a bend), as in 殳

Write these strokes, paying attention to the movement of the stroke as indicated.

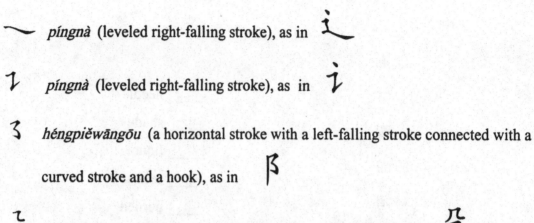

B. Character Structures 汉字结构

In Chapter 11, you learned three major types of Chinese character structures. They are 1) the T-B Structure, 2) the L-R Structure, and 3) the T-Wrap Structure. You also learned the $T_{(L-R)}$-B Structure, which is a subcategory of the T-B Structure, and the $L-R_{(T-B)}$ Structure, which is a subcategory of the L-R Structure. Let's review these structures by doing the following exercises:

1. Match the character structures with their corresponding structure diagrams.

(1)   T-B Structure   a.   ⊓

(2)   T(L-R) -B Structure   b.

(3)   L-R Structure   c.

(4)   L-R(T-B) Structure   d.

(5)   T-Wrap Structure   e.

Answers:
(1) d
(2) e
(3) b
(4) c
(5) a

2. Put each of the following characters after the type of character structure it belongs to.

相 穿 双 尖 多 从 秋 香 好 分 明 雷 烦 取 鲜 男 解 哭 间 罚

a.

b.

c.

d.

e.

Answers:
a. 间
b. 相双从秋好
   明烦取鲜解
c. 解
d. 穿尖多香
   分雷男
e. 哭

The purpose of recognizing the character structures is to know how a new character is constructed; furthermore, this knowledge will enable you to write multicomponent characters in the conventionally accepted order and to memorize multicomponent characters with relative ease.

In this chapter, there are two new types of character structures as shown in (1) and (2), and a new subcategory of the T-B Structure as show in (3):

(1) The L-M-R (Left-Middle-Right) Structure: 狱

(2) The B-L-Wrap (Bottom-Left-Wrap) Structure: 道

(3) The T-B(L-R) Structure: 罚

C. *Stroke Order Analysis* 笔顺分析

These new character structures, like those learned in Chapter 11, should be written in the sequence indicated by the numbers. They follow the same basic rules for stroke order: from top to bottom, from left to right, and from outside to inside. If you have learned all the basic characters in the previous chapters, you will know how to write a multicomponent character in the proper sequence. Can you separate the following multicomponent characters into their component characters in the sequence in which they should be written?

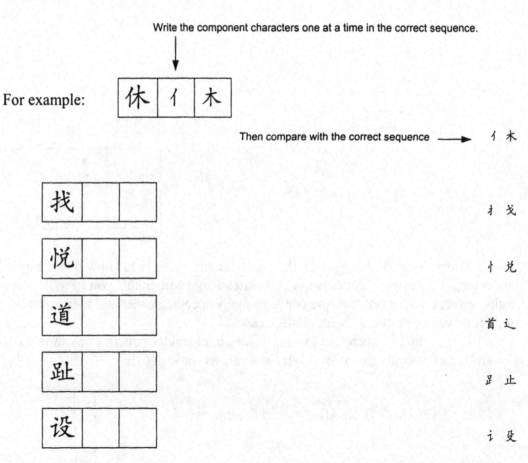

Write the component characters one at a time in the correct sequence.

For example: 休 亻 木

Then compare with the correct sequence ⟶ 亻 木

找   扌 戈

悦   忄 兑

道   首 辶

趾   足 止

设   讠 殳

饮		
祝		
初		
纱		
酒		
焦		
针		
苗		
笔		
那		
阴		
狱		
利		
罚		

饣 欠

礻 兄

衤 刀

纟 少

氵 酉

隹 灬

钅 十

艹 田

竹 毛

刐 阝

阝 月

犭 訁 犬

禾 刂

罒 訁 刂

D. Write with a Pencil 动手动笔

Now that you know the sequence for writing the components in multicomponent characters, it is time to practice writing these characters. Use the following "well" boxes to write each character.

While writing, carefully observe the model character and keep the component characters in mind. Try to write without referring to the model again. Pay attention to the changes in some strokes in order to keep the balance of each character within the box. Each time you finish writing the character, you can compare it with the model. Correct any mistakes and write until you can form the character correctly without looking at the model. It is actually not enough just to write in the boxes provided in the book. You should also practice writing each character on a piece of paper.

亻木   *piě, shù; héng, shù, piě, nà.*   rest
休

扌戈   *héng, shùgōu, tí; héng, xiégōu, piě, diǎn.*   seek
找

丷忄 or 丷忄 兑   *diǎn, diǎn, shù or diǎn, shù, diǎn; diǎn, piě, shù, héngzhé, héng, piě, shùwāngōu.*   pleased
悦

首 丶讠辶   *diǎn, piě, héng, piě, shù, héngzhé, héng, héng, héng; diǎn, hénpiěwān, píngnà.*   way
道

⻊止   *shù, héngzhé, héng, shù, héng, shù, tí; shù, héng, shù, héng.*   toe
趾

讠殳   *diǎn, héngzhétí; piě, héngzhéwān, héngpiě, nà.*   display/set up
设

饣欠   *piě, hénggōu, shùtí; piě, hénggōu, piě, nà.*   to drink
饮

礻兄   *diǎn, héngpiě, shù, diǎn; shù, héngzhé, héng, piě, shùwāngōu.*   to wish
祝

ネ 刀 diǎn, héngpiě, shù, piě, diǎn; héngzhégōu, piě. — beginning

初

纟 少 piězhé, piězhé, tí; shù, diǎn, diǎn, piě. — gauze

纱

氵 酉 diǎn, diǎn, tí; héng, shù, héngzhé, piě, shùwān, héng, héng. — liquor

酒

隹 灬 piě, shù, diǎn, héng, héng, héng, shù, héng; diǎn, diǎn, diǎn, diǎn. — burned

焦

钅 十 piě, héng, héng, héng, shùtí; héng, shù. — needle

针

艹 田 héng, shù, shù; shù, héngzhé, héng, shù, héng. — seedling

苗

竹 毛 piě, héng, diǎn, piě, héng, diǎn; piě, héng, héng, shùwāngōu. — pen

笔

乛乛习刃阝那 héngzhégōu, héng, héng, piě; héngpiěwāngōu, shù. — that

那

阝 月 héngpiěwāngōu, shù; piě, héngzhégōu, héng, héng. — shade

阴

犭 讠 犬 piě, wāngōu, piě; diǎn, héngzhétí; héng, piě, nà, diǎn. — lawsuit/jail

狱

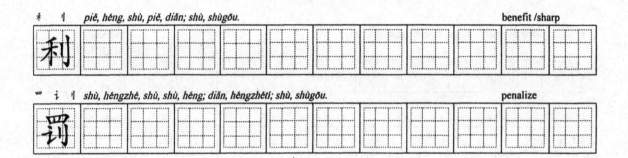

利   禾 刂   *piě, héng, shù, piě, diǎn; shù, shùgōu.*   benefit /sharp

罚   罒 讠 刂   *shù, héngzhé, shù, shù, héng; diǎn, héngzhétí; shù, shùgōu.*   penalize

III. Challenge 2: Apply Your Knowledge 挑战二: 举一反三

A. Know Many Things by Learning One 闻一知十

1. Can you form twelve characters that you have learned in this chapter with the following reduced forms of characters and basic characters as components? Write them in the square boxes below.

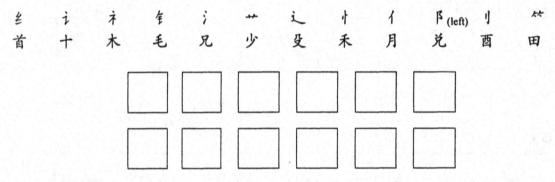

纟   讠   礻   钅   氵   艹   辶   忄   亻   阝(left)   刂   竹
首   十   木   毛   兄   少   殳   禾   月   兑   酉   田

2. With knowledge of the basic characters and the reduced forms of characters used as components, you can also understand characters you have not yet learned.   The reduced forms of Chinese characters are mostly used as semantic components in forming new characters. Therefore, knowing the meanings of the reduced forms of Chinese characters can help you guess the meanings of the characters you have not yet learned.

Exercise 1. Judging from the meanings of the reduced forms, can you guess what the new characters below most likely mean?   Choose one answer for each character.

说   a. speak   b. laugh   c. write

汁   a. number   b. plan   c. juice

打   a. jog   b. hit   c. sing

细   a. slender   b. cloudy   c. sick

裤   a. warehouse   b. plate   c. pants

进　　a. observe　　　　b. enter　　　　　c. dig

银　　a. silver　　　　　b. road　　　　　c. lake

灯　　a. pencil　　　　　b. hammer　　　　c. lamp

Answers: 说 a. 寸 c. 打 b. 细 a. 裤 c. 进 b. 银 a. 推 c

Exercise 2. Can you figure out what the following characters mean by using your knowledge of the reduced forms of Chinese characters?

怕　　a. afraid　　　　　b. expensive　　　c. fast

讲　　a. talk　　　　　　b. kick　　　　　c. cut

神　　a. person　　　　　b. deity　　　　　c. table

锐　　a. happy　　　　　b. sharp　　　　　c. talkative

花　　a. table　　　　　b. river　　　　　c. flower

拉　　a. watch　　　　　b. sleep　　　　　c. pull

都　　a. tunnel　　　　　b. city　　　　　c. ocean

汽　　a. steam　　　　　b. silver　　　　　c. cliff

Answers: 怕 a. 讲 a. 神 b. 锐 b. 花 c. 拉 c. 都 b. 汽 a.

3. The following two-syllable words and phrases are formed with the characters you have learned in this chapter and previous chapters. Can you figure out what they mean?

Group 1:

悦耳＿＿＿＿＿　　1. the manners and morals of the time

悦目＿＿＿＿＿　　2. propose a toast

车道＿＿＿＿＿　　3. junior high school

人道＿＿＿＿＿　　4. beginning of a month

世道＿＿＿＿＿　　5. food and drink

设立＿＿＿＿＿　　6. humanism

饮食＿＿＿＿＿　　7. pleasing to the ear

祝酒_____   8. establish

初中_____   9. traffic (vehicle) lane

月初_____   10. pleasing to the eye

Answers:
悦耳 7.
悦目 10.
车道 9.
人道 6.
世道 1.
设立 8.
饮食 5.
祝酒 2.
初中 3.
月初 4.

Group 2:

工休_____   1. hour hand

面纱_____   2. rice wine

白酒_____   3. scorched earth

米酒_____   4. anxious

果酒_____   5. veil

罚酒_____   6. work break

焦土_____   7. minute hand

焦心_____   8. white spirits

时针_____   9. penalty wine (in a drinking game)

分针_____   10. fruit wine

Answers:
工休 6.
面纱 5.
白酒 8.
米酒 2.
果酒 10.
罚酒 9.
焦土 3.
焦心 4.
时针 1.
分针 7.

Group 3:

禾苗_____   1. cloudy day

火苗_____   2. sharp edge

鱼苗_____   3. seedlings of cereal crops

毛笔_____   4. imprisonment

石笔_____   5. edgily

阴天_____   6. fine

下狱_____   7. newly hatched fish

尖利_____   8. slate pen

利刃_____   9. brush pen

罚金_____   10. flame

Answers: 禾苗 3. 火苗 10. 鱼苗 7. 毛笔 9. 石笔 8. 阴天 1. 下秋 4. 尖利 5. 利刃 2. 罚金 6.

B. Be Perceptive of the Slightest Differences 明察秋毫

1. Which character in each group have you not yet learned? Circle it.
   a. Group 1
          i. 休   ii. 道   iii. 国   iv. 悦

   b. Group 2
          i. 初   ii. 纱   iii. 饮   iv. 疼

   c. Group 3
          i. 公   ii. 针   iii. 酒   iv. 苗

   d. Group 4
          i. 阴   ii. 利   iii. 罚   iv. 画

   e. Group 5
          i. 找   ii. 须   iii. 设   iv. 焦

   f. Group 6
          i. 狱   ii. 那   iii. 印   iv. 笔

Answers: a. iii. b. iv. c. i. d. iv. e. ii. f. iii.

2. Which of the characters in each group is different?

   a. Which character does not have the L-R Structure?
          i. 找   ii. 焦   iii. 悦   iv. 趾

   b. Which character does not have the T-B Structure?
          i. 苗   ii. 笔   iii. 焦   iv. 休

   c. Which character has the B-L-Wrap Structure?
          i. 酒   ii. 狱   iii. 道   iv. 罚

   d. Which character has a slightly different structure from that of the others?
          i. 狱   ii. 那   iii. 针   iv. 阴

e. Which character does not contain a reduced form as a semantic component on its left side?

      i. 饮   ii. 初   iii. 纱   iv. 利

f. Which character does not contain a reduced form as a semantic component?

      i. 好   ii. 那   iii. 祝   iv. 设

Answers:
a.ii b.iv c.iii d.i e.iv f.i

3. Which stroke is that?

a. Which stroke in 纱 is *tí*? It is the _____ stroke.

      i. 1st   ii. 3rd   iii. 5th   iv. 7th

b. Which stroke in 道 is *héngzhéwānpiě*? It is the _____ stroke.

      i. 3rd   ii. 4th   iii. 11th   iv. 12th

c. Which stroke in 道 is *píngnà*? It is the _____ stroke.

      i. 1st   ii. 10th   iii. 11th   iv. last

d. Which stroke in 狱 is *héngzhétí*? It is the _____ stroke.

      i. 5th   ii. 6th   iii. 7th   iv. 8th

e. Which stroke in 那 is *héngpiěwāngōu*? It is the _____ stroke.

      i. 6th   ii. 5th   iii. 4th   iv. 3rd

f. Which stroke in 设 is *héngzhéwān*? It is the _____ stroke.

      i. 3rd   ii. 5th   iii. 2st   iv. 4th

Answers:
a.ii b.iii c.iv d.i e.iii f.iv

C. Be Aware of the Complex Counterpart 学简知繁

If you do not wish to learn the complex forms now, at the beginning level, you may skip this section and go on to the next section for Challenge 3.

1. Comparison. In this chapter, there are four reduced forms that are simplified in the normalized script. Look at the following table and compare the simplified forms with their complex counterparts:

	Simplified Form	Complex Form	Meaning
1	讠	言	speech
2	饣	食	food
3	纟	糸	silk/fabric
4	钅	金	metal/gold
5	艹	艸	grass

2. The following table lists the characters in this chapter that contain the reduced forms listed above as components. Please compare them with their complex counterparts.

	Simplified Form	Complex Form	Meaning
1	设	設	display/set up
2	饮	飲	drink
3	纱	紗	yarn
4	针	針	needle
5	苗	苗	seedling
6	狱	獄	lawsuit/jail
7	罚	罰	penalize

3. In this chapter, there are two characters that have the other components simplified in the normalized script. Look at the following table and compare the simplified forms of these two characters with their complex counterparts:

	Simplified Form	Complex Form	Meaning
1	笔	筆	pen
2	阴	陰	shade

4. Explanation.

言. This comes from the character 言, and can be used as a component on the left side of a character. To accommodate the component on the right, its first horizontal stroke is shortened on the right side, and the last stroke goes upward a little bit to the right side.

饣. This is the reduced form of the character 食. It is used as a component on the left side of a character. To accommodate the component on its right, the falling stroke at the top becomes a dot, and a small left-falling stroke on the right is omitted.

纟. This is a reduced form of 糸, and it is used as component on the left side of a character. The vertical stroke with a hook in 糸 becomes a dot in the reduced form, and the three dots at the bottom are lined up in an upward-slanting manner.

钅. This is actually the character 金, which is used as a component on the left. To achieve a balance with the component on the right, some strokes have changed their original shapes. The right-falling stroke on top is changed to a dot, the first two horizontal strokes are shortened on the right, and the last horizontal stroke becomes a right upward stroke (i.e., *tí*.)

艹. This is a reduced form of the character 艸, and is used as a component at the top of a character.

設, 飲, 紗, 針, 苗, 獄, 罰. Each of these seven characters uses a semantic component explained above.

筆. This is the traditional form of the character for "pen." Under the reduced form of the character 竹 (bamboo) is the component 聿, which depicts a hand grasping a brush pen, as seen in its seal script form: 霜.

陰. This is the traditional form of the character for "shade." It is formed with 阝 (earth mound) on the left and 侌 on the right. 侌 does not mean anything, but it indicates the pronunciation of the whole character. Close observation reveals that 舍 is formed with 今 at the top and 云 at the bottom.

5. Writing. Write this character in its traditional form.

言 殳   *diǎn, héng, héng, héng, shù, héngzhé, héng; piě, héngzhéwān, héngpiě, nà.*   display/set up

設

食 欠   *piě, diǎn, diǎn, héngzhé, héng, héng, shùtí, diǎn; piě, hénggōu, piě, nà.*   to drink

飲

纟 少   *piězhé, piězhé, diǎn, diǎn, diǎn, diǎn; shù, diǎn, diǎn, piě.*   gauze

紗

釒 十   *piě, diǎn, héng, héng, shù, diǎn, piě, tí; héng, shù.*   needle

針

艹 田   *héng, shù, héng, shù; shù, héngzhé, héng, shù, héng.*   seedling

苗

犭 言 犬   *piě, wāngōu, piě; diǎn, héng, héng, héng, shù, héngzhé, héng; héng, piě, nà, diǎn.*   lawsuit/jail

獄

罒 言 刂   *shù, héngzhé, shù, shù, héng; diǎn, héng, héng, héng, shù, héngzhé, héng; shù, shùgōu.*   penalize

罰

⺮ 聿   *piě, héng, diǎn, piě, héng, diǎn; héngzhé, héng, héng, héng, héng, shù.*   pen

筆

阝 舍   *héngpiěwāngōu, shù; piě, nà, diǎn, héngpiě, héng, héng, piězhé, diǎn.*   shade

陰

D. Simplification Method (4): Regularize the Cursive Forms 简化方法 (四): 草书楷化

In the normalized script, some characters were simplified by regularizing their cursive forms.

Traditional	Regularize the Cursive Forms	Simplified	Traditional	Regularize the Cursive Forms	Simplified
東	⟶	东	絲	⟶	丝
車	⟶	车	魚	⟶	鱼
頁	⟶	页	言	⟶	讠
貝	⟶	贝	食	⟶	饣
見	⟶	见	糸	⟶	纟
門	⟶	门	金	⟶	钅
長	⟶	长	艹	⟶	艹
頭	⟶	头			

IV. Challenge 3: Pronounce the Characters 挑战三: 见形发音

After you have firmly established the link between the shape and the meaning of each of the twenty new characters introduced in this chapter, you are ready to establish the link between the shape and the pronunciation of each of these characters.

If you are not ready for this challenge, you can skip this section and go to the next section to practice writing characters or go on to the next chapter to learn to recognize more Chinese characters. After you learn to speak some Chinese, you can return to this section.

1. Listen and read (choose the form you prefer):

(In the traditional form)

Xiū zhǎo yuè dào zhǐ,
休找悦道趾,

Shè yǐn zhù chū shā,
設飲祝初紗,

Jiǔ jiāo zhēn miáo bǐ,
酒焦針苗筆,

Nà yīn yù lì fá.
那陰獄利罰。

(In the normalized form)

Xiū zhǎo yuè dào zhǐ,
休找悦道趾,

Shè yǐn zhù chū shā,
设饮祝初纱,

Jiǔ jiāo zhēn miáo bǐ,
酒焦针苗笔,

Nà yīn yù lì fá.
那阴狱利罚。

2. Read aloud by looking only at the characters:

(In the traditional form)	*(In the normalized form)*
休找悅道趾，	休找悦道趾，
設飲祝初紗，	设饮祝初纱，
酒焦針苗筆，	酒焦针苗笔，
那陰獄利罰。	那阴狱利罚。

3. Guess the answers to the following riddles using the characters in the list. Answer the riddle in Chinese aloud to yourself or to someone who can help with pronunciation, and write the character in the box and its *pinyin* transliteration outside the box after each riddle. Note that in each group there are nine riddles for nine of the ten characters in the list provided at the beginning.

Group 1: 休找悦道趾设饮祝初纱

a) What do people need to do after working for a long time?

b) What do people do when they express good wishes?

c) When you misplace something that you need, what do you do?

d) It is something that can be weaved into cloth.

e) What is the state of mind people have when they smile?

f) What do people do when they feel thirsty?

g) Everybody has ten of them unless some are lost or gained as a result of accidents or birth defects.

h) It is underneath your feet, and you use it when you start a journey.

☐

i) What do people do when they lose things?

☐

Group 2: 酒焦针苗笔那阴狱利罚

a) What instrument can be used to write words on paper?

☐

b) What do people use to sew?

☐

c) What happens to beef if it is left on the barbecue for too long?

☐

d) What would you call very young plants in Chinese?

☐

e) If one has too much of it, one will get drunk.

☐

f) If a criminal is not to be rewarded, what should be done?

☐

g) What is under a big tree on a sunny day?

☐

h) What condition is preferable for a knife to be effective?

☐

i) It is not a name for anything but can be used to refer to anything.

☐

V. Challenge 4: Dictation 挑战四：听音书形知义

1. By now, you should be able to recite the character verse for this chapter. Write the verse in Chinese characters and the meaning for each character in the spaces provided below:

Xiū	zhǎo	yuè	dào	zhǐ	,

Shè	yǐn	zhù	chū	shā	,

Jiǔ	jiāo	zhēn	miáo	bǐ	,

Nà	yīn	yù	lì	fǎ	.

2. Look at the meaning, write its character in the first box, then say it aloud in Chinese before putting its *pinyin* transliteration in the second.

meaning	character	pinyin	meaning	character	pinyin
toe			punishment		
pen			yarn		
sharp			way		
beginning			seedling		
pleased			jail		

needle			wish		
shade			seek		
drink			burned		
rest			set up		
liquor			that		

3. Have your instructor dictate the characters or words covered in Chapter 12.

Chapter 13 第十三章
Other Semantic Components 其它形旁

I. Fundamental Knowledge 基础知识

When forming multicomponent characters, not only basic characters and their reduced forms can be used, but other semantic components can as well. Many of these semantic components, unlike the reduced forms introduced in Chapter 12, did not originate from basic characters; some were once basic characters, but they are not used independently any more. In this chapter, you will learn some of these semantic components.

A. Shapes and Meanings 见形思义

First, let's look at the shapes and meanings of these components:

	Component	Meaning
1.	口	enclosure
2.	宀	roof
3.	夂	downward foot
4.	爫 [1]	claw/upper hand
5.	冫	ice
6.	廴	long stride
7.	彳	street / left step
8.	攵	hand with a stick
9.	廾	two hands

---

[1] Unlike the majority of the semantic components introduced in this chapter, 爫 is a reduced form of the character 爪 (hand/claw).

10.	疒	bed
11.	冖	cover
12.	勹	wrapping
13.	彡	long hair
14.	厶	private
15.	卩	kneeling person
16.	匚	enclosure with an opening on the right / container
17.	凵	enclosure with an opening at the top / pit
18.	冂	enclosure with an opening at the bottom / environs
19.	虍 [2]	tiger
20.	豸	beast

B. Character Formation 组字方式

Let's see how the components listed above are used with other basic characters or components to form new characters.

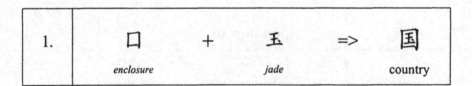

1.	口	+	玉	=>	国
	enclosure		*jade*		*country*

---

[2] Unlike the majority of the semantic components introduced in this chapter, 虍 is the reduced from of the character 虎 (tiger).

2.	宀 *roof*	+	女 *woman*	=>	安 secure		
3.	夂 *downward foot*	+	冫 *ice*	=>	冬 winter		
4.	爫 (爪) *hand*	+	冖 *cover*	+	友 *friend*	=>	爱 love
5.	冫 *ice*	+	水 *water*	=>	冰 ice		
6.	彳 *street / left step*	+	亍 *right step*	=>	行 go		
7.	聿 *hand holding a pen*	+	廴 *long stride*	=>	建 construct		
8.	己 *self*	+	攵 *hand with a stick*	=>	改 alter		
9.	竹 *bamboo*	+	目 *eye*	+	廾 *hands*	=>	算 calculate
10.	疒 *bed*	+	冬 *winter*	=>	疼 painful		
11.	冖 *cover*	+	车 *vehicle*	=>	军 army		
12.	勹 *wrapping*	+	巳 *fetus*	=>	包 bag		

13.	彡 *long hair*	+	页 *head*	=>	须 *beard/must*		
14.	八 *separate*	+	厶 *private*	=>	公 *public*		
15.	爫 (爪) *claw/hand*	+	卩 *kneeling person*	=>	印 *print*		
16.	匚 *container*	+	矢 *arrow*	=>	医 *doctor/medical treatment*		
17.	一 *one*	+	田 *field*	+	凵 *pit*	=>	画 *drawing*
18.	虍 *tiger*	+	几 *standing legs*	=>	虎 *tiger*		
19.	豸 *beast*	+	勺 *ladle*	=>	豹 *leopard*		
20.	冂 *environs*	+	一 *one*	+	口 *mouth*	=>	同 *same*

C. Forms and Meanings 知形会意

国   The earliest form of this character in the oracle-bone inscriptions was a drawing of a dagger ax, which is an ancient weapon, on the right and a 口 on the left representing a city-state. The form in the bronze inscriptions had four lines added around 口, the city-state, indicating armed forces used to protect the state. In the seal script, the "territories" were expanded, and both the city-state and the dagger-ax were enclosed in 口. In the normalized script, 或 inside the enclosure is replaced by 玉 (jade), which is a precious stone treasured by

Chinese people. The meaning of the character is "country" or "nation." Characters that contain the component 口 are all related to something with boundaries.

Oracle	Bronze	Seal	Clerical	Regular	Normal-ized	Semi-cursive	Cursive
吘	哎	國	國	國	国	囯	国

安 This character is formed with the component 宀 (roof) on top and the character 女 (woman) at the bottom. The idea is that when a woman is under the roof in a house, there is security. Therefore, the meaning conveyed by the character 安 is "secure." Characters that have the component 宀 are related to buildings with roofs in one way or another.

Oracle	Bronze	Seal	Clerical	Regular	Normal-ized	Semi-cursive	Cursive
宭	宩	宩	安	安	安	安	安

冬 The oldest form of this character in the oracle-bone inscriptions was a drawing of a rope with a knot on each end. People in ancient times tied knots on a rope to aid their memory of certain events. When a rope has a knot on both ends, it implies "end." Later the character represented winter, the last season of the year. The form in the seal script has a horizontal line across the rope indicating the knots at both ends of the rope. In addition, the component 仌 was added. After the clerical change, the rope with knots was replaced by the component 夂 (downward foot), suggesting a foot on ice. The character 冬 now is used exclusively for "winter"; whereas "end" is represented by a newly created character, 终, in which 纟 is added to the left side of 冬. Characters that have 夂 as a component usually have something to do with "foot."

Oracle	Bronze	Seal	Clerical	Regular	Normal-ized	Semi-cursive	Cursive
𠔾	𠆢	寒	冬	冬	冬	冬	冬

爱 The oldest form of this character was in the seal script. The character had three parts: 旡 at the top indicated the pronunciation, 心 (heart) in the middle indicated "kindness," and 夂 (foot) indicated "behavior." After the clerical change, the component 旡 at the top became 爫 (hand) and 冖 (cover). The normalized form borrows from the cursive script. Instead of 心 (heart) and 夂 (foot) as the lower part, the more easily written 友 (friend) is used. 友 is in fact formed of two hands: 𠂇 (hand) and 又 (hand). "Hand in hand" represents friendship. In the normalized script, the character 爱 implies the concept of love by showing a hand passing a towel, represented by 冖, to a friend.

Oracle	Bronze	Seal	Clerical	Regular	Normal-ized	Semi-cursive	Cursive
		憂	愛	愛	爱	爱	爱

冰　This character means "ice." The oldest form of the character for ice in the oracle-bone inscriptions had two arrows pointing upward, the idea being that the surface of water becomes rugged after it is frozen. The form in the bronze inscriptions had two pieces of "ice" on the right and "water" on the left indicating that ice comes from water. The seal script has "ice" on the left and "water" on the right. Since the clerical change, the rugged surface of frozen water on the left no longer looks like ice but is just two strokes. Many characters that have the component 冫 are related to "iciness." However, the character 次 is an exception because its component 冫 came from 二 (two).

Oracle	Bronze	Seal	Clerical	Regular	Normal-ized	Semi-cursive	Cursive
仌	冰	冰	冰	冰	冰	冰	冰

行　This character in its earliest forms in the oracle-bone and bronze inscriptions looked like an intersection of roads. Therefore, the meaning of the character is related to what people do on roads—"go." The two components 彳 and 亍 may also be used independently to form a two-character concept: 彳 亍, meaning "walk slowly." The characters that contain the component 彳 very often have something to do with "road" or "stroll."

Oracle	Bronze	Seal	Clerical	Regular	Normal-ized	Semi-cursive	Cursive
行	行	行	行	行	行	行	行

建　This character is formed by 聿 (hand holding a pen) and the component 廴 (long stride) in the lower left corner. The combination of these two components indicates the action of drawing up laws and decrees and has come to mean "establish" or "build."

Oracle	Bronze	Seal	Clerical	Regular	Normal-ized	Semi-cursive	Cursive
	建	建	建	建	建	建	建

改 This character is formed with the character 己 (self) and the component 攵 (hand with a stick). Notice that the last stroke in 己 is changed from ㄥ to ㇀ to accommodate the component on the right. The idea conveyed by the combination of the two components is "to beat oneself for mistakes one has made." The meaning of the character, therefore, is "to alter" or "to correct." Characters that contain the component 攵 appear to have something to do with moralizing in one way or another.

Oracle	Bronze	Seal	Clerical	Regular	Normal-ized	Semi-cursive	Cursive
		改	改	改	改	改	改

算 This character means "calculate." It has three components: ⺮ (bamboo) at the top stands for the materials used to make calculating instruments in China; 目 (eye) in the middle does not mean "eye" but represents an abacus, which consists of a frame with parallel rods and beads sliding along them; and 廾 is a depiction of two hands using the calculator. 廾 is always used as a component at the bottom of a character. Characters that contain this component all have something to do with activities related to hands.

Oracle	Bronze	Seal	Clerical	Regular	Normal-ized	Semi-cursive	Cursive
		算	算	算	算	算	算

疼 This character means "painful" or "ache." The component that occupies the upper and left part of the character is 疒, which in its oldest form in the oracle-bone inscriptions represented a person lying on a bed: 疒. In the seal script, the form became 疒. After the clerical change, it began to take on the form 疒, which is still used. Any character that has 疒 as a component is related to physical discomfort. However, the meaning of the character 疼 did not result from the combination of the meanings of the two components; rather, the component 疒 indicates that the meaning of the character is related to physical discomfort, and the other component, 冬, indicates the pronunciation of the whole character. It does not convey meaning but only distinguishes this character from other characters sharing the same semantic component 疒. As this character has one component indicating meaning and another component indicating pronunciation, it is different from associative characters, the type of multicomponent characters you have learned so far. We will deal with this type of character in the next chapter, Chapter 14.

Oracle	Bronze	Seal	Clerical	Regular	Normal-ized	Semi-cursive	Cursive
		㿠	疼	疼	疼	疼	疼

军   The earliest form of this character in the bronze inscriptions had two parts: one was 勹 (wrapping or surrounding) and the other was 車 (vehicle or chariot). The combination of the two components indicated a military camp and meant "army." After the clerical change, the component 勹 became 冖. The component 車 became 车 in the normalized script. The component 冖 in characters is often used to mean "cover."

Oracle	Bronze	Seal	Clerical	Regular	Normal-ized	Semi-cursive	Cursive
	軍	軍	軍	軍	军	军	军

包   This character means "bag." The earliest form of this character in the seal script depicted a fetus inside a womb, or a pregnancy. The top component indicated the womb, and the enclosed component indicated the fetus. After the clerical change, the shape of the component 𠂤 (womb) became 勹, and the component 𢀖 (fetus) became 巳. The component 勹 does not necessarily mean "womb" specifically; it is often used to refer to a wrapper.

Oracle	Bronze	Seal	Clerical	Regular	Normal-ized	Semi-cursive	Cursive
		包	包	包	包	包	包

须   The character has two components: On the right side is 頁 (head), and on the left is the component 彡, indicating long hair. The meaning derived from the combination of these two components is "hair on the face" or "beard."

However, this character has also been borrowed to mean "must." To distinguish the two different meanings, the character 鬚 was created by adding 長 (long) and 彡 on top of 須. In the normalized script, 鬚 is eliminated, and the character 须 is used to mean "beard" as well as "must."

Oracle	Bronze	Seal	Clerical	Regular	Normal-ized	Semi-cursive	Cursive
𩑋	須	須	須	须	须	汤
			鬚	鬚			

公 This character has two components. One is 八 (divide) at the top, and the other is 厶 (private) at the bottom. The idea of the two combined is to divide evenly and fairly, and by extension, the character conveys the idea of fairness or being aboveboard, public, just the opposite of "private." The component 厶 used in other characters does not necessarily mean "private."

Oracle	Bronze	Seal	Clerical	Regular	Normal-ized	Semi-cursive	Cursive
㕣	公	公	公	公	公	公	公

印 The earliest form of this character in the oracle-bone inscriptions showed a hand over a kneeling person. The idea was that the hand was forcing someone to kneel. The meaning conveyed by the character is "to press down." After the clerical change, that character began to take on the L-R structure. On the left is the component 𠂢 (hand), and on the right is the component 卩 (kneeling person). This character also means "seal" or "chop." A seal is made of a hard material with one's name engraved on it so that it can be printed on paper or other material by pressing. The extended meaning of this character is "to print."

Oracle	Bronze	Seal	Clerical	Regular	Normal-ized	Semi-cursive	Cursive
𢑑	印	印	印	印	印	印	印

医 The earliest form of this character in the bronze inscriptions had three components: 医 at the top left consisted of 匚 (container) and 矢 (arrow), representing a container that stores arrows; 殳 at the top right represented an ancient weapon held in a hand, and the combination of 医 and 殳 indicated the sound of being hit; and 酉 at the bottom is a jar for holding liquor, which, being alcoholic, was often used to treat wounds or pain. The combination of the three components means "medical treatment." It also means "doctor," the person who gives medical treatment. The normalized script keeps only the first component 医 and omits the other two.

Oracle	Bronze	Seal	Clerical	Regular	Normal-ized	Semi-cursive	Cursive
	醫	醫	醫	醫	医	医	医

画 This character means "to draw." Its earliest form in the oracle-bone inscriptions showed a hand holding a pen and drawing a pattern. In the bronze inscriptions, the pattern looked a lot more like 田 (farmland). In the seal script, the "farmland" had borders. The normalized script adopts the form that first appeared in a book in the early 14th century. It does not have the "hand holding a pen" but only the "field with borderlines." 凵 means not only "borderline" but also "pit," when it is used as a component in other characters.

Oracle	Bronze	Seal	Clerical	Regular	Normal-ized	Semi-cursive	Cursive
	畫	畫	畫	畫	画	画	画

虎 This character means "tiger." It has two components: 虍 depicts the stripes on a tiger's head and body, and 几 represents the legs. The component 虍 used in other characters often indicates something associated with tigers, such as "fearsome" and "ferocious."

Oracle	Bronze	Seal	Clerical	Regular	Normal-ized	Semi-cursive	Cursive
		虎	虎	虎	虎	虎	虎

豹 This character means "leopard," a meat-eating wild beast that runs very fast. On the left side of the character, 豸 depicts a beast with a long spine and big teeth. On the right, 勺 indicates the pronunciation of the whole character and does not contribute to the meaning as a semantic component. This character, like the character 疼 (painful), is a picto-phonetic character, and they are discussed in Chapter 14.

Oracle	Bronze	Seal	Clerical	Regular	Normal-ized	Semi-cursive	Cursive
	豹	豹	豹	豹	豹	豹	豹

同 This character means "gather together" or "the same." The meaning of this character comes from the combination of its components. In the oracle-bone and bronze inscriptions, this character had two components: 凡 (a plate/every) and 口 (mouth). In the seal script, the top component becomes 冂 (environs) and 一 (one).

Oracle	Bronze	Seal	Clerical	Regular	Normal-ized	Semi-cursive	Cursive
同	同	同	同	同	同	同	同

D. Recognition Reinforcement 辨认巩固练习:

1. Being able to recognize the semantic component in a character helps one to recognize the meaning of the character as a whole. Link each semantic component with the meaning it represents:

a. 口　宀　冖　冫　疒

ice　cover　roof　bed　enclosure

b. 艹　廾　攵　夊　又

two-hands　long stride　downward foot　hand with a stick　hand

c. 彳　卩　彡　匚　冂

long hair　container　environs　a kneeling person　left foot

d. 凵　勹　厶　虍　豸

private　beast　pit　tiger　wrapping

2. Link each character on the first line with its corresponding meaning in English on the second line:

a.　国　　安　　冬　　爱　　冰

　　winter　country　love　ice　secure

b.　行　　建　　改　　算　　疼

　　alter　go　construct　painful　calculate

c.　军　　包　　须　　公　　印

　　bag　print　public　army　beard/must

d.　医　　画　　虎　　豹　　同

　　leopard　drawing　doctor　same　tiger

3. There are ten characters on the left side and eleven words in English on the right side.　Put the letter for each character in the blank for the correct English word.　In each group, there is an extra blank that should be left empty.

Group 1:

a. 算	_____ painful
b. 冰	_____ love
c. 安	_____ country
d. 建	_____ go
e. 爱	_____ secure
f. 改	_____ doctor
g. 行	_____ calculate
h. 疼	_____ alter
i. 国	_____ construct
j. 冬	_____ winter
	_____ ice

Group 2:

| a. 画 | _____ print |
| b. 豹 | _____ same |

c. 包　　　　　_____ doctor

d. 印　　　　　_____ calculate

e. 医　　　　　_____ drawing

f. 须　　　　　_____ public

g. 公　　　　　_____ army

h. 同　　　　　_____ leopard

i. 军　　　　　_____ beard/must

j. 虎　　　　　_____ tiger

　　　　　　　　_____ bag

4. Provide the meaning in English for each of the following characters:

国_____　　安_____　　冬_____　　爱_____　　冰_____

行_____　　建_____　　改_____　　算_____　　疼_____

军_____　　包_____　　须_____　　公_____　　印_____

医_____　　画_____　　虎_____　　豹_____　　同_____

II. Challenge 1: Write the Characters 挑战一: 知义书形

A. Strokes in Characters 详说笔画:　乛

In the semantic components you have learned in this chapter, there is one new stroke:

乛　*héngzhézhépiě* (a horizontal stroke with two turns and a left-falling stroke),

as in 又

Write this stroke and pay attention to the direction of the stroke movement as indicated.

B. Character Structures 汉字结构

Let's review all the characters structures you have learned in the previous two chapters by doing the following exercises first:

1. Match the character structures with their corresponding structure diagrams.

(1)   L-R Structure   a.

(2)   T-B Structure   b.

(3)   T$_{(L-R)}$-B Structure   c.

(4)   L-M-R Structure   d.

(5)   T-B$_{(L-R)}$ Structure   e.

(6)   T-Wrap Structure   f.

(7)   L-R$_{(T-B)}$ Structure   g.

(8)   B-L-Wrap Structure   h.

Answers:
(1) c (2) g (3) h (4) f (5) a (6) b (7) e (8) d

2. Put each of the following characters after the type of character structure each belongs to.

相 穿 双 狱 多 罚 秋 香 纱 分 道 雷 烦 取 指 鲜 男 解 哭 间

a.

b.

c.

d. ⊟

e. ⊟

f. |||

g. ⊟

h. ⊔

Answers:
a. 问
b. 相双秋明 顷取轩解
c. 解
d. 穿尖多 香分雷男
e. 哭
f. 狄
g. 讨
h. 道

3. Put a number in each component space of a character structure type to show that you know how to write each component in a multicomponent character in the conventionally accepted order.

Check answers on pages 218-219 and 249-250.

In this chapter, there are six new types of character structure as shown below; the numbers given in each structure indicate the writing sequence.

(1) The T-M-B (Top-Middle-Bottom) Structure: 爱

(2) The C-Wrap (Complete-Wrap) Structure: 国

(3) The T-R-Wrap (Top-Right-Wrap) Structure: 包

(4) The T-L-Wrap (Top-Left-Wrap) Structure: 病

(5) The L-Wrap (Left-Wrap) Structure: 医

(6) The B-Wrap (Bottom-Wrap) Structure: 画

C. *Stroke Order Analysis 笔顺分析*

The writing sequence of the new character structures in this chapter follows the same basic rules for stroke order: from top to bottom, left to right, outside to inside. Therefore, if you have learned all the basic characters in the previous chapters, you should know how to write a multicomponent character in the proper sequence. Can you separate the following multicomponent characters into their components by writing them in the proper sequence?

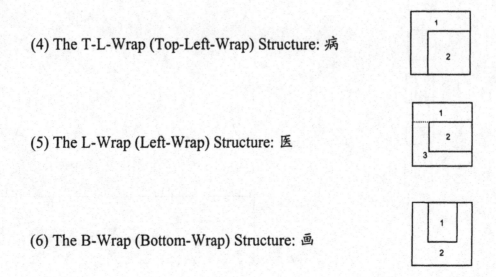

Write the components one at a time in the proper sequence.

For example:

安 宀 女

Then compare with the correct sequence ⟶ 宀 女

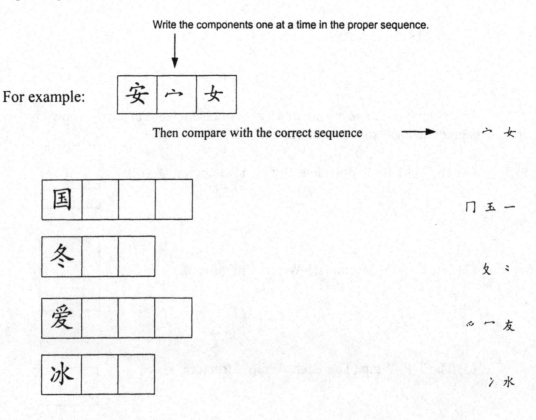

国   冂 玉 一

冬   夂 冫

爱   爫 冖 友

冰   冫 水

行			彳　亍
建			聿　又
改			己　攵
算			竹　目　廾
疼			疒　冬
军			冖　车
包			勹　巳
须			彡　页
公			八　厶
印			𠂇　卩
医			匚　矢　乚
画			一　田　凵
虎			虍　几
豹			豸　勺
同			冂　一　口

D. Write with a Pencil 动手动笔

Now that you know the meaning and the standard stroke order for each of the characters, it is time to practice writing balanced and well-proportioned characters. Use the following "well" boxes to write each character. It is not enough just to write in the boxes provided in the book. You should also practice writing each character on a piece of paper. Take a good look at the model character and try to write it by heart without referring to the model. Each time you finish writing the character, compare it with the model. Correct any mistakes, and write until you do it correctly without looking at the model.

口玉 (冂 玉 一) shù, héngzhé; héng, héng, shù, héng, diǎn; héng.   country

国

宀 (丶 丶 宀) 女 diǎn, diǎn, hénggōu; piědiǎn, piě, héng.   secure

安

夂 冫 piě, héngpiě, nà; diǎn, diǎn.   winter

冬

爫 一 友 piě, diǎn, diǎn, piě; shù, hénggōu; héng, piě, héngpiě, nà.   love

爱

冫 水 diǎn, tí; shùgōu, héngpiě, piě, nà.   ice

冰

彳 亍 piě, piě, shù; héng, héng, shùgōu.   go

行

聿 廴 héngzhé, héng, héng, héng, héng, shù; héngzhézhépiě, píngnà.   construct

建

阝 攵 héngzhé, héng, shùtí; piě, héng, piě, nà.   alter

改

⺮ 目 廾　*piě, héng, diǎn, piě, héng, diǎn; shù, héngzhé, héng, héng, héng; héng, shùpiě, shù.*　　calculate

算

疒 冬　*diǎn, héng, piě, diǎn, tí; piě, héngpiě, nà; diǎn, diǎn.*　　painful

疼

冖 车　*diǎn, hénggōu; héng, piězhé, héng, shù.*　　army

军

勹 巳　*piě, héngzhégōu; héngzhé, héng, shùwāngōu.*　　bag

包

彡 页　*piě, piě, piě; héng, piě, shù, héngzhé, piě, diǎn.*　　beard/must

须

八 厶　*piě, nà; piězhé, diǎn.*　　public

公

⻏ 卩　*piě, shùtí, héng; héngzhégōu, shù.*　　print

印

匚 矢（一 矢 ㇄）　*héng; piě, héng, héng, piě, diǎn; shùzhé.*　　doctor/medical treatment

医

一 田 凵　*héng; shù, héngzhé, héng, shù, héng; shùzhé, shù.*　　drawing

画

⻁ 几　*shù, héng, hénggōu, piě, héng, shùwāngōu; piě, héngzhéwāngōu.*　　tiger

虎

豸 勹　*piě, diǎn, diǎn, piě, wāngōu, piě, piě; piě, héngzhégōu, diǎn.*　　leopard

豹

冂	一	口	shù, héngzhé; héng; shù, héngzhé, héng.							same	
同											

III. Challenge 2: Apply Your Knowledge 挑战二：举一反三

A. Know Many Things by Learning One 闻一知十

1. With the semantic components in the first row and the other component characters in the second row, can you form twelve characters learned in this chapter? Write them in the square boxes below.

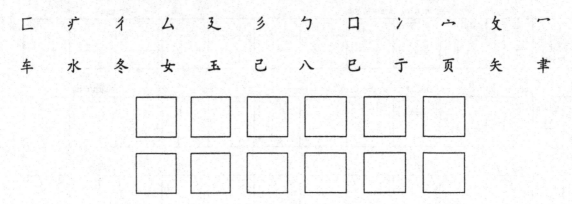

匚　疒　彳　厶　又　彡　勹　口　冫　宀　攵　一

车　水　冬　女　玉　己　八　巴　丁　页　矢　聿

2. Judging from the meaning of the semantic component in each new character below, can you guess what the character most likely means? Choose one answer for each character.

困	a. break	b. stranded	c. cut
家	a. table	b. leg	c. home
冷	a. hot	b. cold	c. warm
病	a. sick	b. thirsty	c. healthy
采	a. jump	b. eat	c. pick
开	a. open	b. kick	c. sing
教	a. smell	b. drink	c. instruct
街	a. hand	b. street	c. person
影	a. fan	b. shadow	c. hammer

凶	a. unlucky	b. happy	c. pleasant
匠	a. nanny	b. nurse	c. craftsman
内	a. slow	b. inner	c. short
虑	a. sleep	b. rest	c. anxious
豺	a. pig	b. jackal	c. worm
冠	a. hat	b. pants	c. socks

Answers: 国 b. 家 c. 冷 b. 满 a. 米 c. 开 a. 救 c. 街 b. 影 a. 凶 c. 匠 c. 内 b. 虑 c. 豺 b. 冠 a.

3. The following two-syllable words and phrases are formed with characters introduced in this chapter and previous chapters. Can you figure out what they mean?

Group 1:

国力 _____	1. establish diplomatic relations
国人 _____	2. found a country
国土 _____	3. spouse
建国 _____	4. national power
爱国 _____	5. love dearly
建交 _____	6. China
天国 _____	7. patriotic
中国 _____	8. compatriot
爱人 _____	9. Kingdom of Heaven
疼爱 _____	10. national territory

Answers: 国力 4. 国人 8. 国土 10. 建国 2. 爱国 7. 建交 1. 天国 9. 中国 6. 爱人 3. 疼爱 5.

Group 2:

安心 _____	1. pedestrian
公安 _____	2. written calculation
欠安 _____	3. mental arithmetic
行人 _____	4. plan

言行_____   5. at ease

改口_____   6. words and deeds

改正_____   7. indisposed

笔算_____   8. withdraw or change one's previous remark

心算_____   9. public security

打算_____   10. correct

Answers: 安心 5. 公安 9. 女安 7. 行人 1. 言行 6. 改口 8. 改正 10. 笔算 2. 心算 3. 打算 4.

Group 3:

军人_____   1. western medicine

军火_____   2. pack

包金_____   3. fair and square

打包_____   4. general holidays

公正_____   5. fingerprint

公休_____   6. army man

手印_____   7. ammunition

中医_____   8. gild

西医_____   9. at the same time

同时_____   10. Chinese medicine

Answers: 军人 3. 军火 10. 包金 7. 打包 9. 公正 8. 公休 1. 手印 4. 中医 5. 西医 2. 同时 6.

Group 4:

爱心_____   1. identical

心爱_____   2. leather bag

国王_____   3. paintbrush

王国_____   4. dear to one's heart

包皮_____   5. strokes of a Chinese character

皮包_____   6. together

画笔_____   7. kingdom

笔画_____   8. king

同一_____   9. compassion

一同_____   10. wrapper

Answers: 爱心 9. 心爱 4. 国王 8. 王国 7. 包皮 10. 皮包 2. 画笔 3. 笔画 5. 同一 1. 一同 6.

B. Be Perceptive of the Slightest Differences 明察秋毫

1. Which character in each group have you not yet learned? Circle it.
    a. Group 1
        i. 冬   ii. 爱   iii. 妈   iv. 安

    b. Group 2
        i. 改   ii. 行   iii. 建   iv. 根

    c. Group 3
        i. 谁   ii. 须   iii. 军   iv. 公

    d. Group 4
        i. 医   ii. 虎   iii. 同   iv. 邮

    e. Group 5
        i. 国   ii. 抱   iii. 算   iv. 疼

    f. Group 6
        i. 印   ii. 画   iii. 想   iv. 豹

    Answers: a. iii.   b. iv.   c. i.   d. iv.   e. ii.   f. iii.

2. Which of the characters in each group is different?

    a. Which character does not have the L-R Structure?
        i. 冰   ii. 建   iii. 行   iv. 须

    b. Which character does not have the T-B Structure?
        i. 冬   ii. 军   iii. 安   iv. 同

    c. Which character has the T-R-Wrap Structure?
        i. 医   ii. 画   iii. 包   iv. 疼

    d. Which character has the C-Wrap Structure?

        i. 国   ii. 建   iii. 医   iv. 虎

    e. Which character contains a semantic component that is in fact the reduced form of a character?

        i. 疼   ii. 军   iii. 冰   iv. 爱

    f. Which character does not contain a semantic component that can also be used as a character in written classical Chinese?

        i. 冬   ii. 豹   iii. 公   iv. 行

Answers: a. ii. b. iv. c. iii. d. i. e. iv. f. i.

3. Which stroke is that?

    a. Which stroke in 改 is *shùtí*? It is the _____ stroke.

        i. 1st   ii. 3rd   iii. 5th   iv. 7th

    b. Which stroke in 建 is *héngzhézhépiě*? It is the _____ stroke.

        i. 1st   ii. 4th   iii. 7th   iv. 8th

    c. Which stroke in 军 is *piězhé*? It is the _____ stroke.

        i. 1st   ii. 2nd   iii. 3rd   iv. 4th

    d. Which stroke in 豹 is *wāngōu*? It is the _____ stroke.

        i. 5th   ii. 6th   iii. 8th   iv. 9th

    e. Which stroke in 那 is *héngpiěwāngōu*? It is the _____ stroke.

        i. 6th   ii. 5th   iii. 4th   iv. 3rd

    f. Which stroke in 虎 is *héngzhéwāngōu*? It is the _____ stroke.

        i. 3rd   ii. 5th   iii. 6th   iv. 8th

Answers: a. ii. b. iii. c. iv. d. i. e. iii. f. iv.

C. Be Aware of the Complex Counterpart 学简知繁

    If you do not wish to learn the complex forms now, at the beginning level, you may skip this section and go on to the next section for Challenge 3.

1. Comparison. In this chapter, six of the characters have been simplified in the normalized script from their complex forms. Look at the following table and compare these six characters in their simplified forms with their complex counterparts:

	Simplified Form	Complex Form	Meaning
1	国	國	country
2	爱	愛	love
3	军	軍	army
4	须	須/鬚	鬚 beard/須 must
5	医	醫	doctor/medical treatment
6	画	畫	drawing

2. Explanation.

國. This is the traditional form of the character 国. It has the component 囗, which represents territories of a country. The character 或, used as a component inside 囗, has two parts: 戈 on the right representing a dagger ax, an ancient weapon, and 口 on the left representing a city-state. 或 indicates that armed forces are used to protect the territories and borders of a state. Originally, 或 meant "country" and then was borrowed to mean "or." To distinguish the two different meanings, 或 was enclosed by the component 囗, forming the character 國 to mean "country."

愛. This traditional form of 爱 is formed not only with 爫 (hand) and 冖 (cover) at the top, but also with 心 (heart) in the middle, indicating "kindness," and 夂 (foot) at the bottom, indicating "behavior."

軍. This is the traditional form of 军. It also has the component 冖, and the other component is the character 車 (vehicle or chariot) in its traditional form. The combination of the two components indicates a military camp, and the character, therefore, means "army."

須/鬚. The first of these two characters has two components: on the right is 頁 (head) and on the left is the component 彡, meaning "long hair." "Beard" is the meaning derived from the combination of these two components. However, this character has been borrowed to mean "must"; therefore, the character 鬚 was created by adding 長 (long) and 彡 on top of 須 to mean "beard" exclusively.

醫. This traditional form of the character has three components: 医 on the top left side is a container that stores arrows; 殳 on the top right side is an ancient weapon held by a hand; 酉 at the bottom is a jar for holding liquor. The combination of the three components refers to medical treatment or the person who performs medical treatment.

畫. This traditional form of the character has the component 聿 at the top, representing a hand holding a pen. The component 田, with 一 at the bottom, represents a pattern that is drawn. The meaning of the character is "drawing."

3. Writing. Write this character in its traditional form.

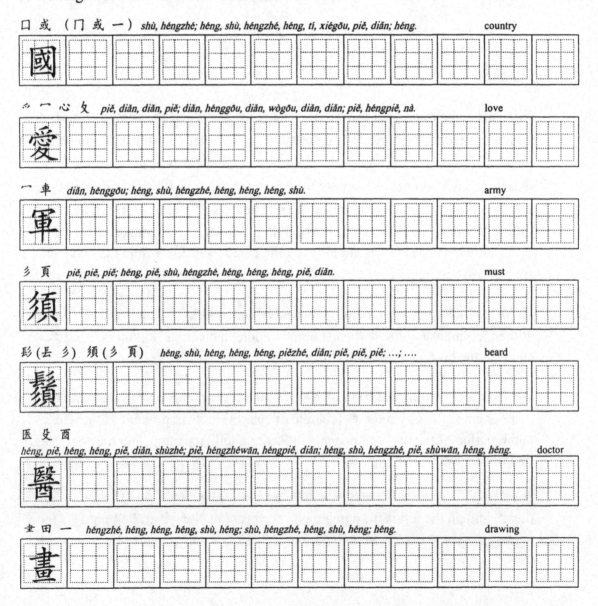

口 或 (冂 或 一) *shù, héngzhé; héng, shù, héngzhé, héng, tí, xiégōu, piě, diǎn; héng.*   country

國

⺫ 一 心 夂 *piě, diǎn, diǎn, piě; diǎn, hénggōu, diǎn, wògōu, diǎn, diǎn; piě, héngpiě, nà.*   love

愛

一 車 *diǎn, hénggōu; héng, shù, héngzhé, héng, héng, héng, shù.*   army

軍

彡 頁 *piě, piě, piě; héng, piě, shù, héngzhé, héng, héng, héng, piě, diǎn.*   must

須

髟 (長 彡) 須 (彡 頁) *héng, shù, héng, héng, héng, piězhé, diǎn; piě, piě, piě; ...; ....*   beard

鬚

医 殳 酉
héng, piě, héng, héng, piě, diǎn, shùzhé; piě, héngzhéwān, héngpiě, diǎn; héng, shù, héngzhé, piě, shùwān, héng, héng.   doctor

醫

聿 田 一 *héngzhé, héng, héng, héng, shù, héng; shù, héngzhé, héng, shù, héng; héng.*   drawing

畫

D. Simplification Method (5): Use a Part for the Whole 简化方法 (五): 以零代整

In the normalized script, some characters were simplified by using a component of the traditional form to represent the whole.

Traditional	Use a component in place of the whole	Simplified
蟲	⟶	虫
醫	⟶	医
廣	⟶	广
廠/厰	⟶	厂
兒	⟶	儿

IV. Challenge 3: Pronounce the Characters 挑战三: 见形发音

Having firmly established the link between the shape and the meaning of each of the 20 new characters introduced in this chapter, you are ready to establish the link between the shape and the pronunciation for each of these characters.

If you are not ready for this challenge, you can skip this section and go to the next section to practice writing characters or go on to the next chapter to learn to recognize more Chinese characters. You can return to this section later.

1. Listen and read (choose the form you prefer):

(In the traditional form)

Guó ān dōng ài bīng,
國安冬愛冰,

Xíng jiàn gǎi suàn téng,
行建改算疼,

Jūn bāo xū gōng yìn,
軍包須公印,

Yī huà hǔ bào tóng.
醫畫虎豹同。

(In the normalized form)

Guó ān dōng ài bīng,
国安冬爱冰,

Xíng jiàn gǎi suàn téng,
行建改算疼,

Jūn bāo xū gōng yìn,
军包须公印,

Yī huà hǔ bào tóng.
医画虎豹同。

2. Read aloud by looking only at the characters:

(In the traditional form)   *(In the normalized form)*

國安冬愛冰，   国安冬爱冰，

行建改算疼，   行建改算疼，

軍包須公印，   军包须公印，

醫畫虎豹同。   医画虎豹同。

3. Guess the answers to the following riddles using the characters in the list. Answer the riddle in Chinese aloud to yourself or to someone who can help with pronunciation and write the character in the box and its *pinyin* transliteration outside the box after each riddle. Note that in each group there are nine riddles for nine of the ten characters in the list provided at the beginning.

    Group 1: 国安冬爱冰行建改算疼

    a) What does water become when it is extremely cold?

    b) What sensation do you have when you get physically hurt?

    c) What is the place of which one can be a citizen?

    d) In which season can people walk on ice outside?

    e) What is the right thing to do when we make a mistake?

    f) What are you expected to do when you are given an arithmetic problem?

    g) How do you feel when you know that you are protected?

    h) It is the feeling that two people have when they are attracted to each other and care about each other.

i) What might people do when they are ready with a plan for a new house?

Group 2: 军包须公印医画虎豹同

a) What does an artist do with a paintbrush?

b) What is an object that you would put things in to carry them?

c) What usually grows on the chin of an adult male?

d) What do almost all the countries in the world believe is necessary for protection?

e) What animal is often considered the king of all animals but is not capable of climbing trees?

f) What beast runs very fast and can climb trees?

g) What is the opposite of "private"?

h) What makes newspapers intelligible?

i) What character expresses the concept of being the same?

V. Challenge 4: Dictation 挑战四: 听音书形知义

1. By now, you should be able to recite the character verse for this chapter. Write the verse in Chinese characters and the meaning for each character in the spaces provided below:

Guó	ān	dōng	ài	bīng	,

Xíng	jiàn	gǎi	suàn	téng	,

Jūn	bāo	xū	gōng	yìn	,

Yī	huà	hǔ	bào	tóng	.

2. Look at the meaning, write its character in the first box, and say it aloud in Chinese before putting its *pinyin* transliteration in the second.

meaning	character	pinyin	meaning	character	pinyin
ice			beard/must		
painful			tiger		
print			bag		
identical			drawing		
leopard			construct		
public			army		
calculate			medical treatment		

love

winter

alter

country

secure

go

3. Have your instructor dictate the characters or words covered in Chapter 13.

Chapter 14 第十四章
Characters Formed with Semantic and Phonetic Components: Picto-Phonetic Characters 由形旁和声旁合成的汉字: 形声字

I. Fundamental Knowledge 基础知识

In the previous three chapters, you have looked at three kinds of multicomponent characters: characters formed by two or more basic characters, introduced in Chapter 11; characters formed by one or more reduced forms of characters with one or more basic characters, introduced in Chapter 12; and characters formed by one or more semantic components with one or more basic characters, introduced in Chapter 13. However, all the multicomponent characters introduced in Chapters 11-13 except for 疼 and 豹 in Chapter 13 share one common feature: all the components of a character contribute to the meaning of the character they form. In Chapter 14, you will look at another kind of multicomponent character, which always contains one (or at least one) component that indicates the meaning and another that indicates the pronunciation. Characters of this kind are, therefore, referred to as picto-phonetic characters. Almost any single-component character may be used in a multicomponent character to indicate the pronunciation of the multicomponent character. Over 90 percent of Chinese characters belong to this category; however, because of developments and changes in pronunciation over the past few thousand years, no more than 30 percent of the picto-phonetic characters used today contain a phonetic component that can accurately represent the pronunciation of the whole character. In Chapter 14, you will look at 20 characters that indicate the pronunciation of the characters they form, and you will see more in the exercises.

A. Meanings and Sounds 形声并举

1.	女 *female*	+	马 *horse* *(Phonetic: **mǎ**)*	=>	妈 mother (**mā**)
2.	门 *door* *(Phonetic: **mén**)*	+	口 *mouth*	=>	问 ask (**wèn**)
3.	车 *vehicle*	+	交 *cross/intersect* *(Phonetic: **jiāo**)*	=>	较 compare (**jiào**)
4.	元 *first/dollar* *(Phonetic: **yuán**)*	+	(辵) 辶 *walking*	=>	远 far (**yuǎn**)

5.	木	+	寸	=>	村
	tree		inch (Phonetic: **cùn**)		village (cūn)
6.	（言）讠	+	隹	=>	谁
	speech		short-tailed bird (Phonetic: **zhuī**)		who (shuí)
7.	（手）扌	+	包	=>	抱
	hand		bag (Phonetic: **bāo**)		embrace (bào)
8.	王	+	里	=>	理
	Jade		Inside (Phonetic: **lǐ**)		jade cutting/manage (lǐ)
9.	相	+	心	=>	想
	mutually (Phonetic: **xiāng**)		heart		think (**xiǎng**)
10.	木	+	艮	=>	根
	tree		look at/tough (Phonetic: **gěn**)		root (gēn)
11.	斤	+	（辵）辶	=>	近
	axe (Phonetic: **jīn**)		walking		near (jìn)
12.	（示）礻	+	见	=>	视
	reveal (Phonetic: **shì**)		see		vision (shì)
13.	女	+	乃	=>	奶
	female		breast/Be (Phonetic: **nǎi**)		breast/milk/grandma (nǎi)
14.	（心）忄	+	白	=>	怕
	heart		white (Phonetic: **bái**)		fear (pà)
15.	尺	+	（辵）辶	=>	迟
	ruler (Phonetic: **chǐ**)		walking		tardy/late (chí)

16.	（人）亻 +	象 =>	像
	person	*elephant* *(Phonetic: xiàng)*	resemble (**xiàng**)
17.	木 +	羊 =>	样
	tree/wood	*goat* *(Phonetic: yáng)*	appearance (**yàng**)
18.	（金）钅 +	中 =>	钟
	metal	*middle* *(Phonetic: zhōng)*	clock (**zhōng**)
19.	由 +	（邑）阝 =>	邮
	through *(Phonetic: yóu)*	*dwelling*	mail (**yóu**)
20.	云 +	（辵）辶 =>	运
	cloud *(Phonetic: yún)*	*walking*	transport (**yùn**)

From the formation of the 20 characters above, the following observations can be made.

Observation 1: Whether a component by itself is a character or a reduced form of a basic character, each of the components in these characters has its own meaning and (except 乃) has been introduced in a previous chapter.

Observation 2: In each character there is always one component that does not really contribute to the meaning of the whole character; instead, it indicates the pronunciation of the character. In other words, one component is borrowed for its sound. This phonetic component may be at the top, on the right, or on the left of a character. Reduced forms of characters are not used for their sounds except in a very few characters. Of the 20 new characters in this chapter, only the character 视 uses a reduced form as the phonetic component; 礻 is the reduced form of 示 (altar table) *shì* and is used to indicate the pronunciation of the whole character 视 (vision) *shì*.

Observation 3: The phonetic component does not always have exactly the same pronunciation as the whole character. The phonetic component 门 *mén* retains only the nasal final sound of the character 问 *wèn*, and the phonetic component 隹 *zhuī* in the character 谁 *shuí* likewise retains only the character's final sounds. In addition, the tones are different. This means that knowing the pronunciation of a phonetic component may help but does not always guarantee knowledge of the exact pronunciation of the character.

Observation 4: While one component indicates the pronunciation, the other component indicates the meaning. However, it does not reveal the exact meaning of the character but only the category of meaning for the whole character.

With these four observations in mind, let's look at each of the characters more closely.

B. Structure Analysis 结构分析

妈　This character has two components: the semantic component 女 (woman) on the left and the phonetic component 马 (horse) *mǎ* on the right. 马 is simplified in the normalized script from the traditional form 馬. Therefore, the traditional form of the whole character is 媽. While 马 does not contribute to the meaning of the whole character, the semantic component 女 indicates only that the meaning of the whole character is related to "woman." The character is pronounced almost the same as the phonetic component; the only difference is the tone. 马 has the low dipping tone, but the character 妈 has the level tone. The meaning of the whole character is "mother."

Oracle	Bronze	Seal	Clerical	Regular	Normal-ized	Semi-cursive	Cursive
		媽	媽	媽	妈	妈	妈

问　The meaning of this character is "to ask." The traditional form of the character in the seal script, the clerical script, and the regular script was formed with two components: 門 (door) *mén* and 口 (mouth). In the normalized form, 門 is simplified to 门 by imitating the form of the character in the cursive script. 门 suggests the pronunciation while 口 indicates the meaning of the whole character is related to "mouth." Although the pronunciation of 问 *wèn* is not exactly the same as that of 门 *mén,* 门 still serves as a reminder of the pronunciation of 问.

Oracle	Bronze	Seal	Clerical	Regular	Normal-ized	Semi-cursive	Cursive
		問	問	問	问	问	问

较　The traditional form of this character is 較. In the normalized script, the component 車 (vehicle) on the left is simplified to 车. 车 is the semantic component for the character, suggesting that the whole character refers to something related to "carriage." The other component, 交 (cross) *jiāo,* indicates the pronunciation of 较. However, the component 交 has the level tone, whereas the character as a whole has the falling tone. The original meaning of 较 is a bronze hook used to decorate the sides of carriages owned by scholar-officials in ancient China. This decoration was not seen on the carts owned by ordinary people; therefore, it marked a contrast between scholar-officials and ordinary people. The character then got its extended meaning, "comparatively," which is what the character most often means.

Oracle	Bronze	Seal	Clerical	Regular	Normal-ized	Semi-cursive	Cursive
		較	較	較	较	较	较

远   The component ⻌ on the bottom left is the reduced form of 辵, which indicates that the meaning of the whole character is related to "walking." On the top right is the component 元 (dollar) *yuán,* which replaced 袁 (a family name) *yuán* as the component representing the pronunciation of the whole character. It means "far."

Oracle	Bronze	Seal	Clerical	Regular	Normal-ized	Semi-cursive	Cursive
次	德	遄	遠	遠	远	远	元

村   The oldest form of this character is in the seal script: 邨. On the left is the component 屯, which is a drawing of grass trying to grow out of the ground, and on the right is 邑, which stands for a residential area. With grass growing around a residential area, the character 邨 indicated a village. However, in the clerical script, a new form of the character was created. On the left, 木 (tree) indicated that a living place for a group of people was often among trees. On the right, the component 寸 (inch) *cùn* represented the pronunciation of the whole the character, although 村 *cūn* now has a level tone rather than a falling tone.

Oracle	Bronze	Seal	Clerical	Regular	Normal-ized	Semi-cursive	Cursive
		邨	村	村	村	村	村

谁   This character has two components: on the left side is 讠, the reduced form of the character 言 (speech); on the right side is the component 隹 (short-tailed bird) *zhuī*, which indicates the pronunciation of the whole character. In fact, 谁 is pronounced *shuí*. The component 隹 represents only the final diphthong of 谁. The character is a question word, "who."

Oracle	Bronze	Seal	Clerical	Regular	Normal-ized	Semi-cursive	Cursive
		雖	誰	誰	谁	谁	活

抱　This character is formed by the component 扌, the reduced form of the character 手 (hand), and the component 包 (bag/wrap) *bāo* on the right. The component 扌 indicates that the character is related to hands, and 包 also appears to have contributed to the meaning of the whole character: "to embrace" or "to hug." However, 包 represents the sound of the whole character except for the tone. While 包 has the first tone, 抱 has the falling tone.

Oracle	Bronze	Seal	Clerical	Regular	Normal-ized	Semi-cursive	Cursive
	抱	抱	抱	抱	抱	抱	

理　This character is formed with 王 (jade) on the left and 里 (inside) *lǐ* on the right. The character for jade, when it stands alone, has a dot stroke on its right side (玉). However, when "jade" is used as component in a character, the dot is not added, and the shape of its last stroke changes from a horizontal stroke to a rightward rising one. (Originally, the character for jade did not have a dot on its right side; the dot was added to distinguish it from the character for king, which as a similar shape.)[1] 王 in the character 理, therefore, suggests that 理 has something to do with jade. As a matter of fact, 理 originally meant "to work on uncut jade." Now its commonly used extended meaning is "to manage." 里 on the right does not contribute to the meaning of the whole character but only indicates its pronunciation: *lǐ*. The pronunciation of the character 理 is exactly the same as that of the component 里.

Oracle	Bronze	Seal	Clerical	Regular	Normal-ized	Semi-cursive	Cursive
		理	理	理	理	理	理

---

[1] For an explanation of why a dot was added to form the new character 玉 for "jade," please refer to the section on the character 王 (king) in Chapter 6.

想　This character can be viewed as being formed by 相 (each other) *xiāng* at the top and 心 (heart) at the bottom. Of course, 相 can be further divided into 木 and 目, but there is no need to do this because you have already learned 相 as a character. Any character that is learned can be treated as one component when it appears in another character. The component 心 indicates that the meaning of the character is related to the heart, which people in ancient times believed is the part of the body where thinking takes place. The character 想 means "to think" or "would like to" and is pronounced *xiǎng* as indicated by the component 相, except that 相 has the level tone, while the tone for 想 is dipping.

Oracle	Bronze	Seal	Clerical	Regular	Normal-ized	Semi-cursive	Cursive
		想	想	想	想	想	转

根　This character is formed with 木 (tree) and 艮 (looking back) *gěn*. The component 木 indicates that the meaning of the whole character is related to tree, and the component 艮 represents the pronunciation of the whole character, except that 艮 has the dipping tone while 根 is pronounced with the level tone. The character 本, introduced in Chapter 9, was first created to mean "root"; however, when it began to be used to mean "origin" more often than its original meaning, the character 根 was created to refer to "root."

Oracle	Bronze	Seal	Clerical	Regular	Normal-ized	Semi-cursive	Cursive
		根	根	根	根	根	柢

近　The oldest form of this character can be found in the seal script. The character had two components: the semantic component 辵 (walking) on the left and 斤 (axe) *jīn* on the right. 辵 in the regular script was reduced to 辶 on the left bottom, and the pronunciation of 斤 is the pronunciation of the whole character, except that the tone is changed from the level tone in 斤 to the falling tone in 近. The meaning of the character is "near."

Oracle	Bronze	Seal	Clerical	Regular	Normal-ized	Semi-cursive	Cursive
		近	近	近	近	近	近

视 This character means "vision" or "to watch." The component that is related to this meaning is 见 (see) on the right, whereas the component 礻, which is a reduced form of the character 示 (reveal) *shì*, represents the pronunciation of the whole character. Picto-phonetic characters mostly use a reduced form to indicate the category of meaning of the whole character, but this character uses the reduced form to indicate its pronunciation.

Oracle	Bronze	Seal	Clerical	Regular	Normal-ized	Semi-cursive	Cursive
示⊘		視	視	視	視	视	视

奶 The basic meaning of this character is "breast." It has two components. 女 (woman) on the left instantly tells us that the meaning of the character is related to "woman." The component 乃 (to be) *nǎi* represents the pronunciation of the whole character 奶 accurately. However, earlier forms of 乃 were ∫ in the oracle-bone inscriptions, ∂ in the bronze inscriptions, and 3 in the seal script. They all somewhat portray a breast; therefore, 乃 in fact also contributes to the meaning of the whole character 奶. The original meaning of 奶 was "breast," and now it often also means "milk." If it is repeated as 奶奶, then the meaning becomes "grandma."

Oracle	Bronze	Seal	Clerical	Regular	Normal-ized	Semi-cursive	Cursive
		奶	奶	奶	奶	奶	奶

怕 This character has two components. 忄 is the reduced form of 心 (heart) on the left, with 白 (white) *bái* on the right. The component 忄 suggests a state of mind. The meaning of the whole character is "fear." The component 白 is supposed to represent the pronunciation of the whole character; however, because of many years of language development and change, the pronunciation of the whole character 怕 is *pà*, which is quite different from the pronunciation of 白 *bái*. However, 白 still serves as a clue to the pronunciation of the character 怕 and distinguishes the shape of 怕 from other characters that contain 忄 such as 忆, 忙, 怀, 忧, 快, 怜, 性, 恨, 悟, 悦, 愧, and so on.

Oracle	Bronze	Seal	Clerical	Regular	Normalized	Semi-cursive	Cursive
		怕	怕	怕	怕	怕	怕

迟 The earliest form of this character in the seal script had two parts: 辵 (walk) on the left and 犀 (rhinoceros) *xī*. 辵 later took the form 辵, which was reduced to 辶, indicating that the meaning of the whole character is related to "walking." Probably because walking is not a fast way of traveling, the meaning of the whole character is "tardy." The pronunciation was represented by 犀 until it was replaced by a different component, 尺 (inch) *chǐ*, in the normalized script. Having four strokes, 尺 is simpler to write, and having the pronunciation of *chǐ*, it represents the pronunciation of the whole character more accurately except for the tone. While the character 迟 is pronounced with the rising tone, the component 尺 by itself is pronounced with the dipping tone.

Oracle	Bronze	Seal	Clerical	Regular	Normalized	Semi-cursive	Cursive
炑	彿	遟	遲	遲	迟	迟	迟

像 The original meaning of this character is "portrait." On the left side of the character is the component 亻, a reduced form of the character 人 (person). On the right is the phonetic component 象 (elephant) *xiàng*, which is the pronunciation of the whole character. As 像 has the connotation of "likeness," it often means "resemble."

Oracle	Bronze	Seal	Clerical	Regular	Normalized	Semi-cursive	Cursive
		像	像	像	像	像	像

样 This character is formed of two components: 木 (tree) on the left and 羊 (goat) *yáng* on the right. The component 木 indicates that the meaning of the whole character is in one way or another related to "tree." Each tree has a distinctive appearance that can make a deep impression on people. Thus the character 样 means appearance. Its earlier forms in the oracle-bone inscriptions, the clerical script, and the regular script had 羕 (long water flow) *yàng* as the phonetic component in the character. 羕 was formed with a tailless 羊 at the top, indicating the pronunciation, and 永 (far reaching water, forever) at the bottom, indicting the meaning. In the normalized script, 羊 is used instead of 羕, making the whole character less complex in structure and number of strokes. However, while 羊 has the rising tone, the whole character 样 has the falling tone.

Oracle	Bronze	Seal	Clerical	Regular	Normal-ized	Semi-cursive	Cursive
		欁	樣	樣	样	样	様

钟   This character means "clock." It has two components. One is 钅, a reduced form of the character 金 (metal). Apart from some very ancient time measuring instruments, no clock is made without "metal." The other component in the character, 中 (middle) *zhōng*, which replaces 童 (child) *tóng* in the normalized script, stands for the pronunciation of the whole character accurately.

Oracle	Bronze	Seal	Clerical	Regular	Normal-ized	Semi-cursive	Cursive
	鐘	鐘	鐘	钟	钟	钟	钟

邮   The meaning of this character is "mail." The older forms in the seal script, the clerical script, and the regular script consist of 垂 (hanging) *chuí* on the left and 阝, the reduced form of the character 邑 (town), on the right. However, 垂 in the character does not indicate the pronunciation of 邮 but rather the meaning of the character 陲[2] (frontiers) *chuí*, even though 垂 alone means hanging and is used in forming the character 邮. The idea is that between town and the frontiers, letters are sent. 邮, therefore, is an associative character, in which both components contribute to the meaning. In the normalized script, the component 垂 is replaced with 由 (through) *yóu*, which indicates the pronunciation of the whole character. Thus, 邮 is a picto-phonetic character pronounced *yóu*, meaning "mail."

Oracle	Bronze	Seal	Clerical	Regular	Normal-ized	Semi-cursive	Cursive
		邨	郵	郵	邮	邮	邮

---

[2] Note that 阝 is on the left of the character 陲. When 阝 is on the left of a character, it is the reduced form of 阜 (mound) rather than of 邑 (town).

运 This character means "to transport." It has two components: 云 on the top right and 辶 on the bottom left. 辶 indicates that the meaning of the character is related to walking or traveling. The meaning of the whole character, "to transport something," involves traveling from one place to another. The other component, 云 (cloud) *yún*, replacing 軍 (army) *jūn* in the older forms of the character, is the phonetic component; however, 运 *yùn* has the falling tone instead of the rising tone.

Oracle	Bronze	Seal	Clerical	Regular	Normal-ized	Semi-cursive	Cursive
		𧗠	運	運	运	运	运

C. Recognition Reinforcement 辨认巩固练习

If you have not taken Challenges 3 and 4 in the previous chapters, it will be difficult to remember these characters by their phonetic components. Therefore, keep using your visual memory to associate the shape of each character with its meaning.

1. Link each character on the first line with its corresponding meaning in English on the second line:

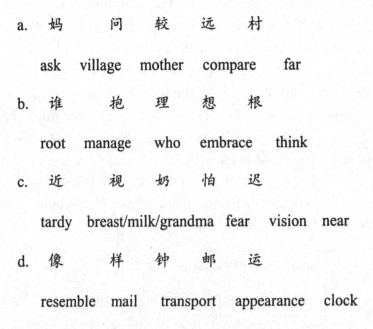

a. 妈   问   较   远   村

ask   village   mother   compare   far

b. 谁   抱   理   想   根

root   manage   who   embrace   think

c. 近   视   奶   怕   迟

tardy   breast/milk/grandma   fear   vision   near

d. 像   样   钟   邮   运

resemble   mail   transport   appearance   clock

2. There are ten characters on the left side and eleven words in English on the right side. Put the letter for each character in the blank next to the corresponding English word. In each group, there is an extra blank that should be left empty.

Group 1:

a. 想

b. 谁

c. 根

d. 远

e. 较

f. 理

g. 问

h. 抱

i. 妈

j. 村

_____ far

_____ embrace

_____ mother

_____ ask

_____ village

_____ near

_____ root

_____ mail

_____ compare

_____ think

_____ manage

Group 2:

a. 样

b. 怕

c. 奶

d. 近

e. 视

f. 邮

g. 钟

h. 迟

i. 运

j. 像

_____ vision

_____ mail

_____ appearance

_____ clock

_____ near

_____ think

_____ transport

_____ resemble

_____ fear

_____ breast/milk

_____ tardy

3. Provide the meaning in English for each of the following characters:

妈_____   问_____   较_____   远_____   村_____

谁_____   抱_____   理_____   想_____   根_____

近_____ 视_____ 奶_____ 怕_____ 迟_____

像_____ 样_____ 钟_____ 邮_____ 运_____

II. Challenge 1: Write the Characters 挑战一：知义书形

A. Strokes in Characters 详说笔画: 乃

In the semantic components you have learned in this chapter, there is one new stroke:

乃 *héngzhézhézhégōu* (a horizontal stroke with three turns and a hook), as

in 乃

Write this stroke paying attention to the direction of the stroke movement as indicated.

B. Character Structures 汉字结构

As you have just learned, every picto-phonetic character has a component that indicates the category of meaning of the whole character (rather than the exact meaning of the character); it provides an important clue to the exact meaning of the character. Every picto-phonetic character also has another component that indicates the pronunciation of the whole character. Being able to identify the major components in a character will help you learn the structure and the meaning of the character.

1. Put each of the following characters after the type of character structure it belongs to, based on the arrangement of the character's two major components.

妈 近 抱 村 想 问 迟 较 理 根 视
奶 远 疼 样 谁 邮 怕 像 钟 运 豹

a. ▢▢

b.	
c.	
d.	
e.	

Answers:
a. 妈较村抱理
根视奶谁怕像
样钟邮豹
b. 疾
c. 想
d. 近迟远运
e. 问

2. Which is the phonetic component in each of the following characters? It will be easy if you know how to pronounce each character. However, if you don't, you can try to identify the semantic component first, thereby isolating the phonetic component.

	Semantic Component	Phonetic Component	Meaning		Semantic Component	Phonetic Component	Meaning
抱				根			
像				视			
问				较			
怕				邮			
谁				近			
妈				奶			
村				钟			
样				运			
远				迟			
想				理			

C. Stroke Order Analysis 笔顺分析

Can you separate the following multicomponent characters into their components in the sequence in which they are supposed to be written?

Write the components one at a time in the proper sequence.
↓

For example:　| 妈 | 女 | 马 |

Then compare with the correct sequence ⟶   女 马

| 问 | | | 门 口

| 较 | | | 车 交

| 远 | | | 元 辶

| 村 | | | 木 寸

| 谁 | | | 讠 隹

| 抱 | | | 扌 包

| 理 | | | 王 里

| 想 | | | 相 心

| 根 | | | 木 艮

| 近 | | | 斤 辶

| 视 | | | 礻 见

| 奶 | | | 女 乃

| 怕 | | | 忄 白

迟 ☐ ☐ 　　　　尺 辶

像 ☐ ☐ 　　　　亻 象

样 ☐ ☐ 　　　　木 羊

钟 ☐ ☐ 　　　　钅 中

邮 ☐ ☐ 　　　　由 阝

运 ☐ ☐ 　　　　云 辶

D. Write with a Pencil 动手动笔

Use the following "well" boxes to write each character. Take a good look at the model character and try to write it by heart without referring to the model. Each time you finish writing the character, you can compare it with the model. Correct any mistakes and write until you do it correctly without looking at the model. Write on a piece of paper if more practice is needed.

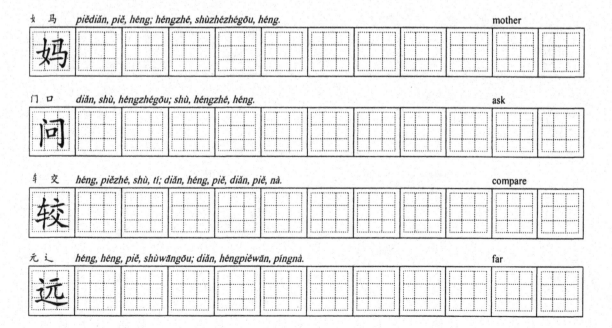

女 马　*piědiǎn, piě, héng; héngzhé, shùzhézhégōu, héng.*　　　　mother

妈

门 口　*diǎn, shù, héngzhégōu; shù, héngzhé, héng.*　　　　ask

问

车 交　*héng, piězhé, shù, tí; diǎn, héng, piě, diǎn, piě, nà.*　　　　compare

较

元 辶　*héng, héng, piě, shùwāngōu; diǎn, héngpiěwān, píngnà.*　　　　far

远

木 寸   *héng, shù, piě, diǎn; héng, shùgōu, diǎn.*   village

村

讠 隹   *diǎn, héngzhégōu; piě, shù, diǎn, héng, héng, héng, shù, héng.*   who

谁

扌 包   *héng, shùgōu, tí; piě, héngzhégōu, héngzhé, héng, shùwāngōu.*   embrace

抱

王 里   *héng, héng, shù, tí; shù, héngzhé, héng, héng, shù, héng, héng.*   jade cutting/manage

理

相 心   *héng, shù, piě, diàn; shù, héngzhé, héng, héng, héng; diǎn, wǒgōu, diǎn, diǎn.*   think

想

木 艮   *héng, shù, piě, diàn; héngzhé, héng, héng, shùtí, piě, nà.*   root

根

斤 辶   *piě, piě, héng, shù; diǎn, héngpiěwān, píngnà.*   near

近

礻 见   *diǎn, héngpiě, shù, diǎn; shù, héngzhé, piě, shùwāngōu.*   vision

视

女 乃   *piědiǎn, piě, héng; hézhézhézhégōu, piě.*   breast/milk/ grandma

奶

丷忄 or 丨忄 白   *diǎn, diǎn, shù* or *diǎn, shù, diǎn; piě, shù, héngzhé, héng, héng.*   fear

怕

尺 辶   *héngzhé, héng, piě, nà; diǎn, héngpiěwān, píngnà.*   tardy

迟

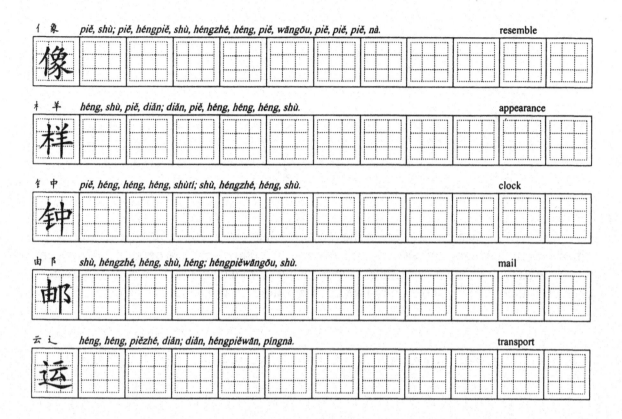

亻象   piě, shù; piě, héngpiě, shù, héngzhé, héng, piě, wāngōu, piě, piě, piě, nà.   resemble

像

木 羊   héng, shù, piě, diǎn; diǎn, piě, héng, héng, héng, shù.   appearance

样

钅中   piě, héng, héng, héng, shùtí; shù, héngzhé, héng, shù.   clock

钟

由 阝   shù, héngzhé, héng, shù, héng; héngpiěwāngōu, shù.   mail

邮

云 辶   héng, héng, piězhé, diǎn; diǎn, héngpiěwǎn, píngnà.   transport

运

III. Challenge 2: Apply Your Knowledge 挑战二: 举一反三

A. Know Many Things by Learning One 闻一知十

1. Most picto-phonetic characters use reduced forms or commonly used semantic components to indicate the category of meaning of the characters. Although it is not easy or necessary for you to learn to tell whether a multicomponent character is an associative character, with all components contributing to the meaning of the whole character, or a picto-phonetic character, with a component suggesting the meaning and a component indicating the pronunciation. However, you must have the ability to separate a character that you have not yet learned into manageable components. Please break the following new characters into two major components:

Example: 他: 亻   也

	Component 1	Component 2			Component 1	Component 2
作				园		
打				钱		
忙				饭		
认				猫		
汽				跳		
点				花		

红			笑		
刚			裤		
冷			败		
很			字		
送			疲		
院			祖		
都			却		

2. All the basic characters in the previous chapters can be used as semantic components, and many can also be used as phonetic components. A phonetic component can be used with different semantic components to form new characters. Can you match each character with the correct definition in the following 11 groups?

A.

1)	妈	*mā*	_____	A.	ants; locusts; leech
2)	码	*mǎ*	_____	B.	mother
3)	吗	*ma*	_____	C.	agate
4)	玛	*mǎ*	_____	D.	character indicating questions
5)	蚂	*mǎ; mà*	_____	E.	dock; code

1) B
2) E
3) D
4) C
5) A

B.

1)	问	*wèn*	_____	A.	stuffy
2)	闻	*wén*	_____	B.	plural ending for people
3)	扪	*mén*	_____	C.	ask
4)	们	*men*	_____	D.	hear
5)	闷	*mèn*	_____	E.	touch

1) C
2) D
3) E
4) B
5) A

C.

1)	较	*jiào*	_____	A.	twist
2)	绞	*jiǎo*	_____	B.	fall
3)	郊	*jiāo*	_____	C.	compare; relatively
4)	跤	*jiāo*	_____	D.	Chinese dumpling
5)	饺	*jiǎo*	_____	E.	suburbs

1) C
2) A
3) E
4) B
5) D

D.

1) 刨 *bào; páo* _____ A. embrace
2) 饱 *bǎo* _____ B. bud
3) 抱 *bào* _____ C. satiated with food
4) 苞 *bāo* _____ D. hail
5) 雹 *báo* _____ E. plane; dig

1) E
2) C
3) A
4) B
5) D

E.

1) 俚 *lǐ* _____ A. carp
2) 锂 *lǐ* _____ B. vulgar
3) 狸 *lí* _____ C. jade cutting
4) 鲤 *lǐ* _____ D. lithium
5) 理 *lǐ* _____ E. racoon dog

1) B
2) D
3) E
4) A
5) C

F.

1) 种 *zhòng* _____ A. clock
2) 钟 *zhōng* _____ B. swollen
3) 忠 *zhōng* _____ C. to plant
4) 盅 *zhōng* _____ D. loyal
5) 肿 *zhǒng* _____ E. handless cup

1) C
2) A
3) D
4) E
5) B

G.

1) 箱 *xiāng* _____ A. oak
2) 湘 *xiāng* _____ B. think
3) 想 *xiǎng* _____ C. resemble
4) 橡 *xiàng* _____ D. the Xiang River
5) 像 *xiàng* _____ E. bamboo case

1) B
2) E
3) D
4) C
5) A

H.

1) 痒 *yǎng* _____ A. pretend
2) 氧 *yǎng* _____ B. ocean
3) 佯 *yáng* _____ C. itch
4) 洋 *yáng* _____ D. appearance
5) 样 *yàng* _____ E. oxygen

1) C
2) E
3) A
4) B
5) D

I.

1)	谁	*shuí*	_____	A.	push
2)	推	*tuī*	_____	B.	pile up
3)	堆	*duī*	_____	C.	who
4)	锥	*zhuī*	_____	D.	stone pestle
5)	碓	*duì*	_____	E.	prick

1) C
2) A
3) B
4) E
5) D

J.

1)	柚	*yòu*	_____	A.	weasle
2)	铀	*yóu*	_____	B.	oil
3)	油	*yóu*	_____	C.	mail
4)	邮	*yóu*	_____	D.	teak
5)	鼬[3]	*yòu*	_____	E.	uranium

1) D
2) E
3) B
4) C
5) A

K.

1)	跟	*gēn*	_____	A.	hate
2)	根	*gēn*	_____	B.	ruthless
3)	狼	*hěn*	_____	C.	root
4)	恨	*hèn*	_____	D.	follow
5)	痕	*hěn*	_____	E.	vestige; scar

1) D
2) C
3) B
4) A
5) E

3. The following two-syllable words and phrases are formed with the characters introduced in this chapter as well as in the previous chapters. Can you figure out what they mean?

Group 1:

后妈_____	1. Near East
大妈_____	2. say hello
奶妈_____	3. stepmother

---

[3] 鼠 means "mouse" and is used here as a semantic component.

问心 _____   4. denounce

近视_____   5. shortcut

近东_____   6. aunty

近道_____   7. wet nurse

问好_____   8. shortsighted

自问_____   9. examine one's conscience

问罪_____   10. ask oneself

Answers:
后怕 3. 大妈 6. 奶妈 7. 问心 9. 近视 8. 近东 1. 近道 5. 问好 2. 自问 10. 问罪 4.

Group 2:

山村_____   1. pathology

渔村_____   2. mentality

理解_____   3. ideal; wishful thinking

理由_____   4. manage by oneself

理想_____   5. electric clock

病理_____   6. fear after the event

心理_____   7. fishing village

自理_____   8. reason

电钟_____   9. comprehend

后怕_____   10. mountain village

Answers:
山村 10. 渔村 7. 理解 9. 理由 8. 理想 3. 病理 1. 电钟 5. 心理 2. 自理 4. 后怕 6.

Group 3:

想像_____   1. TV

像样_____   2. imagine

好像_____   3. portrait

人像_____   4. resemble each other

相像_____   5. farsighted

病根_____   6. visual angle

邮包_____   7. root cause of illness or trouble

电视_____   8. seem like

远视_____   9. presentable; up to the standard

视角_____   10. mailbag

Answers: 想象 2. 像样 9. 好像 8. 人像 3. 相像 4. 病根 7. 邮包 10. 电视 1. 远视 5. 视角 6.

Group 4:

奶牛_____   1. the same

奶牙_____   2. in that way

远东_____   3. foresight

远见_____   4. cow

长远_____   5. baby tooth

那样_____   6. be in motion

多样_____   7. water transport

一样_____   8. Far East

运行_____   9. long-term

水运_____   10. varied

Answers: 奶牛 4. 奶牙 5. 远东 8. 远见 3. 长远 9. 那样 2. 多样 10. 一样 1. 运行 6. 水运 7.

B. Be Perceptive of the Slightest Differences 明察秋毫

1. Which component do the characters in each group share? Write it, and match it with the meaning category it indicates. (An English translation is provided under each character; however, keep in mind many characters may have more than one meaning.)

A.

					Shared Semantic Component		Meaning Category

Group 1 　悟 realize　快 quick　情 feeling　慢 slow　懂 understand　_____　1. ___　a. hand

Group 2 　细 slender　织 weave　给 supply　经 warp　纸 paper　_____　2. ___　b. fire

Group 3 　照 shine　然 like that　热 hot　熟 ripe　烈 strong　_____　3. ___　c. mind

Group 4 　进 enter　迎 greet　这 this　遍 all over　还 give back　_____　4. ___　d. silk/fiber

Group 5 　报 report　把 hold　提 lift　挂 hang　挤 squeeze　_____　5. ___　e. walk

Group 6 　让 let　讲 say　词 word　请 invite　谢 thank　_____　6. ___　f. town

Group 7 　街 street　得 gain　往 toward　律 rule　征 journey　_____　7. ___　g. intersection

Group 8 　别 other　刮 scrape　到 arrive　刻 engrave　剩 surplus　_____　8. ___　h. mountain

Group 9 　阳 bright　阴 dark　除 remove　附 attach　险 danger　_____　9. ___　i. knife

Group 10 　部 part　邦 nation　邻 neighbor　邪 evil　郎 man　_____　10. ___　j. speech

Answers:
1. c
2. d
3. b
4. e
5. a
6. j
7. g
8. i
9. h
10. f

B.

					Shared Semantic Component		Meaning Category

Group 1 　你 you　作 do　住 live　体 body　伟 great　_____　1. ___　a. ice

Group 2 　没 not　河 river　洗 wash　游 swim　渴 thirsty　_____　2. ___　b. bamboo

Group 3 　净 clean　凉 cool　冷 cold　况 situation　冻 freeze　_____　3. ___　c. animal

Group	Characters					Shared Semantic Component	#	Meaning Category
Group 4	囚 prisoner	困 stranded	图 chart	圆 round	围 enclose	_____	4. ___	d. water
Group 5	银 silver	钢 steel	铅 lead	错 fault	锻 forge	_____	5. ___	e. people
Group 6	饱 full	饿 hungry	饺 dumpling	饼 pancake	馆 hall	_____	6. ___	f. grass/plant
Group 7	狼 ruthless	狂 crazy	猪 pig	狗 dog	狐 fox	_____	7. ___	g. food
Group 8	跟 follow	跳 jump	跑 run	踢 kick	路 road	_____	8. ___	h. metal
Group 9	茶 tea	菜 vegetable	草 grass	药 medicine	苦 bitter	_____	9. ___	i. foot
Group 10	第 order	等 wait	答 reply	篮 basket	简 brief	_____	10. ___	j. enclosure

Answers: 1. e 2. d 3. a 4. j 5. h 6. g 7. c 8. i 9. f 10. b

C.

Group	Characters					Shared Semantic Component	#	Meaning Category
Group 1	被 quilt	袜 socks	补 patch	衬 liner	袖 sleeve	_____	1. ___	a. sickness
Group 2	政 politics	故 former	敢 dare	数 count	教 teach	_____	2. ___	b. roofed house
Group 3	家 home	室 room	富 wealthy	客 guest	寒 cold	_____	3. ___	c. two hands
Group 4	病 sick	痛 pain	疯 insane	疗 cure	瘾 addiction	_____	4. ___	d. clothing
Group 5	神 deity	礼 rite	祖 ancestor	祥 auspicious	福 happiness	_____	5. ___	e. long beard or shape
Group 6	开 open	异 different	弄 play with	弃 discard	弊 fraud	_____	6. ___	f. wrapping
Group 7	形 shape	彩 color	影 shadow	彪 hefty	彦 man of virtue	_____	7. ___	g. case/container

Group 8	采 pick	觅 look for	妥 proper	受 accept	舀 scoop	＿＿	8.＿	h. hand with a stick
Group 9	区 section	匠 craftsman	匣 case	匪 bandit	匡 rectify	＿＿	9.＿	i. altar
Group 10	匀 even	勾 tick off	句 sentence	旬 a period of ten days or years	訇 loud noise	＿＿	10.＿	j. claw/upper hand

Answers:
1. d
2. h
3. b
4. a
5. i
6. c
7. e
8. j
9. g
10. f

2. Which component do the characters in each group share? Write it, and then figure out which sound they share regardless of tones.

						Shared Phonetic Component	Shared Pronunciation
1)	bǎ 把 hold	ba 吧 a question word	bà 爸 dad	bā 疤 scar	bǎ 靶 target	＿＿	＿＿
2)	cǎi 彩 color	cài 菜 vegetable	cǎi 踩 trample	cǎi 睬 pay attention		＿＿	＿＿
3)	fàn 饭 meal	fǎn 返 return	fàn 贩 resell			＿＿	＿＿
4)	bān 扳 pull to turn	bǎn 版 edition	bǎn 板 board	bǎn 舨 sampan	bǎn 坂 hillside	＿＿	＿＿
5)	fāng 芳 fragrant	fáng 防 defend	fáng 房 house	fǎng 访 visit	fàng 放 discharge	＿＿	＿＿
6)	fú 福 happiness	fú 富 wealthy	fú 幅 breadth	fú 辐 spoke	fù 副 deputy	＿＿	＿＿
7)	gāng 刚 just	gāng 钢 steel	gāng 纲 outline	gāng 岗 hillock		＿＿	＿＿

8)
gū	gū	gú	gù	gù
姑	估	轱	固	故
aunt	estimate	wheel	solid	former

_____   _____

9)
qīng	qíng	qíng	qǐng	qīng
清	晴	情	请	氰
clear	sunny	feeling	invite	cyanogen

_____   _____

10)
jīng	jīng	jīng	jìng	jìng
精	睛	菁	静	靖
extract	eyeball	lush	quiet	pacify

_____   _____

11)
kē	kē	kē	kē	kè
棵	窠	颗	稞	课
a measure word for plants	nest	a measure word for round articles	barley	lesson

_____   _____

12)
jīng	jīng	jīng	jǐng
惊	兢	鲸	景
shock	cautious	whale	scene

_____   _____

13)
liáng	liàng	liàng
凉	谅	晾
cool	forgive	to dry in the air

_____   _____

14)
líng	lǐng	lǐng	líng	líng
零	领	岭	铃	玲
zero	lead	ridge	bell	tinkling

_____   _____

15)
màn	màn	mán	màn	màn
慢	漫	馒	蔓	幔
slow	overflow	steamed bun	tendril	curtain

_____   _____

16)
piāo	piāo	piáo	piáo	piáo
漂	飘	剽	瓢	嫖
float	wave to and fro	rob	gourd ladle	visit prostitutes

_____   _____

17)
qī	qī	qí	qí	qí
期	欺	棋	旗	祺
period	deceive	chess	flag	auspicious

_____   _____

18)
qiáo	qiáo	qiáo
桥	侨	荞
bridge	live abroad	buckwheat

_____   _____

19)
jiāo	jiāo	jiǎo	jiào
骄	娇	矫	轿
proud	charming	rectify	sedan

_____   _____

20)
jī	jī	jī	jī	jī
机	肌	饥	矶	讥
machine	muscle	starve	rock that sticks out	mock

_____   _____

	jiàn	*jiàn*	*jiān*	*jiàn*	
21)	践	贱	笺	饯	_____ _____
	tread	cheap	annotation	give a farewell dinner	

	qián	*qiǎn*		
22)	钱	浅	_____ _____
	money	shallow	

	jù	*jù*	*jù*	*jù*	*jù*	
23)	据	剧	锯	踞	倨	_____ _____
	rely on	drama	saw	crouch	haughty	

	tóng	*tóng*	*tǒng*	*tóng*	
24)	铜	桐	筒	酮	_____ _____
	copper	tung	canister	ketone	

	yǒng	*yǒng*	*yǒng*	*yǒng*	*yǒng*	
25)	涌	勇	俑	蛹	踊	_____ _____
	gush	brave	tomb figure	pupa	jump up	

	tōng	*tǒng*	*tǒng*	*tòng*	
26)	通	桶	捅	痛	_____ _____
	through	barrel	poke	pain	

	wěi	*wéi*	*wéi*	*wěi*	*wěi*	
27)	伟	围	违	纬	苇	_____ _____
	great	enclose	disobey	latitude	reed	

	jiǎn	*jiǎn*	*jiǎn*	*jiǎn*	*jiàn*	
28)	检	捡	俭	硷	剑	_____ _____
	check up	pick up	frugal	alkali	sword	

	yōu	*yōu*	*yóu*	*yóu*	*yóu*	
29)	优	忧	犹	疣	鱿	_____ _____
	excellent	worry	just as	wart	squid	

	yú	*yú*	*yú*	*yù*	*yù*	
30)	愉	逾	榆	愈	喻	_____ _____
	pleasant	exceed	elm	heal	metaphor	

	zhàn	*zhàn*	*zhān*	*zhān*	*zhān*	
31)	站	战	沾	粘	毡	_____ _____
	stand	battle	moisten	glue	felt	

	zhāng	*zhàng*	*zhàng*	*zhàng*	
32)	张	帐	胀	账	_____ _____
	sheet	canopy	swell	account	

	zhēn	*zhēn*	*zhěn*	*zhěn*	*zhěn*	
33)	珍	胗	诊	疹	畛	_____ _____
	treasure	gizzard	diagnose	rash	path	

	zhēng	zhěng	zhèng	zhèng	zhèng		
34)	征	整	证	政	症	_____	_____
	go on a journey	tidy	prove	politics	disease		

	zhí	zhí	zhí	zhí	zhì		
35)	值	植	殖	埴	置	_____	_____
	value	plant	breed	clay	place		

	zū	zǔ	zǔ	zǔ	zǔ		
36)	租	组	祖	阻	诅	_____	_____
	rent	group	ancestor	block	curse		

Answers:

1. 巴 ba	2. 采 cai	3. 反 fan	4. 反 ban	5. 方 fang	6. 畐 fu	7. 冈 gang	8. 古 gu	9. 青 qing
10. 青 jing	11. 果 ke	12. 京 jing	13. 京 liang	14. 令 ling	15. 曼 man	16. 票 piao	17. 其 qi	18. 乔 qiao
19. 乔 jiao	20. 几 ji	21. 戋 jian	22. 戋 qian	23. 居 ju	24. 同 tong	25. 甬 yong	26. 甬 tong	27. 韦 wei
28. 佥 jian	29. 尤 you	30. 俞 yu	31. 占 zhan	32. 长 zhang	33. 乡 zhen	34. 正 zheng	35. 直 zhi	36. 且 zu

C. Be Aware of the Complex Counterpart 学简知繁

If you do not wish to learn the complex forms now because you are still at the beginning level, you may skip this section and go to the next section for Challenge 3.

1. Comparison. In this chapter, eleven of the characters have been simplified in the normalized script from their complex forms. Look at the following table and compare the simplified forms of these eleven characters with their complex counterparts:

	Simplified Form	Complex Form	Meaning
1	妈	媽	mother
2	问	問	ask
3	较	較	compare
4	远	遠	far
5	谁	誰	who
6	视	視	to watch
7	迟	遲	tardy

8	样	樣	appearance
9	钟	鐘	clock
10	邮	郵	mail
11	运	運	transport

2. Explanation.

媽, 問, 較, 視, 誰. Each of these five characters has a component that is simplified in the normalized script: 馬 in 媽 becomes 马, 門 in 問 becomes 门, 車 in 較 becomes 车, 見 in 視 becomes 见, and 言 in 誰 becomes 讠. Therefore, the simplified forms of these characters in the normalized script are 妈, 问, 较, 视, and 谁. As mentioned in the previous chapters, the simplification of these characters and components was achieved through the regularization of their forms in the cursive script.

遲. This is the traditional form of the character 迟 (tardy) *chí*. The component 犀 (rhinoceros) *xī* indicates how the whole character was pronounced a long time ago. The pronunciation of the character is no longer *xī* but *chí* now.

遠. This is the traditional form of the character 远 (far) *yuǎn*. The traditional form of the character uses 袁 (a family name) *yuán* to represent the pronunciation of the whole character.

樣. This is the traditional form of the character 样. The phonetic component in the traditional form is 羕 (long water flow) *yàng*, which is composed of 羊 (goat) *yáng* and 永 (far reaching water, forever). Therefore, 羕 itself is also a picto-phonetic character that is used as a phonetic component in the character 樣.

鐘. This is the traditional form of the character 钟. The component 釒 (metal) indicates that the meaning of the character is related to metal, and the component 童 (child) *tóng* indicates that the whole character 鐘, is pronounced *zhōng*.

郵. The traditional form of the character 邮 is not a picto-phonetic character but an associative character, in which both components contribute to the meaning of the whole character. 垂 means "frontiers," and 阝 is the reduced form of the character 邑, meaning "town."   The combination of these two components suggests the idea of delivering documents and letters between cities and frontiers.

運．This is the traditional form of the character 运. However, the phonetic component 軍 (army) *jūn* represents the pronunciation of the whole character 運 (transport) *yùn* only partially.

3. Writing. Write these characters in their traditional forms.

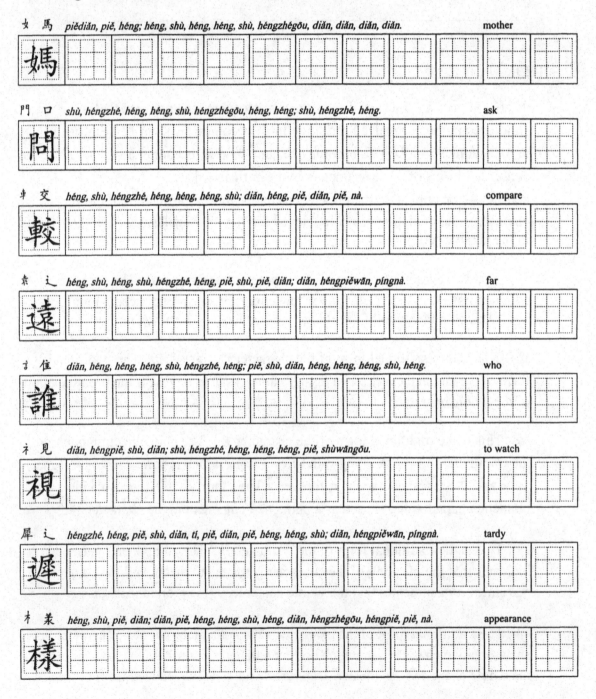

女 馬　*piědiǎn, piě, héng; héng, shù, héng, héng, shù, héngzhégōu, diǎn, diǎn, diǎn, diǎn.*　mother

媽

門 口　*shù, héngzhé, héng, héng, shù, héngzhégōu, héng, héng; shù, héngzhé, héng.*　ask

問

車 交　*héng, shù, héngzhé, héng, héng, héng, shù; diǎn, héng, piě, diǎn, piě, nà.*　compare

較

袁 辶　*héng, shù, héng, shù, héngzhé, héng, piě, shù, piě, diǎn; diǎn, héngpiěwān, píngnà.*　far

遠

言 隹　*diǎn, héng, héng, héng, shù, héngzhé, héng; piě, shù, diǎn, héng, héng, héng, shù, héng.*　who

誰

礻 見　*diǎn, héngpiě, shù, diǎn; shù, héngzhé, héng, héng, héng, piě, shùwāngōu.*　to watch

視

犀 辶　*héngzhé, héng, piě, shù, diǎn, tí, piě, diǎn, piě, héng, héng, shù; diǎn, héngpiěwān, píngnà.*　tardy

遲

木 羕　*héng, shù, piě, diǎn; diǎn, piě, héng, héng, shù, héng, diǎn, héngzhégōu, héngpiě, piě, nà.*　appearance

樣

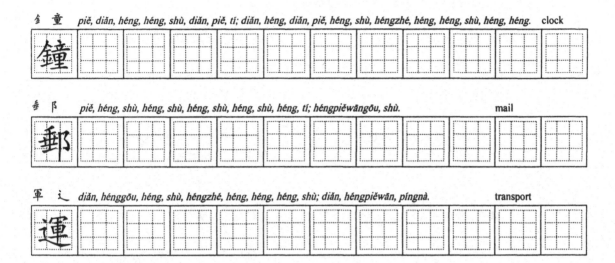

金 童　*piě, diǎn, héng, héng, shù, diǎn, piě, tí; diǎn, héng, diǎn, piě, héng, shù, héngzhé, héng, héng, shù, héng, héng.*　clock

钟

垂 阝　*piě, héng, shù, héng, shù, héng, shù, héng, shù, héng, tí; héngpiěwāngōu, shù.*　mail

邮

軍 辶　*diǎn, hénggōu, héng, shù, héngzhé, héng, héng, héng, shù; diǎn, héngpiěwān, píngnà.*　transport

运

D. Simplification Method (6): Replace a Complex Component with a Simple One
简化方法 (六): 删繁就简

In the normalized script, some characters have been simplified by replacing complex components with relatively simple ones.

Traditional	Replace the complex component	Simplified	Traditional	Replace the complex component	Simplified
樣	⟶	样	國	⟶	国
鐘	⟶	钟	筆	⟶	笔
運	⟶	运	陰	⟶	阴
遲	⟶	迟	雙	⟶	双
遠	⟶	远	時	⟶	时
億	⟶	亿	畫	⟶	画

IV. Challenge 3: Pronounce the Characters　挑战三: 见形发音

Having firmly established the link between the shape and the meaning for each of the 20 new characters introduced in this chapter, you are ready to establish the link between the shape and the pronunciation for each of these characters.

Again, if you are not ready for this challenge, you can skip this section and go to the next to practice writing characters. You may also consider taking a Chinese language class to learn to speak Chinese, while continuing to learn to read and write Chinese characters.

1. Listen and read (choose the form you prefer):

(In the traditional form)	*(In the normalized form)*
Mā wèn jiào yuǎn cūn, 媽問較遠村，	Mā wèn jiào yuǎn cūn, 妈问较远村，
Shuí bào lǐ xiǎng gēn, 誰抱理想根，	Shuí bào lǐ xiǎng gēn, 谁抱理想根，
Jìn shì nǎi pà chí, 近視奶怕遲，	Jìn shì nǎi pà chí, 近视奶怕迟，
Xiàng yàng zhōng yóu yùn. 像樣鐘郵運。	Xiàng yàng zhōng yóu yùn. 像样钟邮运。

2. Read aloud by looking only at the characters:

(In the traditional form)	*(In the normalized form)*
媽問較遠村，	妈问较远村，
誰抱理想根，	谁抱理想根，
近視奶怕遲，	近视奶怕迟，
像樣鐘郵運。	像样钟邮运。

3. Guess the answers to the riddles using the characters in the list. Answer the riddle in Chinese aloud to yourself or to someone who can help with pronunciation, and write the character in the box and its *pinyin* outside the box after each riddle. Note that there are nine riddles for the ten characters in each group.

Group 1:   妈问较远村谁抱理想根

a) It is the main part of a tree that absorbs water.

b) What should you do if you have questions?

c) How is the distance between one's house and a school described if it takes four hours to drive from the house to the school?

d) It is often the very first word a baby can say to his/her mother.

e) It is the action of holding somebody or something with both arms.

f) What do we do with our brains?

g) It is a place that has houses and shops but is smaller than a town.

h) It is the action of putting things in order.

i) People say it when trying to find out who someone is.

Group 2: 近视奶怕迟像样钟邮运

a) It has hands, but they do not hold anything. It has a face but not a mouth; yet, it tells people the time.

b) How is the distance between one's house and a school described if it takes only two minutes to walk from the house to the school?

c) It is a situation in which someone arrives in class ten minutes after it started.

d) It is the action of carrying things from one place to another.

e) It is the action of delivering letters and parcels.

f) It is the action of using eyes.

g) All babies nurse at it in order to grow.

h) It is the feeling that people normally have when they are in a dangerous and helpless situation.

i) It is the situation in which two people share a lot of similarities in appearance.

V. Challenge 4: Dictation 挑战四：听音书形知义

1. By now, you should be able to recite the character verse for this chapter. If not, continue to practice until you feel confident. When you are ready, write the verse in Chinese characters and the meaning for each character in the spaces provided below:

Mā	wèn	jiào	yuǎn	cūn	,

Shuí	bào	lǐ	xiǎng	gēn	,

Jìn	shì	nǎi	pà	chí	,

Xiàng	yàng	zhōng	yóu	yùn	.

2. Look at the meaning, write its character in the first box, and say it aloud in Chinese before putting its *pinyin* transliteration in the second.

meaning	character	pinyin		meaning	character	pinyin
transport				manage		
far				compare		

root			ask		
village			mother		
near			embrace		
think			tardy		
fear			vision		
mail			appearance		
clock			resemble		
who			breast/milk		

3. Have your instructor dictate the characters or words covered in Chapter 14.

Chapter 15 第十五章
Questions and Answers About Learning Chinese Characters
有关汉字学习的问答

Congratulations on having learned the basic knowledge of Chinese characters presented in the previous 14 chapters. More congratulations to you if you have met all four challenges in these chapters. The previous 14 chapters were designed to help you lay a solid foundation of basic knowledge of Chinese characters, so you can learn to read and write Chinese with confidence. If you have already started to take a regular Chinese language course and have learned the Chinese phonetic system but have not yet taken Challenges 3 and 4 in each chapter, you should go back to Chapters 3-14 and take on Challenges 3 and 4. If you have not yet taken a Chinese language course, it is time for you to do so. This last chapter of the book addresses some important questions related to learning Chinese characters before you continue your Chinese language learning.

I. How should an unknown Chinese character be looked up in a Chinese dictionary?

There are two major kinds of Chinese dictionaries: Chinese character dictionaries and Chinese word dictionaries.[1] A character dictionary has characters as entries with pronunciation transcription, definition, and usage for each character. A word dictionary also has characters as entries, but under each character, all the words that start with the character are also listed as subentries, with pronunciation transcriptions, definitions, and usages. As these two major kinds of Chinese dictionaries both have characters as entries, they can be consulted in the same way.

The entries in these two major kinds of dictionaries are arranged alphabetically according to the *pinyin* spelling of the characters. Therefore, if you do not know how it looks or how to pronounce a character but know how to transcribe the pronunciation in *pinyin*, you can use the alphabetical order method. However, if you come across an unknown character and don't know how it sounds and what it means, you should then look it up by using the radical index provided in the dictionary.

Radicals are the strokes and side components by which the entries in a dictionary are categorized. The first Chinese dictionary, *An Analysis and Explanation of Characters* (《说文解字》), which was compiled by Xu Shen in the first century, had 540 radicals. *Jade Book* (《玉篇》), which as compiled by Gu Yewang in the fourth century by using characters in the regular script, had 542 radicals. However, *Collections of Characters* (《字汇》), which Mei Yingzuo completed compiling in 1615, reduced the number of

---

[1] A good example of a character dictionary is *Xinhua Dictionary* (《新华字典》), which is the most popular character dictionary used by native Chinese speakers. *Xinhua Dictionary with English Translation* (《汉英双解新华字典》) was first published by the Commercial Press International Co., LTD in China in 2000. A good example of a word dictionary is *The Contemporary Chinese Dictionary* (《现代汉语词典》), compiled by the Dictionary Department of the Institute of Linguistics at the Chinese Academy of Social Sciences. The Chinese-English Edition of *The Contemporary Chinese Dictionary* (《汉英双语现代汉语词典》) was·published by Foreign Language Teaching and Research Press in China in 2002.

radicals to 214 and for the first time ordered the characters for each radical based on stroke count. *Kangxi Dictionary* (《康熙字典》), which Zhang Yushu, Chen Tingjing, and others completed compiling in 1716, adopted this 214-radical system created by Mei Yingzuo. Dictionaries compiled since then have all used a similar system with about 200 radicals. *Xinhua Dictionary* (《新华字典》), the most popular character dictionary in China, and *The Contemporary Chinese Dictionary* (《现代汉语词典》), the most popular word dictionary in China, both have 189 radicals listed in their radical indexes according to the number of strokes each radical contains. Here are the 189 radicals:

一丨丿丶乙二十厂匚刂卜冂亻八人勹儿几亠冫冖讠卩阝²阝³凵刀
力厶又叒士土工扌艹寸廾大尢弋小口囗山巾彳彡犭夕夂饣忄广门氵忄
宀辶彐尸己弓子屮女马纟幺巛王韦木犬歹车戈比瓦止攴日曰贝水见牛
手毛气攵片斤爪父月欠风殳文方火斗灬户礻心聿毋示石龙业目田罒皿
钅矢禾白瓜用鸟疒立穴衤疋皮矛耒老耳臣西页虍虫缶舌竹臼自血舟衣
羊米艮羽糸麦走赤豆酉辰豕卤里足身采谷豸角言辛青其雨齿黾隹金鱼
革骨鬼食音門髟麻鹿黑鼠鼻 (189)

You can see that not all radicals are characters. Among the 189 radicals, 141 can be used alone as characters:

一乙二十厂卜八人儿几刀力厶又士土工寸大弋小口山巾广门尸己
弓子女马幺王韦木犬歹车戈比瓦止日曰贝水见牛手毛气片斤爪父月欠
风殳文方火斗户心毋示石龙业目田皿矢禾白瓜用鸟立穴疋皮矛耒老耳
臣页虫缶舌竹臼自血舟衣羊米艮羽糸麦走赤豆酉辰豕卤里足身采谷豸
角言辛青其雨齿黾隹金鱼革骨鬼食音門髟麻鹿黑鼠鼻 (141)

The remaining 48 are not used alone as characters since they are either strokes or dependent components (including the reduced forms of characters):

丨丿丶勹匚冂叒廾刂亻亠冫冖讠卩阝阝凵彐巛扌艹尢囗彳彡犭夕
夂饣忄氵忄宀辶纟屮攴灬礻聿罒钅疒衤西虍 (48)

Five of the 189 radicals are strokes, regardless of whether they can be used as characters or not:
1) The horizontal stroke (*héng*): 一
2) The vertical stroke (*shù*): 丨

---

² A reduced form of the character 阜 (mound) used as a left side component in a character.
³ A reduced form of the character 邑 (town) used as a right side component in a character.

3) The left-falling stroke (*piě*): 丿
4) The dot stroke (*diǎn*): 丶
5) A stroke with a turn (*zhé*), including: 乙, 乛, 亅, 𠃊

The 189 radicals in these two popular modern Chinese dictionaries head 189 sections in which characters containing those radicals are grouped.

Generally speaking, you look up an unknown character by going to the radical index, which will direct you to the appropriate page or entry in the character entry index. Then you must go to the character entry index and find the radical in question. For each radical in the character entry index, there is a list of characters that have the radical as part of their structure and the page number each character can be found in the dictionary.

A more detailed procedure for looking up an unknown Chinese character is as follows:

Step 1: Analyze the character and decide whether it is a single-component character or a multicomponent character. With the knowledge of characters you have learned so far, you have the ability to identify components in a character. If you can divide a character into two, it is a multicomponent character. There is no need to separate a character into more than two components, even though there can be more than two components. If you cannot break a character into two components, it is a single-component character.

Example: Are these characters single-component characters or multicomponent characters?

半, 用, 弋, 习, 药, 志, 点, 怎, 欢, 到, 退, 题, 坐, 因, 能.

Single-component Characters	
Multicomponent Characters	

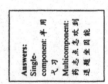

If you are sure the character you are trying to look up is a single-component character, then go to *Step 2a*; otherwise, go to *Step 2b*.

Step 2a: If you have a single-component character, then count the number of strokes it has. Look for this character in the radical index among the radicals with the same number of strokes. If it is indeed a radical in the dictionary, get the number next to it and go to *Step 6*. If not, go to *Step 3a*.

Example: What is the number of strokes for each of these single-component characters? Is each one of them listed as a radical in the *Xinhua Dictionary with English Translation*?[4] What step should be taken next for each of them?

---
[4] *Xinhua Dictionary with English Translation*, Commercial Press International Co., LTD, 2000.

	半	用	弋	习
Number of Strokes				
Radical or Not				
If it is a radical, the number next to it				
Go to Step#				

Answers:
半 5 No – 3a
用 5 Yes 70 6a
弋 3 Yes 46 6a
习 3 No – –

Step 3a: For those single-component characters that are not listed as radicals, you need to identify which is the first stroke in these characters because their first stroke will be their radical. Then go to *Step 4a*. If you do not know which is the first stroke, then go to *Step 7*.

Example: In *Step 2a*, you found that 习 and 半 were not listed as radicals in the dictionary. Now find out which is the first stroke in each of these two characters.

	半	习
The 1st stroke		

Answers:
半 丶 (diǎn)
习 乛 (zhé)

After you identify the first stroke, go to the next step: *Step 4a*. If you are not sure which is the first stroke, go directly to *Step 7*.

Step 4a: The first stroke serves as the radical for a single-component character that is not listed as a radical. Therefore, look for this one-stroke radical in the radical index and get the number next to it. With this number, go to *Step 5a*.

Example: As identified in *Step 3a*, the first stroke for 半 is 丶, and the first stroke for 习 is 乛. What is the page number given for each of these two one-stroke radicals in the radical index of the *Xinhua Dictionary with English Translation*?

Radical	丶	乛
Page number in the radical index		

Answers:
丶 34
乛 35

Step 5a: How many strokes are there left in a single-component character excluding the first stroke? For a character that uses its first stroke as its radical, you need to know the answer to the question. Then go to the next step: *Step 6*.

Example: How many strokes are there in 半 and 习 respectively, excluding the first stroke that is used as a radical?

	半	习
Number of strokes excluding the first stroke		

Answers:
半 4
习 2

After you answer the question, go to the next step: *Step 6*.

Step 2b: If a character is identified as a multicomponent character in *Step 1*, you must decide which component is a radical used in the dictionary. Most of the characters you have learned in Chapters 4-9 and the reduced forms of characters in Chapter 12 and other semantic components in Chapter 13 are listed as radicals in Chinese dictionaries. You already have the ability to tell which component might be a radical. The rule of thumb is that if a component looks familiar, it is very likely a radical. If you can see one radical in a character, go to *Step 4b*. If you see that the two components in a character can both be radicals, then go to *Step 3b*. If you find it difficult to identify a radical, even guided by what you have learned in this book, go to *Step 7*.

Example: You found, in *Step 1*, the following characters contain more than one component. Can you break each of the following characters into two major components? Can you also identify which component in each of the following characters is a radical? Finally, which step should you take next?

	药	志	点	怎	欢	到	退	题	坐	回	能
Component 1											
Component 2											
Radical 1											
Radical 2											
Go to Step#											

Answers:	药	志	点	怎	欢	到	退	题	坐	回	能
Component 1	艹	士	占	乍	又	至	艮	页	?	口	?
Component 2	约	心	灬	心	欠	刂	辶	是	?	口	?
Radical 1	艹	士	灬	心	又	刂	艮	页	?	口	?
Radical 2		心			欠		辶			口	?
Go to Step#	*4b*	*3b*	*4b*	*4b*	*3b*	*4b*	*3b*	*4b*	*7*	*3b*	*7*

Step 3b: If you divide a character into only two components and go no further, there can be three major layouts: top-bottom, left-right, outer-inner. When both components in a character can be radicals, you need to choose one according to the following rules: 1) choose the top component rather than the bottom, 2) choose the left component rather than the right, and 3) choose the outer component rather than the inner. Then go to *Step 4b*.

Example: Which is the radical in the following characters?

	志	欢	退	回	因
Component 1					
Component 2					
Which to choose?					

Answers:	志	欢	退	回	因
Component 1	士	又	艮	口	口
Component 2	心	欠	辶	口	大
Which to choose?	士	又	辶	口	口

After you answer the question, go to the next step: *Step 4b*.

Step 4b: Count the number of strokes in a radical, look it up in the radical index, and note the page number on the right. With this page number, go to *Step 5b*.

Example: How many strokes are there in each of the following radicals? What are the page numbers on the right of each in the *Xinhua Dictionary with English Translation*?

	药	志	点	怎	欢	到	退	题	回
Radical	艹	士	灬	心	又	刂	辶	页	口
Number of Strokes									
Page Number									

Answers:	药	志	点	怎	欢	到	退	题	回
Radical	艹	士	灬	心	又	刂	辶	页	口
# of Strokes	3	3	4	4	2	2	3	6	3
Page#	44	41	66	66	41	35	55	72	49

After you answer the questions, go to *Step 5b*.

Step 5b: Turn to the page you have found in *Step 4b*. Find the radical section on the page, and then count the number of strokes in the character, excluding the radical. Keep this number in mind and go to *Step 6*.

Step 5b is similar to *Step 5a* discussed earlier, and the only difference is that in *Step 5b*, you count the number of strokes in a multicomponent character, excluding the component that is the radical, while in *Step 5a*, you count the number of strokes in a single-component character, excluding the first stroke that serves as a radical.

Example: How many strokes are in each of the following characters, excluding the radical?

	药	志	点	怎	欢	到	退	题	回
Radical	艹	士	灬	心	又	刂	辶	页	口
Number of Strokes excluding the radical									

Answers:	药	志	点	怎	欢	到	退	题	回
Radical	艹	士	灬	心	又	刂	辶	页	口
# of Strokes excluding the radical	6	4	5	5	4	6	6	9	3

After you answer the question, go to the next step: *Step 6.*

Step 6: Turn to the page in the character entry index according to the page number you found in *Step 2a, Step 5a, or Step 5b*. Find the correct radical section on the page, and look for the character in the relevant subsection. In the character entry index, all characters are categorized by radical. The characters with the same radical are organized into subsections according to the number of strokes in the characters, excluding the radical. (If only a few characters share the same radical, there may be no subsections.) Once you find the character, observe the number to its right. This is the page number for the entry of the character in the dictionary. On that page, you can see pronunciation, definitions, and usage information for the character.

Example 1: If you use the *Xinhua Dictionary with English Translation,* on which page can you see the entry for each of the following single-component characters?

	半	用	弋	习
Page number for the character entry in the dictionary				

Answers:
半 18
用 780
弋 764
习 692

Example 2: On which page can you see the entry for each of the following characters in the *Xinhua Dictionary with English Translation?*

	药	志	点	怎	欢	到	退	题	回
Page number for the character entry in the dictionary									

Answers:	药	志	点	怎	欢	到	退	题	回
Page number for the character entry in the dictionary	754	846	129	814	263	118	659	640	269

Now you have learned to look up unknown single-component and multicomponent characters. If you have difficulty distinguishing the stroke or the radical, go to *Step 7.*

Step 7: When you do not know which is the first stroke in a single-component non-radical character, or when you come across a multicomponent character in which the radical is difficult to identify, you can use the stroke index provided after the character entry index. The characters in this index are arranged according to the number of strokes each character contains. Simply count the number of strokes in a character and look for it under the section for characters with the same number of strokes, but note the page number to the right. The entry for the character will appear on that page. Be careful not to jump to the conclusion that the character has no radical; the stroke index contains only some characters that are difficult to categorize, it does not have all the characters in the stroke index. Therefore, use the stroke index as the last resort.

Example: Assume that you do not know the first stroke or radical for the following characters: 半, 习, 也, 北, 能, 坐.   How many strokes are in each of the characters? Using the *Xinhua Dictionary with English Translation*, look up the character in the stroke index and find the page number for each of the character entries.

	半	习	也	北	能	坐
Number of strokes						
Page number for the character entry in the dictionary						

Answers:
半 5 18
习 3 692
也 3 756
北 5 26
能 10 476
坐 7 882

The following diagram shows the procedure for looking up a new character in a Chinese dictionary by using the radical index:

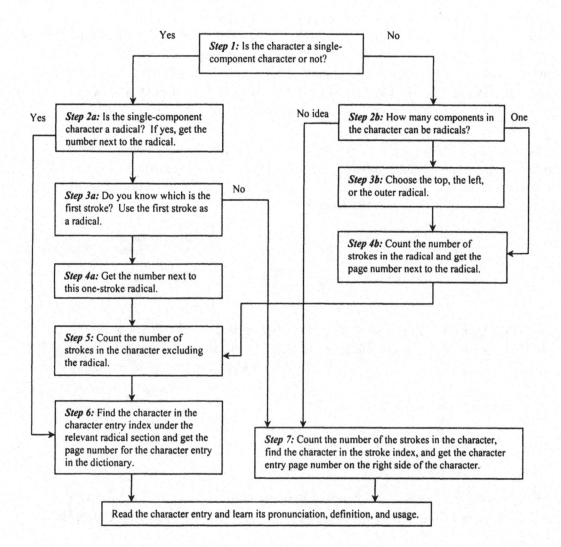

Yes   **Step 1:** Is the character a single-component character or not?   No

Step 2a: Is the single-component character a radical? If yes, get the number next to the radical.

No idea   **Step 2b:** How many components in the character can be radicals?   One

Step 3a: Do you know which is the first stroke? Use the first stroke as a radical.

No

Step 3b: Choose the top, the left, or the outer radical.

Step 4a: Get the number next to this one-stroke radical.

Step 4b: Count the number of strokes in the radical and get the page number next to the radical.

Step 5: Count the number of strokes in the character excluding the radical.

Step 6: Find the character in the character entry index under the relevant radical section and get the page number for the character entry in the dictionary.

Step 7: Count the number of the strokes in the character, find the character in the stroke index, and get the character entry page number on the right side of the character.

Read the character entry and learn its pronunciation, definition, and usage.

II. Are the printed forms of Chinese characters the same as the handwritten forms?

The printed forms of Chinese characters are different from their handwritten forms, even though the printed forms developed from the handwritten forms. Chinese characters were written by hand for thousands of years before they were carved on wood blocks and printed on paper. The normalized script, which is also referred to as "model script," is the style that most often resembles the forms written with a pointed Chinese brush pen. Chinese textbooks for elementary school pupils or books for childeren are all printed in the normalized regular script. However, newspapers, magazines, most books, and even dictionaries are printed in the Song style characters, first developed in the Song Dynasty (960-1279 A.D.) in China. The Song style characters have thick vertical strokes and slender horizontal strokes, and each character is printed in a precise square shape. Because Song style characters are commonly believed to cause less eye weariness than any other style, they are the most popular printed form today.

However, Song style characters should not be used as models for learning to write because they are typeset forms and not suited for handwriting. Although the two styles appear not to cause any recognition difficulty, they do confuse some learners when it comes to writing characters. The following seven major differences should be taken note of to eliminate possible confusion caused by the two different styles:

1) The horizontal stroke. In Song style characters, the horizontal stroke has a tiny yet noticeable triangle at the right end. The horizontal stroke in the model script (i.e., the normalized regular script) has no triangle at the end, and its left end is slightly lower than its right. Look at the following examples and compare:

Song Style	Model Script	Song Style	Model Script	Song Style	Model Script
一	一	王	王	立	立

2) The vertical stroke. In the Song style, the long vertical stroke is not as pointed as it is in the model script, and some short vertical strokes in the Song style appear as left-falling strokes in the model script. Look at the following examples and compare:

Song Style	Model Script	Song Style	Model Script	Song Style	Model Script	Song Style	Model Script
十	十	中	中	卅	艹	要	要

3) The left dot stroke. The left dot stroke in many characters in the model script becomes a left-falling stroke in the Song style. Look at the following examples and compare:

Song Style	Model Script	Song Style	Model Script	Song Style	Model Script
小	小	东	东	示	示

4) The horizontal stroke with a turn. The horizontal stroke with a turn in the Song style has a 90-degree angle formed by a horizontal stroke and a verticle stroke; whereas, in the model script, the angle formed by the horizontal and verticle strokes is often less than 90 degrees.

Song Style	Model Script	Song Style	Model Script	Song Style	Model Script
口	口	田	田	西	西

5) The horizontal stroke with a left-falling stroke and a curve. In the model script, this is the second stroke in the radical 辶. However, it becomes a horizontal stroke with a turn 辶 in Song style characters. Look at the following examples and compare:

Song Style	Model Script	Song Style	Model Script	Song Style	Model Script
辶	辶	近	近	远	远

6) Strokes inside a frame. In the model script, the radical 雨 (rain) has four dot strokes in its frame, whereas in the Song style, this radical has four short horizontal strokes. In the model script, the right end of the horizontal strokes in a frame are not linked with the right side of the frame as they are in Song style characters. Look at the following examples and compare:

Song Style	Model Script	Song Style	Model Script	Song Style	Model Script	Song Style	Model Script
雪	雪	雹	雹	目	目	月	月

7) The right rising stroke. In the model script, the radicals 氵 and 冫 both have a right-rising stroke. However, in the Song style, the right-rising stroke in these two radicals becomes somewhat like a tick or check mark.

Song Style	Model Script	Song Style	Model Script	Song Style	Model Script	Song Style	Model Script
氵	氵	冫	冫	酒	酒	冰	冰

III. What is calligraphy? Can my handwriting in Chinese be considered calligraphy?

Calligraphy is the art of beautiful handwriting. Chinese characters originated from drawings and are now formed by lines, dots, turns, and hooks. Writing with pointed brush pens, which were invented more than two thousand years ago in China, people may use different degrees of thickness, darkness, and firmness for strokes, and different degrees of density, size, and arrangement for characters in writing a piece in order to express themselves. Since the 18th century, people have also been using pencils, fountain pens, and ballpoint pens to write Chinese characters. If someone's handwriting is viewed as beautiful and is well liked and even imitated by a lot of people, he or she is a calligrapher. The handwriting of many noted calligraphers in Chinese history led to the creation and development of the seal script, the clerical script, the regular script, the normalized script, the semi-cursive script, and the cursive script, and they still influence the way we write Chinese characters today. Let's enjoy looking at some examples of beautiful handwriting.

(Normalized style with a hard pen)

休我悦道趾，

设饮祝初纱，

酒焦针苗笔，

那阴狱利罚。

(Semi-cursive style with a hard pen)

休我悦道趾，

设饮祝初纱，

酒焦针苗笔，

那阴狱利罚。

(Normalized style with a brush pen)

休找悦道趾，

设饮祝初纱，

酒焦针苗笔，

那阴狱利罚。

(Semi-cursive style with a brush pen)

休找悦道趾，

设饮祝初纱，

酒焦针苗笔，

那阴狱利罚。

　　You may have noticed that the same character verse has been written four times. The first two verses were written with a fountain pen, and the last two verses with a brush pen. If you look again, you can also see that all the characters in the first and third verses were written one stroke after another while the second and fourth verses have characters in which some strokes were connected. The writing style for the second and fourth verses is semi-cursive, as some strokes are connected and many others are not. In everyday life, Chinese people often write their letters, messages, memos, and even articles in this semi-cursive style. Some may even write some characters in a cursive style, in which almost all the strokes in a character are linked. What needs to be pointed out here is that writing characters in a cursive style remains of interest mostly to calligraphers, and its value is mainly artistic rather than practical today. Few people in China can recognize all characters written in a cursive style.

　　If you have learned to write characters in the standardized stroke order, you will be able to recognize semi-cursive characters with considerable ease, as strokes in a character are often naturally linked together when writing. However, if you wish to learn to write in the semi-cursive style, you should still imitate a model first because strokes cannot always be linked at will. When you practice writing characters, your handwriting is not calligraphic. However, after years of imitating a model and practicing, you can develop your own style. If your handwriting in your own style is viewed as beautiful and liked by many people, it will be considered calligraphy. Except for a few Japanese and Koreans, no one from countries other than China has attained the honor of being a recognized Chinese character calligrapher. I sincerely hope that you will become a Chinese character calligrapher, if not the first one. A lot of people can sing, but very few eventually become singers. Likewise, a lot of people can write Chinese characters, but few can become Chinese calligraphers.

IV. How should a new Chinese character be learned?

With the fundamental knowledge and basic skills for reading and writing Chinese characters you have acquired, you can learn new Chinese characters faster than those who have no such fundamental knowledge and skills.

The **fundamental knowledge** of Chinese characters you have learned from this book includes:

1) Knowledge of the origin and construction of Chinese characters (Chapter 1)
2) Knowledge of the historical development of Chinese characters (Chapter 1)
3) Knowledge of the characteristics of Chinese characters (Chapter 2)
4) Knowledge of all the basic and compound strokes used in writing Chinese characters (Chapters 2, 3)
5) Knowledge of the semantic components commonly used in Chinese characters (Chpaters 12, 13)
6) Knowledge of all the 229 characters covered in the book (Chapters 3-14)

The **basic skills** you have acquired by using this book include:

1) The ability to recognize and discuss the different scripts of Chinese characters
2) The ability to say the names of all strokes and write them correctly
3) The ability to recognize and write all of the 229 characters in the standardized stroke order;
4) The ability to recognize the semantic component (including reduced forms of basic characters) in an unfamiliar multicomponent character
5) The ability to separate an unfamiliar multicomponent character into at least two major components
6) The ability to figure out the stroke order for an unfamiliar Chinese character

If you already have the ability to speak some Chinese or if you are learning to speak Chinese while you are using this book, you are expected to have taken Challenge 3 and Challenge 4 in Chapters 3-14, and you should be able to say the 12 character verses aloud with correct pronunciation and intonation, and write these verses without referring to the models. If you can truly do that, learning more new Chinese characters should no longer be difficult. However, here are a few suggestions to help you learn more Chinese characters more efficiently and effectively, especially if you have not taken Challenge 3 and Challenge 4 in Chapters 3-14:

1) If you have not yet started to learn how to speak Chinese, you should start now. Every character has three important elements associated with it: sound, shape, and meaning. If you know what a character means and how it is written, that is great, but without knowing how it should be pronounced, your knowledge of the character is not complete. About 90 percent of Chinese characters are picto-phonetic, and 30 percent of these picto-phonetic characters still have accurate phonetic components. Knowing how to pronounce a character will facilitate learning other unfamiliar characters that contain the same phonetic component. Once you have learned the Chinese sound system and the *pinyin* (i.e., the Chinese phonetic alphabet), you should come back to take Challenge 3 and Challenge 4 in Chapters 3-14.

2) A new character should always be learned in context rather than in isolation. You have already learned enough basic characters to help you analyze and memorize other characters. In Chinese, a character may have more than one meaning; when you learn a character in context, it will help you remember the meaning of the character. A character learned out of context is more easily forgotten and has to be learned again. In modern Chinese, most words are formed with two characters; awareness of the relationship between the two characters, and of the meaning of the word in relation to the individual characters, will help you remember the meaning of the word and the characters that make it up.

3) Computer software programs may help you learn new Chinese characters. Well-designed computer software programs with multimedia features can often help learners memorize the pronunciation, shape, and meaning of new characters more effectively. Hearing how a character is pronounced frequently encourages one to pronounce the character in exactly the same way. Seeing how a character is structured and written stimulates one's desire to write it correctly in the same way. However, keep in mind that to be able to pronounce a character you must open your mouth to actually say it, and to be able to write a character you must use your hand to actually write it.

4) It is now quite popular to input Chinese characters on a computer screen by using an English keyboard. One can type the pronunciation in *pinyin* and choose the desired character from among the homonyms appearing on the screen. One can also type in Chinese characters by keying in the first letter of the name of a stroke or a side component in *pinyin*, or numbers that represent strokes and side components. However, if you want to learn to write Chinese characters, you should hold a pen in your hand and write it one stroke after another. Keyboard input methods were first developed for people who already know how to write Chinese characters. One may argue that it is increasingly common to use a keyboard to type Chinese characters, and that learning to write Chinese characters by hand is a waste of time. However, writing by hand remains a very useful skill. There is no doubt that computers can help us write efficiently and effectively, but they have not proved to be handy in many situations in our daily life such as filling out a paper form, leaving a note, writing an intimate letter, or writing at all

if the electric power fails. If the keyboard could eliminate writing by hand, elementary schools in the United States would have excluded handwriting from their curriculums a long time ago; however, there is no report of any elementary school abolishing writing in English by hand from their basic education. Writing Chinese characters by hand is a process, and going through this process facilitates the retention of learned Chinese characters. The experience of writing characters enhances the ability to use the keyboard to input Chinese characters. If you agree that the ability to write basic Chinese characters is the "horse" and that the ability to use the keyboard to input Chinese characters is the "cart," then you know which comes first.

Attached at the end of this book is the "List of Frequently Used Chinese Characters" issued by the Department of Chinese Characters of the National Language Commission of China in 1988. It contains the 2,500 most frequently used characters. The day you can recognize them, say them, write them, and use them is the day you can proudly say that you have become a master of the modern Chinese language. Good luck on your journey to learning the Chinese language!

Appendix: A List of 2,500 Frequently Used Characters
2,500 常用字表

This list is based on the "List of Frequently Used Chinese Characters" issued by the Department of Chinese Characters of the National Language Commission of China in 1988.

1 Stroke	Normalized Script	Complex Form	Semi-Cursive
yī	一		一
yǐ	乙		乙

2 Strokes	Normalized Script	Complex Form	Semi-Cursive
bā	八		八
bǔ (bo)	卜	(蔔)	卜
chǎn	厂	廠	厂
dāo	刀		刀
dīng	丁		丁
ér	儿	兒	儿
èr	二		二
jǐ (jǐ)	几	(幾)	几
jiǔ	九		九
le, liǎo (liào)	了	(瞭)	了
lì	力		力
nǎi	乃		乃
qī	七		七
rén	人		人
rù	入		入
shí	十		十
yòu	又		又

3 Strokes	Normalized Script	Complex Form	Semi-Cursive
cái	才	(纔)	才

	Normalized Script	Complex Form	Semi-Cursive
chā, chá, chǎ, chà	叉		叉
chuān	川		川
cùn	寸		寸
dà, dài	大		大
fán	凡		凡
fēi	飞	飛	飞
gān, gàn	干	(乾/幹)	干
gè	个	個	个
gōng	工		工
gōng	弓		弓
guǎng	广	廣	广
jí	及		及
jǐ	己		己
jīn	巾		巾
jiǔ	久		久
kǒu	口		口
kuī	亏	虧	亏
mǎ	马	馬	马
me	么	麼	么
mén	门	門	门
nǚ	女		女
qǐ	乞		乞
qiān	千		千
rèn	刃		刃
sān	三		三

Pinyin	Normalized Script	Complex Form	Semi-Cursive
shān	山		山
shàng	上		上
sháo	勺		勺
shī	尸	(屍)	尸
shì	士		士
tǔ	土		土
wán	丸		丸
wàn	万	萬	万
wáng	亡		亡
wèi	卫	衛	卫
xī	夕		夕
xí	习	習	习
xià	下		下
xiāng	乡	鄉	乡
xiǎo	小		小
yě	也		也
yǐ	已		已
yì	亿	億	亿
yì	义	義	义
yú	于	(於)	于
yǔ, yù	与	與	与
zhàng	丈		丈
zhī	之		之
zǐ, zi	子		子

4 Strokes

Pinyin	Normalized Script	Complex Form	Semi-Cursive
bā	巴		巴
bàn	办	辦	办
bèi	贝	貝	贝
bǐ	比		比
bì	币	幣	币

Pinyin	Normalized Script	Complex Form	Semi-Cursive
bù	不		不
cāng	仓	倉	仓
cháng, zhǎng	长	長	长
chē, jū	车	車	车
chǐ	尺		尺
chóu, qiú	仇		仇
chǒu	丑	(醜)	丑
cóng	从	從	从
dān	丹		丹
dìng	订	訂	订
dòu, dǒu	斗	(鬥)	斗
duì	队	隊	队
fá	乏		乏
fǎn	反		反
fāng	方		方
fēn, fèn	分		分
fēng	丰	(豐)	丰
fēng	风	風	风
fèng	凤	鳳	凤
fū	夫		夫
fù	父		父
gāng	冈	岡	冈
gōng	公		公
gōu	勾		勾
hù	互		互
hù	户		户
huà, huā	化		化
huàn	幻		幻
huǒ	火		火
jì	计	計	计
jiàn	见	見	见

Pinyin	Character	(Traditional)
jiè	介	
jīn	斤	
jīn	今	
jǐn	仅	僅
jǐng	井	
jù	巨	
kāi	开	開
kǒng	孔	
lì	历	歷/曆
liù	六	
máo	毛	
mù	木	
nèi	内	
niú	牛	
pǐ	匹	
piàn	片	
pú	仆	僕
qì	气	氣
qiàn	欠	
qiē, qiè	切	
qū, ōu	区	區
quǎn	犬	
quàn	劝	勸
rén	仁	
rèn	认	認
réng	仍	
rì	日	
shǎo, shào	少	
shén, shí	什	
shēng	升	(昇/陞)
shì	氏	

Pinyin	Character	(Traditional)
shǒu	手	
shū	书	書
shuāng	双	雙
shuǐ	水	
tài	太	
tiān	天	
tīng	厅	廳
tún	屯	
wǎ	瓦	
wáng	王	
wéi, wèi	为	為
wén	文	
wū	乌	烏
wú	无	無
wǔ	五	
wǔ	午	
wù	勿	
xīn	心	
xiōng	凶	(兇)
yá	牙	
yǐ	以	
yì	艺	藝
yì	忆	憶
yǐn	引	
yóu	尤	
yǒu	友	
yú	予	
yuán	元	
yuè	月	
yún	云	雲
yún	匀	

Pinyin	Normalized Script	Complex Form	Semi-Cursive
yǔn	允		允
zā, zhā	扎		扎
zhī	支		支
zhǐ	止		止
zhōng, zhòng	中		中
zhuǎ, zhǎo	爪		爪
zhuān	专	專	专

5 Strokes

Pinyin	Normalized Script	Complex Form	Semi-Cursive
bā, pá	扒		扒
bái	白		白
bàn	半		半
bāo	包		包
běi	北		北
běn	本		本
bì	必		必
biān	边	邊	边
bǐng	丙		丙
bù	布	(佈)	布
cè	册		册
chì	斥		斥
chū	出	(齣)	出
chù, chǔ	处	處	处
cōng	匆		匆
cóng	丛	叢	丛
dǎ, dá	打		打
dài	代		代
dàn	旦		旦
dāo	叨		叨
diàn	电	電	电
diāo	叼		叼

Pinyin	Normalized Script	Complex Form	Semi-Cursive
dīng	叮		叮
dōng	东	東	东
dōng	冬		冬
duì	对	(鑿)對	对
fā, fà	发	發/髮	发
fàn	犯		犯
fù	付		付
gān	甘		甘
gōng	功		功
gǔ	古		古
guā	瓜		瓜
guī	归	歸	归
hàn	汉	漢	汉
hào, háo	号	號	号
hé	禾		禾
hū	乎		乎
huì	汇	匯/彙	汇
jī	饥	飢/(饑)	饥
jí	击	擊	击
jì	记	記	记
jiā	加		加
jiǎ	甲		甲
jiào	叫		叫
jié	节	節	节
jiū	纠	糾	纠
jiù	旧	舊	旧
jù	句		句
kǎ, qiǎ	卡		卡
kān	刊		刊
kě	可		可
lán	兰	蘭	兰

Pinyin	Simplified	Traditional
lè, yuè	乐	樂
lǐ	礼	禮
lì	厉	厲
lì	立	
liáo	辽	遼
lìng	另	
lìng	令	
lóng	龙	龍
máo	矛	
men	们	們
miè	灭	滅
mín	民	
mò	末	
mǔ	母	
mù	目	
nǎi	奶	
ní	尼	
niǎo	鸟	鳥
níng, nìng	宁	寧
nú	奴	
pí	皮	
píng	平	
pū	扑	撲
qiǎo	巧	
qiě	且	
qiū	丘	
qù	去	
ràng	让	讓
rēng	扔	
shǎn	闪	閃
shēn	申	

Pinyin	Simplified	Traditional
shēng	生	
shèng	圣	聖
shī	失	
shí	石	
shǐ	史	
shì	示	
shì	世	
shì	市	
shù	术	術
shuǎi	甩	
shuài	帅	帥
sī	司	
sī	丝	絲
sì	四	
tā	他	
tā	它	(牠)
tái	台	(臺/檯/颱)
tàn	叹	嘆
tǎo	讨	討
tián	田	
tóu	头	頭
wài	外	
wèi	未	
wù	务	務
xiān	仙	
xiě	写	寫
xiōng	兄	
xué	穴	
xùn	训	訓
xùn	讯	訊

Pinyin	Normalized Script	Complex Form	Semi-Cursive
yāng	央		央
yè	业	業	业
yè	叶		叶
yí	仪	儀	仪
yì	议	議	议
yìn	印		印
yǒng	永		永
yòng	用		用
yóu	由		由
yòu	右		右
yòu	幼		幼
yù	玉		玉
yùn	孕		孕
zhá, yà	轧	(軋)	轧
zhàn, zhān	占	(佔)	占
zhàng	仗		仗
zhào	召		召
zhèng, zhēng	正		正
zhī	汁		汁
zhǐ, zhī	只	(隻/衹)	只
zhǔ	主		主
zǐ, zǎi	仔		仔
zuǒ	左		左

6 Strokes	Normalized Script	Complex Form	Semi-Cursive
ān	安		安
bǎi	百		百
bì	毕	畢	毕
bì	闭	閉	闭
bīng	冰		冰
bìng	并		并

Pinyin	Normalized Script	Complex Form	Semi-Cursive
chǎn	产	産	产
chǎng, cháng	场	場	场
chén	臣		臣
chén	尘	塵	尘
chéng	成		成
chī	吃		吃
chí	池		池
chí	驰	馳	驰
chōng, chòng	冲	衝/沖	冲
chōng	充		充
chóng	虫	蟲	虫
chuán, zhuàn	传	傳	传
chuǎng	闯	闖	闯
chuàng, chuāng	创	創	创
cǐ	此		此
cì	次		次
cún	存		存
dá	达	達	达
dāng, dàng	当	當/噹	当
dǎo	导	導	导
dēng	灯	燈	灯
dì, de	地		地
diào	吊		吊
diū	丢		丢
dòng	动	動	动
duō	多		多
duó	夺	奪	夺
duǒ	朵		朵
ér	而		而
ěr	耳		耳

fá	伐		伐
fān	帆		帆
fáng	防		防
fǎng	仿		仿
fǎng	访	訪	访
fèn	份		份
fěng	讽	諷	讽
fú	伏		伏
fù	负	負	负
fù	妇	婦	妇
gāng	刚	剛	刚
gè, gě	各		各
gǒng	巩	鞏	巩
gòng	共		共
guān	关	關	关
guān, guàn	观	觀	观
guāng	光		光
guǐ	轨	軌	轨
guò	过	過	过
hàn	汗		汗
hǎo, hào	好		好
hé	合	(閤)	合
hóng	红	(紅)	红
hòu	后	(後)	后
huá, huà	划	(劃)	划
huá, huà	华	華	华
huān	欢	歡	欢
huī	灰		灰
huí	回	(迴)	回
huì, kuài	会	(會)	会
huǒ	伙	(夥)	伙

jī	机	機	机
jī	肌		肌
jī	圾		圾
jí	吉		吉
jí	级	級	级
jì	纪	紀	纪
jiā, jiá	夹	夾	夹
jià	价	價	价
jiān	尖		尖
jiān	奸	(姦)	奸
jiàn	件		件
jiāng	江		江
jiǎng	讲	講	讲
jiàng	匠		匠
jiāo	交		交
jiē	阶	階	阶
jǐn, jìn	尽	儘/盡	尽
jué	决	決	决
jūn	军	軍	军
káng	扛		扛
kǎo	考		考
kòu	扣		扣
kuā	夸	誇	夸
kuò	扩	擴	扩
lǎo	老		老
liè	列		列
liè	劣		劣
liú	刘	劉	刘
lùn, lún	论	論	论
mā	妈	媽	妈
ma, má, mǎ	吗	嗎	吗

pinyin				pinyin			
mǎi	买	買	买	shī	师	師	师
mài	迈	邁	迈	shì	式		式
máng	芒		芒	shōu	收		收
máng	忙		长	shǒu	守		守
mǐ	米		米	sǐ	死		死
míng	名		名	sì	寺		寺
nà, nèi	那		那	sì, shì	似		似
nián	年		年	suì	岁	歲	岁
nóng	农	農	农	sūn	孙	孫	孙
pāng	兵		兵	tā	她		她
pīng	乒		乒	tāng	汤	湯	汤
pǔ, piáo, pō, pò	朴	(樸)	朴	tóng	同		同
qí	齐	齊	乔	tǔ, tù	吐		吐
qǐ	岂	豈	岂	tuán	团	團/糰	团
qì	企		企	tuō	托		托
qiān	迁	遷	近	wǎng	网	網	网
qiáo	乔	喬	乔	wàng	妄		妄
qìng	庆	慶	庆	wēi	危		危
qǔ, qū	曲		曲	wěi	伟	偉	伟
quán	权	權	权	wěi	伪	偽	伪
quán	全		全	wèn	问	問	问
rèn, rén	任		任	wū	污		污
ròu	肉		肉	wǔ	伍		伍
rú	如		如	xī	西		西
sǎn	伞	傘	伞	xī	吸		吸
sǎo, sào	扫	掃	扫	xì	戏	戲	戏
sè, shǎi	色		色	xià, hè	吓	嚇	吓
shā	杀	殺	杀	xiān	先		先
shāng	伤	傷	伤	xiān, qiàn	纤	纖/縴 (嬼)	纤
shé	舌	舌	舌	xiàng	向		向
shè	设	設	设	xié	协	協	协

Pinyin	Normalized Script	Complex Form	Semi-Cursive
xié	邪		邪
xíng	刑		刑
xíng, háng	行		行
xìng, xīng	兴	興	兴
xiū	休		休
xiǔ	朽		朽
xǔ	许	許	许
xuè, xiě	血		血
xún	旬		旬
xún	寻	尋	寻
xún	巡		巡
xùn	迅		迅
yā	压	壓	压
yà	亚	亞	亚
yán	延		延
yàn	厌	厭	厌
yáng	扬	揚	扬
yáng	羊		羊
yáng	阳	陽	阳
yǎng	仰		仰
yé	爷	爺	爷
yè	页	頁	页
yī	衣		衣
yì	亦		亦
yì	异		异
yīn	因		因
yīn	阴	陰	阴
yōu	优	優	优
yǒu	有		有
yǔ	屿	嶼	屿
yǔ	宇		宇

Pinyin	Normalized Script	Complex Form	Semi-Cursive
yǔ	羽		羽
yuē	约	約	约
zá	杂	雜	杂
zài	再		再
zài	在		在
zǎo	早		早
zé	则	則	则
zhái	宅		宅
zhào	兆		兆
zhēn	贞	貞	贞
zhèn	阵	陣	阵
zhēng	争	爭	争
zhī	芝		芝
zhí	执	執	执
zhǐ	旨		旨
zhì	至		至
zhòng	众	眾	众
zhōu	舟		舟
zhōu	州		州
zhū	朱		朱
zhú	竹		竹
zhuāng	庄	莊	庄
zhuàng	壮	壯	壮
zì	自		自
zì	字		字

7 Strokes	Normalized Script	Complex Form	Semi-Cursive
ā, ē	阿		阿
bǎ, bà	把		把
bà	坝	壩	坝
ba	吧		吧

Pinyin	简	繁
bàn	扮	
bàn	伴	
bào	报	報
bié, biè	别	
bīng	兵	
bó	伯	
bó	驳	駁
bǔ	补	補
bù	步	
cái	材	
cái	财	財
càn	灿	燦
cāng	苍	蒼
céng	层	層
chà	岔	
cháng	肠	腸
chāo	抄	
chǎo	吵	
chě	扯	
chè	彻	徹
chén	辰	
chén	沉	
chén	陈	陳
chéng	呈	
chí	迟	遲
chì	赤	
chū	初	
chuàn	串	
chuáng	床	
chuī	吹	
chún	纯	純

Pinyin	简	繁
cí	词	詞
	(獸)	
cūn	村	
dāi	呆	
dàn	但	
dǎo	岛	島
dī	低	
dì	弟	
dīng	盯	
dīng, dìng	钉	釘
dòng	冻	凍
dǒu	抖	
dòu	豆	
dù	杜	
dù, dǔ	肚	
dūn	吨	噸
fǎn	返	
fàn	饭	飯
fàn	泛	
fāng	芳	
fāng	坊	
fǎng	妨	
fǎng	纺	紡
fēn	芬	
fēn	吩	
fēn	纷	紛
fēn	坟	墳
fó, fú	佛	
fǒu	否	
fú	扶	
fǔ	抚	撫
fù	附	

拼音	简体	繁体
gǎi	改	
gān, gǎn	杆	
gān	肝	
gāng	岗	崗
gāng	纲	綱
gàng	杠	
gào	告	
gèng, gēng	更	
gōng	攻	
gòng	贡	貢
gōu	沟	溝
gū	估	
gǔ	谷	(穀)
guī	龟	龜
hái, huán	还	還
hán	含	
hàn	旱	
hé	何	
hóng	宏	
hǒu	吼	
hù	护	護
huā	花	花
huái	怀	懷
huài	坏	壞
jī	鸡	雞
jí	极	極
jí	即	
jì	技	
jì	忌	
jì	际	際
jiān	歼	殲

拼音	简体	繁体
jiān	坚	堅
jiān, jiàn	间	間
jiǎo, jué	角	
jié	劫	
jiè	戒	
jìn	进	進
jìn	近	
jìn	劲	勁
jiù	究	
jú	局	
jù	拒	
jūn	均	
jūn	君	
kàng	抗	
ké, qiào	壳	殼 (剋)
kè	克	
kēng	坑	
kù	库	庫
kuài	块	塊
kuài	快	
kuáng	狂	
kuàng	旷	曠
kuàng	况	況 (眍)
kuàng	况	
kùn	困	
lái	来	來
láo	劳	勞
láo	牢	
lěng	冷	
lǐ	李	
lǐ	里	(裏/裡)
lì	丽	麗

pinyin	简	繁
lì	励	勵
lì	利	利
lián	连	連
liáng	良	良
liǎng	两	兩
liáo	疗	療
lín	邻	鄰
líng	伶	伶
líng	灵	靈
lú	芦	蘆
lù	陆	陸
lú	驴	驢
luǎn	卵	卵
luàn	乱	亂
mài	麦	麥
méi, mò	没	沒
měi	每	每
mèn, mēn	闷	悶
miǎn	免	免
miào	妙	妙
mǔ	亩	畝
nà	纳	納
nán	男	男
nǐ	你	你
niào	尿	尿
niǔ	扭	扭
niǔ	纽	紐
nòng, lòng	弄	弄
nǔ	努	努
pàn	判	判
pāo	抛	抛

pinyin	简	繁
pī	批	批
píng	评	評
qǐ	启	啟
qì	弃	弃
qì	汽	汽
qiǎng	抢	搶
qín	芹	芹
qióng	穷	窮
qiú	求	求
qū	驱	驅
què	却	卻
rǎo	扰	擾
rěn	忍	忍
shā	沙	沙
shā	纱	紗
shān	删	刪
shè	社	社
shēn	伸	伸
shēn	身	身
shěn	沈	沈
shēng	声	聲
shí	时	時
shí	识	識
shòu	寿	壽
shù	束	束
sī	私	私
sòng	宋	宋
sū	苏	蘇
sù	诉	訴
tán	坛	壇/罎
tǐ	体	體

tiáo	条		條	余	yán	言	言
tīng	听		廳	听	yáng	杨	杨
tóu	投			投	yāo	妖	妖
tū	秃			秃	yě	冶	冶
tūn	吞			吞	yī	医	醫 医
tuǒ	妥			妥	yì	役	役
wán	完			完	yì	译	譯 译
wāng	汪			汪	yì	饮	飲 饮
wàng	忘			忘	yǐn, yìn	应	應 应
wéi	违	違		违	yīng, yìng	迎	迎
wéi	围	圍		围	yíng	佣	傭 佣
wěi	尾			尾	yòng	忧	憂 忧
wèi	位			位	yōu	邮	郵 邮
wén	纹	紋		纹	yóu	犹	猶 犹
wǒ	我			我	yóu	余	(餘) 余
wò	沃			沃	yú	园	園 园
wū	呜	嗚		呜	yuán	员	員 员
wú	吴			吴	yuán	远	遠 远
xī	希			希	yuǎn	运	運 运
xì, jì	系	(係/繫)		系	yùn	灾	灾
xián	闲	閒		闲	zāi	皂	皂
xiàn	县	縣		县	zào	灶	竈 灶
xiào	孝			孝	zào	张	張 张
xīn	辛			辛	zhāng	帐	帳 帐
xíng	形			形	zhàng	找	找
xìng	杏			杏	zhǎo	折	折
xiù	秀			秀	zhé, shé, zhē	这	這 这
xù	序			序	zhè, zhèi	针	針 针
ya, yā	呀			呀	zhēn	诊	診 诊
yá	芽	芽		芽	zhēn	证	證 证
yán	严	嚴		严	zhèng	址	址
					zhǐ		

Pinyin	Normalized Script	Complex Form	Semi-Cursive
zhǐ	纸		纸
zhì	志		志
zhù	助		助
zhù	住		住
zhuā	抓		抓
zhuàng	状	狀	状
zòng	纵	縱	纵
zǒu	走		走
zú	足		足
zǔ	阻		阻
zuò, zuō	作		作
zuò	坐		坐

8 Strokes

Pinyin	Normalized Script	Complex Form	Semi-Cursive
àn	岸		岸
áng	昂		昂
bá	拔		拔
bà	爸		爸
bài	败	敗	败
bǎn	板		板
bǎn	版		版
bàn	拌		拌
bǎo	饱	飽	饱
bǎo	宝	寶	宝
bào	抱		抱
bēi	杯		杯
bèi	备	備	备
bēn, bèn	奔		奔
bǐ	彼		彼
biàn	变	變	变
biǎo	表		表

Pinyin	Normalized Script	Complex Form	Semi-Cursive
bō	拨	撥	拨
bō	波		波
bó	泊		泊
bù	怖		怖
cǎi	采		采
cān, cēn, shēn	参	參	参
cè	厕	廁	厕
cè	侧	側	侧
chāi	拆		拆
chāng	昌		昌
chàng	畅	暢	畅
chǎo	炒		炒
chèn	衬	襯	衬
chéng	诚	誠	诚
chéng	承		承
chǐ	齿	齒	齿
chōu	抽		抽
chuī	炊		炊
chuí	垂		垂
cì	刺		刺
dān, dàn	担	擔	担
dān, shàn, chán	单	單	单
dàn	诞	誕	诞
dào	到		到
de, dì	的		的
dǐ	抵		抵
dǐ	底		底
diǎn	典		典
diàn	店		店
diào	钓	釣	钓

Pinyin	Simplified	Traditional
dǐng	顶	
dìng	定	
fǎ	法	
fàn	范	(範)
fàn	贩	販
fǎng	房	
fàng	放	
fēi	非	
féi	肥	
fèi	肺	
fèi	废	廢
fèi	沸	
fèn	奋	奮
fēng	奉	
fū	肤	膚
fú	服	
fǔ	斧	
fǔ	府	
fù	咐	
gāi	该	該
gǎn	秆	
gōng, gòng	供	
gǒu	狗	
gòu	构	構
gòu	购	購
gū	孤	
gū	姑	
gǔ	股	
gù	固	
guā	刮	(颳)
guāi	乖	

Pinyin	Simplified	Traditional
guǎi	拐	
guài	怪	
guān	官	
guàn	贯	貫
guī	规	規
guì	柜	櫃
guó	国	國
guǒ	果	
hé, hè, huó, huò, hú	和	
hé	河	
hōng	轰	轟
hū	呼	
hū	忽	
hú	狐	
hǔ	虎	
huà	画	畫
huà	话	話
huán	环	環
hūn	昏	
huò	或	
huò	货	貨
jì	季	
jì	剂	劑
jiā	佳	
jià	驾	駕
jiān	肩	
jiān	艰	艱
jiǎn	拣	揀
jiàn	建	
jiàng, xiáng	降	

pinyin				pinyin			
jiāo	郊		郊	liàn	练	練	练
jié	杰	(傑)	杰	lín	林		林
jiě	姐		姐	lǐng	岭	嶺	岭
jiè	届		届	lǒng	拢	攏	拢
jīn	金		金	lǒng	垄	壟	垄
jīng	茎	莖	茎	lú	炉	爐	炉
jīng	京		京	lǔ	虏	虜	虏
jīng	经	經	经	lù	录	錄/彔	录
jìng	径	徑	径	lún	轮	輪	轮
jìng	净	淨	净	luó	罗	羅	罗
jū	拘		拘	mǎ	码	碼	码
jū	居		居	mài	卖	賣	卖
jù	具		具	máng	盲		盲
juàn, juǎn	卷	(捲)	卷	máo	茅	茅	茅
kǎi	凯	(凱)	凯	mào	茂	茂	茂
kàng	炕		炕	mèi	妹		妹
kè	刻		刻	mèng	孟		孟
kěn	肯		肯	miáo	苗	苗	苗
kōng	空		空	miào	庙	廟	庙
kǔ	苦	苦	苦	míng	明		明
kuàng	矿	礦	矿	míng	鸣	鳴	鸣
kūn	昆		昆	mìng	命		命
lā	拉		拉	mǒ, mò, mā	抹		抹
lā	垃		垃	mò	沫		沫
lán	拦	攔	拦	mù	牧		牧
láng	郎		郎	nào	闹	鬧	闹
lèi	泪		泪	ne, ní	呢		呢
lì	例		例	ní	泥		泥
lì	隶	(隸)	隶	niàn	念		念
lián	帘	(簾)	帘	ōu	欧	歐	欧
lián	怜	憐	怜	pá	爬		爬

pà	怕		怕	shào	绍	紹
pāi	拍		拍	shě, shè	舍	(捨)
pào, pāo	泡		泡	shěn	审	審
pèi	佩		佩	shèn	肾	腎
péng	朋		朋	shī	诗	詩
pī	披		披	shí	实	實
pín	贫	貧	貧	shǐ	使	使
píng	苹	(蘋)	苹	shǐ	始	始
píng	凭	憑	凭	shǐ	驶	駛
pō	坡		坡	shì	势	勢
pō	泼	潑	泼	shì	事	事
pò, pǎi	迫		迫	shì	侍	侍
qī	妻		妻	shì	饰	飾
qí	其		其	shì	试	試
qí, jī	奇		奇	shì	视	視
qiǎn	浅	淺	浅	shòu	受	受
qiāng	枪	槍	枪	shú	叔	叔
qiáo	侨	僑	侨	shù	述	述
qié, jiā	茄	茄	茄	shuā	刷	刷
qīng	青		青	sì	饲	飼
qǐng	顷	頃	顷	sōng	松	(鬆)
qū	屈		屈	sù	肃	肅
qǔ	取		取	suǒ	所	所
quàn	劝		劝	tái	抬	抬
rǔ	乳		乳	tài	态	態
ruǎn	软	軟	软	tān	贪	貪
ruò	若	若	若	tǎn	坦	坦
sàng	丧	喪	丧	tiē, tiě, tiè	帖	帖
shān	衫	衫	衫	tú	图	圖
shǎn	陕	陝	陕	tù	兔	兔
shàng	尚		尚	tuō	拖	拖

pinyin	字	变体	行书
tuó	驼	骆	驼
wán	玩		玩
wǎng	往		往
wàng	旺		旺
wěi	委		委
wèi	味		味
wò	卧		卧
wǔ	武		武
wù	物		物
xī	析		析
xì	细	细	细
xián	贤	贤	贤
xián	弦		弦
xiàn	现	现	现
xiàn	限		限
xiàn	线	綫	线
xiáng	详	详	详
xiǎng	享		享
xiē	些		些
xié	胁		胁
xiè	泄		泄
xiè	泻	瀉	泻
xīn	欣		欣
xìng	幸		幸
xìng	性		性
xìng	姓		姓
xué	学	學	学
xún	询	詢	询
yā	押		押
yán	岩		岩
yán	炎		炎

pinyin	字	变体	行书
yán	沿		沿
ye	夜		夜
yī	依		依
yí	宜		宜
yì	易		易
yīng	英	英	英
yōng	拥	擁	拥
yǒng	咏		咏
yǒng	泳		泳
yóu	油		油
yú	鱼	鱼	鱼
yǔ	雨		雨
yù	育		育
zǎo	枣	棗	枣
zé	责	责	责
zé	择	择	择
zé	泽	泽	泽
zhá	闸	闸	闸
zhān	沾		沾
zhǎn	斩	斩	斩
zhàng	胀	脹	胀
zhāo	招		招
zhě	者		者
zhēn	侦	侦	侦
zhěn	枕		枕
zhēng	征		征
zhèng	郑	(徵)郑	郑
zhī	枝		枝
zhī	知		知
zhī	肢		肢
zhī	织	織	织

	Normalized Script	Complex Form	Semi-Cursive		Normalized Script	Complex Form	Semi-Cursive
zhí	直		直	biāo	标	標	标
zhí	侄		侄	bǐng	柄		柄
zhì	质	質	质	bǐng	饼	餅	饼
zhì	帜	幟	帜	bō	玻		玻
zhì	制	(製)	制	cán	残	殘	残
zhì	治		治	cǎo	草		草
zhōng	忠		忠	cè	测	測	测
zhōng	终	終	终	chá	茶		茶
zhǒng	肿	腫	艸	chá	查		查
zhōu	周	(週)	周	chà, chā, cì	差		差
zhòu	宙		宙	cháng	尝	嘗	尝
zhù	注	(註)	注	chāo	钞	鈔	钞
zhù	驻	駐	驻	chéng	城		城
zhuǎn	转	轉	转	chí	持		持
zōng	宗		宗	chú	除		除
zǔ	组	組	组	chuān	穿		穿
				chuāng	疮	瘡	疮
9 Strokes				chūn	春		春
āi	哀		哀	cù	促		促
àn	按		按	dài	带	帶	带
ǎo	袄	襖	袄	dài	贷	貸	贷
bā	疤		疤	dài	待		待
bǎi, bó	柏		柏	dài	怠		怠
bài	拜		拜	dǎn	胆	膽	胆
bāng	帮	幫	帮	dǎng	挡	擋	挡
bǎng	绑	綁	绑	dàng	荡	蕩	荡
bāo	胞		胞	dì	帝		帝
bǎo	保		保	diǎn	点	點	点
bèi, bēi	背		背	diàn	垫	墊	垫
biǎn	扁		扁	dòng	栋	棟	栋
biàn, pián	便		便	dòng	洞		洞

pinyin			pinyin		
dǒu	陡		hěn	很	
dú	毒		hěn	狠	
dú	独	獨	hèn	恨	
dù, duó	度		héng	恒	
duàn	段		hóng	虹	
dùn	盾		hóng	洪	
fá	罚	罰	hǒng, hōng	哄	
fá	阀	閥	hòu	厚	
fèi	费	費	hú	胡	
fēng	封		huá	哗	(嘩)
fēng	疯	瘋	huāng	荒	
fú	俘		huáng	皇	
fù	赴		huī	挥	揮
fù	复	(復/複)	huī	恢	
gān	竿		huì	绘	繪
gāng	钢	鋼	hún	浑	渾
gāng	缸		huó	活	
gé	革		jí	急	
gé	阁	閣	jǐ	挤	擠
gěi, jǐ	给	給	jì	迹	(跡/蹟)
gōng	宫		jì, jǐ	济	濟
gōu	钩	鈎	jì	既	
gú	骨		jià	架	
gù	故		jiǎn	茧	繭
guà	挂		jiǎn	俭	儉
guān, guàn	冠		jiàn	荐	薦
guǐ	鬼		jiàn	贱	賤
guì	贵	貴	jiàn	剑	劍
hā, hǎ	哈		jiāng	将	將 (薑)
hái	孩		jiāng	姜	
hè	贺	賀	jiǎng	奖	獎

pinyin				pinyin			
jiāo	浇		浇	lèi	类	類	类
jiāo	娇	嬌	娇	lí	厘		厘
jiāo	骄	驕	骄	liàn	炼	(鏨)煉	炼
jiǎo	狡		狡	liǎng, liǎ	俩	倆	俩
jiǎo	饺	餃	饺	liàng	亮		亮
jiǎo	绞	絞	绞	lín	临	臨	临
jiē	皆		皆	liǔ	柳		柳
jié	洁	潔	洁	luò	络	絡	络
jié	结	結	结	luò	骆	駱	骆
jiè	界		界	lù	律		律
jīn	津		津	mǎ, mà	蚂	螞	蚂
jǔ	矩		矩	mà	骂	罵	骂
jǔ	举	舉	举	mài	脉		脉
jué, jiào	觉	覺	觉	máng	茫		茫
jué	绝	絕	绝	mào	冒		冒
jùn	俊		俊	mào	贸	貿	贸
kǎn	砍		砍	méi	眉		眉
kàn, kān	看		看	měi	美		美
kē	科		科	mí	迷		迷
ké, hāi	咳		咳	miǎn	勉		勉
kè	客		客	miàn	面	(麵)	面
kěn	垦	墾	垦	miǎo	秒		秒
kū	枯		枯	mǒu	某		某
kuǎ	垮		垮	nǎ, něi, na, né	哪		哪
kuà	挎		挎	nài	耐		耐
kuò	括		括	nán	南		南
lán	栏	欄	栏	náo	挠	撓	挠
lǎn	览	覽	览	nǎo	恼	惱	恼
làn	烂	爛	烂	nì	逆		逆
lǎo	姥		姥	nóng	浓	濃	浓
lěi	垒	壘	垒	nù	怒		怒

nuó	挪	挪		shěng, xǐng	省	省
pā	趴	趴		shèng	胜	胜
pài	派	派		shī	狮	狮
pàn	盼	盼		shī	施	施
pàn	叛	叛		shí	拾	拾
pàng, pán	胖	胖		shí	食	食
pào	炮	炮		shí	蚀	蚀
pén	盆	盆		shì	柿	柿
pīn	拼	拼		shì	是	是
pǐn	品	品		shì	室	室
qì	砌	砌		shì	适	适 (適)
qià	洽	洽		shǒu	首	首
qià	恰	恰		shù	树	树
qiān	牵	牵		shù	竖	竖
qián	前	前		shuǎ	耍	耍
qiè	窃	窃		shuān	拴	拴
qīn	侵	侵		shùn	顺	顺
qīn, qìng	亲	親	亲	shuō, shuì	说	说
qīng	轻	輕	轻	sī	思	思
qiū	秋	秋		sòng	送	送
quán	泉	泉		sòng	诵	诵
rǎn	染	染		sú	俗	俗
ráo	饶	饶		suī	虽	虽
rào	绕	繞	绕	tàn	炭	炭
róng	荣	榮	荣	táo	逃	逃
róng	绒	絨	绒	tì	剃	剃
róu	柔	柔		tiāo, tiǎo	挑	挑
sǎ	洒	灑	洒	tiē	贴	贴
shén	神	神		tíng	亭	亭
shèn	甚	甚		tíng	庭	庭
shēng	牲	牲		tǐng	挺	挺

Pinyin	Simplified	Traditional
tǒng	统	統
tū	突	
tuì	退	
wā	挖	
wá	娃	
wāi	歪	
wān	弯	彎
wēi	威	
wèi	畏	
wèi	胃	
wén	闻	聞
wū	屋	
wǔ	侮	
wù	误	誤
xǐ	洗	
xiā	虾	蝦
xiá	峡	峽
xiá	狭	狹
xián	咸	(鹹)
xiǎn	显	顯
xiǎn	险	險
xiàn	宪	憲
xiāo, xuē	削	
xiāng, xiàng	相	
xiāng	香	
xiǎng	响	響
xiàng	项	項
xiàng, hàng	巷	
xiè	卸	
xìn	信	
xīng	星	

Pinyin	Simplified	Traditional
xíng	型	
xiū	修	
xū	须	須/鬚
xù	叙	
xuān	宣	
xuǎn	选	選
yā	鸦	鴉
yǎ	哑	
yán	研	
yān, yàn, yè	咽	
yāng	殃	
yáng	洋	
yǎng	养	養
yǎo	咬	
yào	药	藥
yào	要	
yào, yuè	钥	钥/鑰
yí	姨	
yǐ	蚁	蟻
yì	疫	
yīn	音	
yīn	姻	
yíng	盈	
yìng	映	
yǒng	勇	
yòu	诱	誘
yǔ	语	語
yù	狱	獄
yuàn	怨	
yuàn	院	

Pinyin	Normalized Script	Complex Form	Semi-Cursive
zán	咱		咱
zěn	怎		怎
zhá, zhà	炸		炸
zhǎ	眨		眨
zhàn	战	戰	战
zhào	赵	趙	赵
zhēn	珍		珍
zhèng	政		政
zhèng	挣	掙	挣
zhǐ	指		指
zhōng	钟	鐘/鍾	钟
zhǒng, zhòng	种	(種)	种
zhòng, chóng	重		重
zhōu	洲		洲
zhòu	昼	晝	昼
zhù	柱		柱
zhù	祝		祝
zhuān	砖	磚	砖
zhuī	追		追
zhuó	浊	濁	浊
zī	姿		姿
zǒng	总	總	总
zòu	奏		奏
zǔ	祖		祖
zuó	昨		昨

10 Strokes	Normalized Script	Complex Form	Semi-Cursive
ā, á, ǎ, à	啊		啊
āi, ái	挨		挨
āi, ài	唉		唉

Pinyin	Normalized Script	Complex Form	Semi-Cursive
ài	爱	愛	爱
àn	案		案
bà	罢	罷	罢
bān	班		班
bān	般		般
bèi	倍		倍
bèi	被		被
bǐ	笔	筆	笔
bì	毙	斃	毙
bīn	宾	賓	宾
bìng	病		病
bō, bāo	剥		剥
bǔ	捕		捕
bù	部		部
cán	蚕	蠶	蚕
cāng	舱	艙	舱
chái	柴		柴
chàng	倡		倡
chēng, chèn	称	稱	称
chéng	乘		乘
chèng	秤		秤
chǐ	耻		耻
chì	翅		翅
chòu	臭		臭
chǔ	础	礎	础
chù, xù	畜		畜
chún	唇		唇
cuì	脆		脆
dān	耽		耽
dǎng	档	檔	档
dǎng	党	黨	党

dǎo, dào	倒		倒	hài	害	害
dí	敌	敵	敌	háng	航	航
dì	递	遞	递	hào	耗	耗
diào, tiáo	调	調	调	hào	浩	浩
diē	爹		爹	hé, hè	荷	荷
dōu, dū	都		都	hé	核	核
dòu	逗		逗	hōng	烘	烘
dú, dòu	读	讀	读	hòu	候	候
dùn	顿	頓	顿	hú	壶	壺	壺
è, ě, wù	恶	恶	恶	huàn	换	换
è	饿	餓	饿	huàn	唤	唤
ēn	恩	恩	恩	huǎng, huàng	晃	晃
fán	烦	煩	烦	huǐ	悔	悔
fěi	匪	匪	匪	huì	贿	賄	贿
fěn	粉	粉	粉	huò	获	獲/穫	获
fēng	峰	峰	峰	jī	积	積	积
féng	逢	逢	逢	jí	脊	脊
fú	浮	浮	浮	jí	疾	疾
fǔ	俯	俯	俯	jì	继	繼	继
gǎn	赶	趕	赶	jiā	家	家
gāo	高	高	高	jiān, jiàn	监	監	监
gē	哥	哥	哥	jiān	兼	兼
gē	胳	胳	胳	jiǎn	捡	撿	捡
gé	格	格	格	jiàn	健	健
gēn	根	根	根	jiàn	舰	艦	舰
gēng	耕	耕	耕	jiāng	浆	漿	浆
gōng	恭	恭	恭	jiǎng	桨	槳	桨
gōng	躬	躬	躬	jiāo	胶	膠	胶
gù	顾	顧	顾	jiào	轿	轎	轿
guì	桂	桂	桂	jiào	较	較	较
hǎi	海	海	海	jiè	借	(藉)	借

jǐn	紧	紧	liè	烈		烈
jìn	晋	晋	líng	铃	铃	铃
jìn	浸	浸	líng	陵		陵
jìng	竞	竞	liú	留		留
jiǔ	酒	竞 酒	liú	流		流
jù	俱	俱	lǔ	旅		旅
jù	剧	剧 剧	lù	虑	虑	虑
juān	捐	捐	mái, mán	埋		埋
juàn	倦	倦	mì	秘		秘
juàn	绢	绢 绢	mián	眠		眠
kǎo	烤	烤	mò	莫	莫	莫
kè	课	课 课	ná	拿		拿
kěn	恳	恳 懇	nán, nàn	难	难	难
kǒng	恐	恐	nǎo	脑	脑	脑
kū	哭	哭	néng	能		能
kuān	宽	宽 宽	niáng	娘		娘
kuàng	框	框	niē	捏		捏
kǔn	捆	捆	páng	旁		旁
láng	狼	狼	páo	袍		袍
lǎng	朗	朗	péi	陪		陪
làng	浪	浪	pèi	配		配
lāo	捞	捞 捞	pí	疲		疲
lào	涝	涝 涝	píng	瓶		瓶
lí	狸	狸	pò	破		破
lí	离	离	pōu	剖		剖
lì	栗	栗	qǐ	起		起
lián	莲	莲 蓮	qiān	铅	铅	铅
liàn	恋	恋 戀	qián	钱	钱	钱
liáng, liàng	凉	凉	qián	钳	钳	钳
liàng	谅	谅 谅	qiāo	悄		悄
liào	料	料 料	qiáo	桥	桥	桥

Pinyin	简	繁	繁
qīng	倾	倾	倾
qǐng	请	請	請
quán	拳	拳	拳
quē	缺	缺	缺
rè	热	熱	熱
róng	容	容	容
rǔ	辱	辱	辱
rùn	润	潤	潤
ruò	弱	弱	弱
sāng	桑	桑	桑
shài	晒	曬	晒
shàn, shān	扇	扇	扇
shǎng	晌	晌	晌
shāo	捎	捎	捎
shāo	烧	燒	烧
shào	哨	哨	哨
shè	射	射	射
shè	涉	涉	涉
shì	逝	逝	逝
shū	殊	殊	殊
shuāi	衰	衰	衰
shuí, shéi	谁	誰	誰
sòng	颂	頌	颂
sù	素	素	素
sù	速	速	速
sǔn	损	損	损
sǔn	笋	笋	笋
suǒ	索	索	索
tài	泰	泰	泰
tán	谈	談	谈
táng	唐	唐	唐

Pinyin	简	繁	繁
tǎng	倘		倘
tàng	烫		烫
tāo	涛		涛
táo	桃		桃
táo	陶		陶
tào	套		套
tè	特		特
téng	疼		疼
tiě	铁	鐵	铁
tōng, tòng	通		通
tóng	桐		桐
tòu	透		透
tú	徒		徒
tú	途		途
tú	涂	(塗)	涂
wà	袜	襪	袜
wán	顽	頑	顽
wǎn	挽		挽
wén	蚊		蚊
wēng	翁		翁
wù	悟		悟
xī	牺	犧	牺
xī	息		息
xí	席	(蓆)	席
xià	夏		夏
xiàn	陷		陷
xiáng	祥		祥
xiāo	消		消
xiāo	宵		宵
xiǎo	晓	曉	晓
xiào, jiào	校		校

xiào	笑		笑	zǎi	宰		宰
xiào	效		效	zǎi, zài	载		载
xiè	屑		屑	zāng, zàng	脏	髒/臟	脏
xiōng	胸		胸	zào	造		造
xiū	羞		羞	zéi	贼	賊	贼
xiù	袖		袖	zhǎi	窄		窄
xiù	绣	绣/繡	绣	zhài	债		债
xú	徐		徐	zhǎn	盏	盞	盏
yā	鸭	鴨	鸭	zhǎn	展		展
yān	烟		烟	zhàn	站		站
yán	盐	鹽	盐	zhǎng, zhàng	涨	漲	涨
yàn	艳	豔	艳	zhé	哲		哲
yàn	宴		宴	zhè	浙		浙
yàn	验	驗	验	zhēn	真		真
yāng	秧		秧	zhèn	振		振
yǎng	氧		氧	zhēng, zhèng	症	癥	症
yàng	样	樣	样	zhī	脂		脂
yǐ	倚		倚	zhí	值		值
yì	谊	誼	谊	zhì	致		致
yì	益		益	zhì	秩		秩
yǒng	涌		涌	zhòu	皱	皺(縐)	皱
yú	娱		娱	zhū	珠		珠
yù	浴		浴	zhū	株		株
yù	预	預	预	zhū	诸	諸	诸
yuān	冤		冤	zhú	逐		逐
yuán	原		原	zhú	烛	燭	烛
yuán	圆	圓	圆	zhǔn	准	準	准
yuè	阅	閱	阅	zhuō	捉		捉
yuè	悦		悦	zhuō	桌		桌
yūn, yùn	晕	暈	晕	zī	资	資	资
zāi	栽		栽	zū	租		租

zuān, zuàn	钻	鑽	钻	děi		
zuò	座		座	dí	笛	笛
				dì	第	第

	Normalized Script	**Complex Form**	**Semi- Cursive**
11 **Strokes**			

				diào	掉	掉
bèn	笨		笨	dǔ	堵	堵
bō	菠	菠	菠	duàn	断	断 断
bó	脖		脖	duī	堆	堆
cāi	猜		猜	fú	符	符
cǎi	彩		彩	fǔ	辅	辅 辅
cài	菜	菜	菜	fù	副	副
cán	惭	慚	惭	gài	盖	盖 盖
cǎn	惨	惨	惨	gǎn	敢	敢 敢
chǎn	铲	剷	铲	gē	鸽	鸽 鸽
cháng	常		常	gòu	够	够
cháng	偿	償	偿	guǎn	馆	馆 馆
chàng	唱		唱	guàn	惯	惯 惯
chén	晨		晨	háo	毫	毫
chí, shì	匙		匙	hé	盒	盒
chóng	崇		崇	hén	痕	痕
chóu	绸	綢	绸	huàn	患	患
chuán	船		船	huáng	黄	黄 黄
còu	凑		凑	huǎng	谎	谎 谎
cū	粗		粗	hūn	婚	婚
dài, dǎi	逮		逮	hùn, hún	混	混
dài	袋		袋	huò	祸	祸
dàn	淡		淡	jī	基	基
dàn, tán	弹	彈	弹	jī	绩	绩 绩
dàn	蛋		蛋	jì	寄	寄
dào	盗	盗	盗	jiǎ, jià	假	假
dào	悼		悼	jiǎn	检	检 检
de, dé,	得		得	jiǎn	减	减 减

Pinyin	Character	Traditional
jiǎn	剪	
jiàn	渐	漸
jiāo, jiào	教	
jiǎo	脚	
jiē	接	
jié	捷	
jīng	惊	驚
jǐng, gěng	颈	頸
jìng	竟	
jiù	救	
jú	菊	
jù, jū	据	據
jù	距	
jù	惧	懼
jué	掘	
jūn, jùn	菌	菌
kāng	康	
kòng	控	
kòu	寇	
lā	啦	
láng	廊	
lè, lēi	勒	
lèi, lěi	累	(壘)
lí	梨	
lí	犁	
lǐ	理	
lì	粒	
liǎn	脸	臉
liáng	梁	
liàng	辆	輛
liè	猎	獵

Pinyin	Character	Traditional
lín	淋	
lǐng	领	領
lóng	聋	聾
lóng	笼	籠
lóng	隆	
lù	鹿	
lù, shuài	率	
lù, lù	绿	綠
lüè	掠	
lüè	略	
luó	萝	蘿 (蔴)
má	麻	
māo, máo	猫	貓
méi	梅	
méng	萌	萌
měng	猛	
mèng	梦	夢
mī	眯	
mí	谜	謎
mì	密	
mián	绵	綿
miáo	描	描
mǐn	敏	
móu	谋	謀
nián	粘	
nín	您	
ǒu	偶	
pái	排	
pán	盘	盤
péi	培	
pěng	捧	

Pinyin	Simplified	Traditional
piān	偏	偏
piào	票	票
píng	萍	萍
pó	婆	婆
qī	戚	戚
qí	骑	騎
qīng	清	清
qíng	情	情
qiú	球	球
qú	渠	渠
quān, juàn, juān	圈	圈
què	雀	雀
shāng	商	商
shāo	梢	梢
shé	蛇	蛇
shēn	深	深
shěn	婶	嬸
shèn	渗	滲
shéng	绳	繩
shèng, chéng	盛	盛
shòu	授	授
shòu	售	售
shòu	兽	獸
shū	梳	梳
shuǎng	爽	爽
sù, xiǔ, xiù	宿	宿
suí	随	隨
tàn	探	探
táng	堂	堂
tāo	掏	掏

Pinyin	Simplified	Traditional
táo	萄	萄
táo	淘	淘
tī	梯	梯
tì	惕	惕
tiān	添	添
tián	甜	甜
tíng	停	停
tóng	铜	銅
tǒng	桶	桶
tōu	偷	偷
tú	屠	屠
tuī	推	推
tuō	脱	脫
wǎn	晚	晚
wàng	望	望
wéi	唯	唯
wéi	维	維
xǐ	悉	悉
xǐ	惜	惜
xí	袭	襲
xiān	掀	掀
xián	衔	銜
xiàn	馅	餡
xiàng	象	象
xié	斜	斜
xiè	械	械
xū	虚	虚
xù	绪	緒
xù	续	續
xuán	悬	懸
xuán	旋	旋

Pinyin	Normalized Script	Semi-Cursive
xuě	雪	雪
yá	崖	崖
yān	淹	淹
yǎn	掩	揞
yǎn	眼	眼
yǎng	痒	痒 (癢)
yáo	窑	窑
yě	野	野
yè	液	液
yí	移	移
yín	银	银 (銀)
yǐn	隐	隐
yíng	营	营
yōng	庸	庸
yōu	悠	悠
yú	渔	渔 (漁)
yù	域	域
yù	欲	欲
yuè	跃	跃 (躍)
zhǎn	崭	崭 (嶄)
zhāng	章	章
zhe, zhāo, zháo, zhuó	着	着
zhēng	睁	睁
zhí	职	职 (職)
zhū	猪	猪
zhù	著	著
zhuó	啄	啄
zú	族	族
zuò	做	做

Pinyin	Normalized Script	Complex Form	Semi-Cursive
12 Strokes			
ào	傲		傲
ào	奥		奥
bān	斑		斑
bàng	棒		棒
bàng	傍		傍
bǎo, bǔ, pù	堡		堡
bēi	悲		悲
bèi	辈		辈
bī	逼		逼
biān	编	編	编
biàn	遍		遍
bó	博		博
cái	裁		裁
cè	策		策
céng, zēng	曾		曾
chā	插		插
chán	馋	饞	馋
chǎng	敞		敞
chāo	超		超
cháo, zhāo	朝		朝
chèn	趁		趁
chéng	程		程
chéng	惩	懲	惩
chú	厨		厨
chú	锄	鋤	锄
chǔ	储	儲	储
chuǎn	喘		喘
chuāng	窗		窗
cōng	葱	蔥	葱

Pinyin	字	字	字
cuàn	竄	窜	窜
dā	搭	搭	搭
dá, dā		答	答
dào		道	道
dēng		登	登
děng		等	等
dī		堤	堤
dié		跌	跌
dǒng	董	董	董
dǔ	賭	赌	赌
dù		渡	渡
duǎn		短	短
duàn	緞	缎	缎
duò		惰	惰
é	鵝	鹅	鹅
fān		番	番
fèn	糞	粪	粪
fèn		愤	愤
fēng	鋒	锋	锋
fú		幅	幅
fù		傅	傅
fù		富	富
gài		溉	溉
gǎng		港	港
gē	擱	搁	搁
gē		割	割
gé, gě	葛	葛	葛
gé		隔	隔
gū		辜	辜
gùn		棍	棍
guō	鍋	锅	锅

Pinyin	字	字	字
hán		寒	寒
hǎn		喊	喊
hē, hè		喝	喝
hēi		黑	黑
hóu		喉	喉
hóu		猴	猴
hú		湖	湖
huá		猾	猾
huá		滑	滑
huǎn	緩	缓	缓
huāng		慌	慌
huī	輝	辉	辉
huì		惠	惠
huò		惑	惑
jí		集	集
jiàn	踐	践	践
jiāo		椒	椒
jiāo		焦	焦
jiǎo	攪	搅	搅
jiē		揭	揭
jiē		街	街
jīn		筋	筋
jǐng		晶	晶
jǐng		景	景
jìng	敬	敬	敬
jiū		揪	揪
jiù		就	就
kǎi		慨	慨
kān		堪	堪
kē		棵	棵
kě		渴	渴

pinyin	字		pinyin	字	
kù	裤	褲	qī	欺	欺
kuǎn	款		qí	棋	棋
kuāng	筐		qiān	谦	謙
kuí	葵	葵	qiāng	腔	腔
kuì	愧	愧	qiáng, jiàng, qiǎng	强	強
kuò	阔	阔	qín	琴	琴
lǎ, lā	喇	喇	qín	禽	禽
là	腊	腊	qíng	晴	晴
lián	联	聯	qū	趋	趨
liàn	链	鏈	què	确	確
liáng, liàng	量	量	qún	裙	裙
liè	裂	裂	rán	然	然
lǒu, lōu	搂	摟	rě	惹	惹
lǔ	鲁	魯	róu	揉	揉
lǔ	屡	屢	ruì	锐	銳
luò, là, lào	落	落	sǎn	散	散
mán	蛮	蠻	sǎo	嫂	嫂
mào	帽	帽	sēn	森	森
mián	棉	棉	shà, xià	厦	厦
pái	牌	牌	shāi	筛	篩
pǎo	跑	跑	shàn	善	善
péi	赔	賠	shǎng	赏	賞
pēn	喷	噴	shāo	稍	稍
péng	棚	棚	shèng	剩	剩
pí	脾	脾	shī	湿	溼
piàn	骗	騙	shì	释	釋
pū, pù	铺	鋪	shū	舒	舒
pú	葡	葡	shū	疏	疏
pǔ	普		shǔ	暑	暑
qī	期		shǔ	属	屬

shuì	税		稅	yàn	焰	焰
sī	斯		斯	yáo	谣	謠 遙
sōu	搜		搜	yí	遗	遺
suǒ	锁	鎖	鎖	yǐ	椅	硬
tǎ	塔	塔	塔	yìng	硬	硬
tǎn	毯		毯	yóu	游 (遊)	游
tí, dī	提		提	yú	愉	愉
tì	替		替	yù	遇	遇
tíng	蜓		蜒	yù	御 (禦)	御
tǐng	艇		艇	yù	裕	裕
tóng	童		童	yuán	援	援
tǒng	筒		筒	yuán	缘 緣	緣
tòng	痛		痛	yuè	越	越
wā	蛙		蛙	zàn	暂	暫
wān	湾 灣		灣	zàng	葬	葬
wèi	喂		喂	zhā	渣	渣
wēn	温		溫	zhǎng	掌	掌
wō	窝 窩		窩	zhēng	筝 箏	箏
wò	握		握	zhí	植	植
xī	稀		稀	zhí	殖	殖
xǐ	喜		喜	zhì	智	智
xì	隙		隙	zhōu	粥	粥
xiàn	羡		羨	zhū	蛛	蛛
xiāo	销 銷		銷	zhǔ	煮	煮
xiè	谢 謝		謝	zhù	铸 鑄	鑄
xióng	雄		雄	zhù	筑 築	築
xiù	锈 銹/鏽		銹	zhuāng	装 裝	裝
xù	絮		絮	zī	滋	滋
xún	循		循	zǐ	紫	紫
yǎ	雅		雅	zōng	棕	棕
yàn	雁		雁	zuì	最	最

	Normalized Script	Complex Form	Semi-Cursive
zūn	尊		尊

13 Strokes

	Normalized Script	Complex Form	Semi-Cursive
ǎi	矮		矮
ài	碍	礙	碍
àn	暗		暗
bǎi	摆	擺/襬	摆
bān	搬		搬
báo	雹		雹
bēi	碑		碑
bǐ	鄙		鄙
bì, pì	辟		辟
bīn	滨	濱	滨
bó	搏		搏
cǎi	睬		睬
chán	缠	纏	缠
chóu	酬		酬
chóu	稠		稠
chóu	愁		愁
chóu	筹	籌	筹
chǔ	楚		楚
chù	触	觸	触
chuí	锤	錘	锤
cí	辞	辭	辞
cí	慈		慈
cuī	催		催
cuò	错	錯	错
diàn	殿		殿
dié	叠		叠
dū	督		督
duǒ	躲		躲

	Normalized Script	Complex Form	Semi-Cursive
é	蛾		蛾
fēng	蜂		蜂
fēng	缝	縫	缝
fú	福		福
fù	腹		腹
gài	概		概
gǎn	感		感
gǎo	搞		搞
gēn	跟		跟
gǔ	鼓		鼓
guì	跪		跪
gǔn	滚		滚
huái	槐		槐
huáng	煌		煌
huǐ	毁		毁
hún	魂		魂
jià	嫁		嫁
jiān	煎		煎
jiǎn	简	簡	简
jiàn	鉴	鑑	鉴
jiàn	键	鍵	键
jiàng	酱	醬	酱
jiě, xiè	解		解
jǐn	锦	錦	锦
jǐn	谨	謹	谨
jìn, jīn	禁		禁
jǐng	睛		睛
jiù	舅		舅
jù	锯	鋸	锯
kuà	跨		跨
lài	赖	賴	赖

lán	蓝	藍	蓝	ruì	瑞		瑞
làn	滥	濫	滥	sāi, sè	塞		塞
léi	雷		雷	sǎng	嗓		嗓
lián	廉		廉	shǎ	傻		傻
liáng	粮	糧	粮	shè	摄	攝	摄
liáng	梁		梁	shèn	慎		慎
líng	零		零	shū	输	輸	输
líng	龄	齡	龄	shǔ	鼠		鼠
liū, liù	溜		溜	shù, shǔ	数	數	数
lóu	楼	樓	楼	shuì	睡		睡
lù	碌		碌	sì	肆		肆
lù	路		路	sù	塑		塑
lù	滤	濾	滤	suàn	蒜	蒜	蒜
luó	锣	鑼	锣	suì	碎		碎
mǎn	满	滿	满	tā	塌		塌
méi	煤		煤	tān	摊	攤	摊
méng, mēng, měng	蒙	(濛/懞/矇)	蒙	tān	滩	灘	滩
méng	盟		盟	tán	痰		痰
mō	摸	摸	摸	táng	塘		塘
mò	漠	漠	漠	tāo	滔		滔
mù	墓	墓	墓	téng	腾	騰	腾
mù	幕	幕	幕	tián	填		填
nuǎn	暖		暖	tiào	跳		跳
péng	蓬	蓬	蓬	tuǐ	腿		腿
pèng	碰		碰	wǎn	碗		碗
qiān	签	簽/籤	签	wēi	微		微
qiǎn	遣		遣	wù	雾	霧	雾
qín	勤		勤	xī	溪		溪
què	鹊		鹊	xī	锡	錫	锡
qún	群		群	xián	嫌		嫌
				xiàn	献	獻	献

Pinyin	Normalized Script	Complex Form	Semi-Cursive
xiǎng	想		想
xiàng	像		像
xiē	歇		歇
xié	携		携
xīn	新		新
xīng	腥		腥
xù	蓄	蓄	蓄
yāo	腰		腰
yáo	摇		摇
yáo	遥		遥
yì	意		意
yú	榆		榆
yú	愚		愚
yù	愈		愈
yù	誉	譽	誉
yuán	源		源
yùn	韵		韵
zhàng	障		障
zhào	照		照
zhào	罩		罩
zhēng	蒸	蒸	蒸
zhì	置		置
zuì	罪		罪

14 Strokes

Pinyin	Normalized Script	Complex Form	Semi-Cursive
bǎng	榜		榜
bǎng, páng	膀		膀
bí	鼻		鼻
bì	碧		碧
bì	蔽	蔽	蔽
bì	弊		弊

Pinyin	Normalized Script	Complex Form	Semi-Cursive
bó	膊		膊
chá	察		察
cí	磁		磁
cuī	摧		摧
cuì	翠		翠
dèng	凳		凳
dī	滴		滴
duān	端		端
duàn	锻	鍛	鍛
fǔ	腐		腐
gāo	膏		膏
gē	歌		歌
guǎn	管		管
guǒ	裹		裹
háo	豪		豪
jiā	嘉		嘉
jié	截		截
jié	竭		竭
jīng	精		精
jìng	静	靜	靜
jìng	境		境
jù	聚		聚
kē	颗	顆	顆
kù	酷		酷
là	辣		辣
là	蜡	蠟	蠟
lí	璃		璃
liáo	僚		僚
liú	榴		榴
lòu	漏		漏
luó	箩	籮	籮

luó	骡	骡	骡	sòu	嗽		嗽
mán	馒	馒	馒	suān	酸		酸
màn	漫		漫	suàn	算		算
màn	慢		慢	suō	缩	縮	縮
mào	貌		貌	wěn	稳		稳
mì	蜜		蜜	wǔ	舞		舞
miè	蔑	(蠛)	蔑	xī	熄		熄
mó	模	模	模	xiān, xiǎn	鲜	鲜	鲜
mó	膜	膜	膜	xióng	熊		熊
mù	慕	慕	慕	xū	需		需
mù	暮	暮	暮	yǎn	演		演
nèn	嫩		嫩	yí	疑		疑
niàng	酿	釀	酿	yíng	蝇	蠅	蝇
piāo, piáo, piǎo	漂		漂	yuàn	愿	(願)	愿
piě	撇		撇	zāo	遭		遭
pò	魄		魄	zhà	榨		榨
pǔ	谱	谱	谱	zhāi	摘		摘
qī	漆		漆	zhài	寨		寨
qí	旗		旗	zhē	遮		遮
qiàn	歉		歉	zhī	蜘		蜘
qiáng	墙	墙	墙	zhuàn	赚	赚	赚
qiāo	锹	锹	锹				
qiāo	敲		敲	**15 Strokes**	**Normalized Script**	**Complex Form**	**Semi-Cursive**
qīng	蜻		蜻	bào, pù	暴		暴
róng	熔		熔	bō	播		播
sài	赛		赛	cǎi	踩		踩
shang	裳		裳	cáo	槽		槽
shì	誓		誓	cháo	潮		潮
shòu	瘦		瘦	chè	撤		撤
shuāi	摔		摔	chēng	撑		撑
				cōng	聪	聪	聪

Pinyin	Normalized Script	Complex Form	Semi-Cursive
cù	醋		醋
dào	稻		稻
dé	德		德
dié	蝶		蝶
dǒng	懂	懂	懂
é	额	额	额
gǎo	稿		稿
héng, hèng	横		横
hú	蝴		蝴
hú, hū	糊		糊
huì	慧		慧
jià	稼		稼
jiàn	箭		箭
jiāng	僵		僵
jiāo	蕉	蕉	蕉
kào	靠		靠
lí	黎		黎
mán	瞒	瞒	瞒
méi	霉		霉
mó	摩		摩
mò	墨		墨
pī, pǐ	劈		劈
pì	僻		僻
piān	篇		篇
piāo	飘		飘
qián	潜		潜
qù	趣		趣
sā, sǎ	撒		撒
shóu, shú	熟		熟
shū	蔬	蔬	蔬
sī	撕		撕

Pinyin	Normalized Script	Complex Form	Semi-Cursive
sōu	艘		艘
tà	踏		踏
táng	膛		膛
tǎng	躺		躺
tàng	趟		趟
tī	踢		踢
tí	题	题	题
wèi	慰		慰
xǐ	膝		膝
xiā	瞎		瞎
xiāng	箱		箱
xiàng	橡		橡
xié	鞋		鞋
yán	颜	颜	颜
yì	毅		毅
yīng	樱	樱	樱
yǐng	影		影
zēng	增		增
zhèn	震		震
zhèn	镇	镇	镇
zhǔ	嘱	嘱	嘱
zhuàng	撞		撞
zōng	踪		踪
zuì	醉		醉
zūn	遵		遵

16 Strokes	Normalized Script	Complex Form	Semi-Cursive
báo, bó, bò	薄	薄	薄
bì	壁		壁
bì	避		避
biàn	辩		辩

	Normalized Script	Complex Form	Semi-Cursive
biàn	辩	辯	辯
cān	餐		餐
cāo	操		操
diān	颠	顛	顛
diāo	雕		雕
gāo	糕		糕
héng	衡		衡
jī	激		激
jiǎo	缴	繳	繳
jìng	镜	鏡	鏡
jú	橘		橘
lán	篮	籃	籃
lǎn	懒	懶	懶
mó, mò	磨		磨
mò	默		默
níng	凝		凝
péng	膨		膨
qì	器		器
rán	燃		燃
róng	融		融
shǔ	薯	薯	薯
táng	糖		糖
tí	蹄		蹄
xīn	薪	薪	薪
xǐng	醒		醒
yàn	燕		燕
yāo	邀		邀
zàn	赞	讚	讚
zǎo	澡		澡
zèng	赠	贈	贈
zhěng	整		整

	Normalized Script	Complex Form	Semi-Cursive
zuǐ	嘴		嘴

17 Strokes

	Normalized Script	Complex Form	Semi-Cursive
bì, bei	臂		臂
biàn	辨	辮	辮
cā	擦		擦
cáng, zàng	藏	藏	藏
dài	戴		戴
dǎo	蹈		蹈
fán	繁		繁
jū	鞠		鞠
kāng	糠		糠
luó	螺		螺
qiáo	瞧		瞧
shuāng	霜		霜
suì	穗		穗
xiá	霞		霞
yì	翼		翼
yíng	赢		赢
zāo	糟		糟
zào	燥		燥
zhòu	骤	驟	驟

18 Strokes

	Normalized Script	Complex Form	Semi-Cursive
bèng	蹦		蹦
biān	鞭		鞭
fān	翻		翻
fù	覆		覆
lián	镰	鐮	鐮
yīng	鹰	鷹	鷹

19 Strokes	Normalized Script	Complex Form	Semi-Cursive
bàn	瓣		瓣
bào	爆		爆
chàn	颤	顫	顫
dūn	蹲		蹲
jiāng	疆		疆
jǐng	警	警	警
pān	攀		攀

20 Strokes	Normalized Script	Complex Form	Semi-Cursive
guàn	灌	灌	灌
jí	籍		籍
jiáo, jué	嚼		嚼
mó	魔		魔
rǎng	壤		壤
rǎng, rāng	嚷		嚷
yào	耀		耀
zào	躁		躁

21 Strokes	Normalized Script	Complex Form	Semi-Cursive
bà	霸		霸
chǔn	蠢		蠢
lòu, lù	露		露

22 Strokes	Normalized Script	Complex Form	Semi-Cursive
náng, nǎng	囊		囊

23 Strokes	Normalized Script	Complex Form	Semi-Cursive
guàn	罐	罐	罐

References 参考书目

Dictionary Department, Institute of Linguistics at the Chinese Academy of Social Sciences: *The Contemporary Chinese Dictionary (Chinese-English Edition)*. Beijing: Foreign Language Teaching and Research Press, 2002. （中国社会科学院语言研究所词典编辑室：《汉英双解现代汉语词典》。北京：外语教学与研究出版社，2002 年。）

Wilder, G. D., and J. H. Ingram. *Analysis of Chinese Characters*. New York: Dover Publications, Inc., 1974.

Xie Guanghui et al. *The Composition of Common Chinese Characters: An Illustrated Account*. Beijing: Peking University Press, 1997. （谢光辉等：《常用汉字图解》。北京：北京大学出版社，1997。）

Xinhua Dictionary with English Translation. Beijing: The Commercial Press International Co., Ltd., 2000. （《英汉双解新华字典》。北京：商务印书馆国际有限公司，2000 年。）

Yin Bingyong, and J. S. Rohsenow. *Modern Chinese Characters*. Beijing: Sinoligngua, 1994. （尹斌庸、罗圣豪：《现代汉字》。北京：华语教学出版社，1994。）

戴汝潜等：《汉字教与学》。济南：山东教育出版社，1999 年。

樊中岳：《金文速查手册》。武汉：湖北美术出版社，1994 年。

国家对外汉语教学顶到小组办公室汉语水平考试部：《汉语水平词汇语汉字等级大纲》。北京：北京语言学院出版社，1992 年。

汉语大字典编辑委员会：《汉语大字典（缩印本）》。武汉：湖北辞书出版社；成都：四川辞书出版社，1995 年。

李大遂：《简明实用汉字学》。北京：北京大学出版社，1993 年。

李大遂：《转注之名的探讨》，《北京师范大学学报》1990 年增刊，第 102-106 页、第 96 页。

李乐毅：《汉字演变五百例》。北京：北京语言文化大学出版社，1993 年。

李乐毅：《简化字源》。北京：华语教学出版社，1996 年。

吕必松等：《汉字与汉字教学研究论文集》。北京：北京大学出版社，1999 年。

苏培成：《现代汉字学纲要》。北京：北京大学出版社，1994 年。

唐兰：《甲骨文自然分类简编》。太原：山西教育出版社，1999 年。

王凤阳：《汉字学》。长春：吉林文史出版社，1989 年。

吴宗济等：《现代汉语语音概要》。北京：华语教学出版社，1991 年。

许慎：《说文解字》。北京：中华书局，1963 年。

杨洪清、朱新兰:《快速识字字典》。南京：江苏古籍出版社，1996 年。

尹黎云：《汉字字源系统研究》。北京：中国人民大学出版社，1998 年。

语言出版社：《语言文字规范手册》（1997 年重排版）。北京：语文出版社，
　　　1997 年。

约斋：《字源》。上海：上海书店，1986。

张书岩等：《简化字溯源》。北京：语文出版社，1997 年。

赵元任：《语言问题》。北京：商务印书馆，1980 年。

邹晓丽等：《甲骨文字学述要》。长沙：岳麓书社，1999 年。

Index 索引